THE BUDDHA AND THE BABY

THE BUDDHA AND THE BABY
Psychotherapy and Meditation in Working with Children and Adults

Maria Pozzi Monzo

KARNAC

First published in 2014 by
Karnac Books Ltd
118 Finchley Road
London NW3 5HT

Copyright © 2014 by Maria Pozzi Monzo

The right of Maria Pozzi Monzo to be identified as the author of this work has been asserted in accordance with §§ 77 and 78 of the Copyright Design and Patents Act 1988.

All rights reserved. No part of this publication may be reproduced, stored in a retrieval system, or transmitted, in any form or by any means, electronic, mechanical, photocopying, recording, or otherwise, without the prior written permission of the publisher.

British Library Cataloguing in Publication Data

A C.I.P. for this book is available from the British Library

ISBN-13: 978-1-78049-081-6

Typeset by V Publishing Solutions Pvt Ltd., Chennai, India

www.karnacbooks.com

CONTENTS

ABOUT THE AUTHOR AND CONTRIBUTORS   ix

FOREWORD   xv
by Mary Twyman

PROLOGUE
Reflections on Buddhism and child psychoanalytic
    psychotherapy   xvii

INTRODUCTION   xxxiii

CHAPTER ONE
A baby is born   1
Dialogue with Claudia Goulder

CHAPTER TWO
Let us allow to arrive: bringing into being   9
Dialogue with Rosalind Powrie

vi CONTENTS

CHAPTER THREE
The Buddha in the sky 29
Dialogue with Stephen Malloch

CHAPTER FOUR
Serendipity in the magic garden 43
Dialogue with Deirdre Dowling

CHAPTER FIVE
The presence of the therapist 53
Dialogue with Monica Lanyado

CHAPTER SIX
The moon allows the sun to shine on it 67
Dialogue with Dorette Engi

CHAPTER SEVEN
Coming home 77
Dialogue with Anonymous

CHAPTER EIGHT
The curative factor 93
Dialogue with Pamela Bartram

CHAPTER NINE
The facilitating silence 109
Dialogue with Sara Leon

CHAPTER TEN
Nothing fixed 121
Dialogue with Akashadevi

CHAPTER ELEVEN
Walking with Buddha 143
Dialogue with friends

CHAPTER TWELVE
The smug Buddha 157
Dialogue with Caroline Helm

CONTENTS vii

CHAPTER THIRTEEN
What works for whom? 169
Dialogue with Myra Berg

CHAPTER FOURTEEN
Mindfulness and meditation in the consulting room 179
Dialogue with Ricky Emanuel

CHAPTER FIFTEEN
Vagal superstars 197
Dialogue with Graham Music

CHAPTER SIXTEEN
Jung and the Buddha 213
Dialogue with Jackie Van Roosmalen

CHAPTER SEVENTEEN
A Burmese noodle soup with Buddha 223
Dialogue with Aye Aye Yee

CHAPTER EIGHTEEN
From the cushion to the couch 233
Dialogue with Nicholas Carroll

CHAPTER NINETEEN
The child in the adult: psychotherapy informed by Buddhism 265
Dialogue with Steven Mendoza

EPILOGUE 287

INDEX 293

ABOUT THE AUTHOR AND CONTRIBUTORS

Akashadevi has recently changed her name from Claudia McLoughlin, through joining the Triratna Buddhist Order. She is a child and adolescent psychotherapist trained at the Tavistock Clinic. After working in the Islington Community CAMHS Service in Inner London for the past ten years, she is about to enter more freelance working contexts. She has a particular interest in working with hard to reach and marginalised children and families, and in developing ways of bringing her meditation practice to her supervisory and consultative work.

Aye Aye Yee was born and raised in Myanmar (previously known as Burma) to Buddhist parents. Aye Aye was instilled with Buddhist values and practice. In her early years as a Buddhist, she simply followed the traditional family practice of Buddhism laid down by her parents without exploring further the true *dhamma* and meditation. She started practising meditation in 2002 and uses this experience to integrate mindfulness in her work as a child psychiatrist.

Pamela Bartram grew up in Glasgow and studied Indian philosophy at university. She trained as a music therapist and worked with children for whom words were not possible using improvised music as a means of communication. Now a psychoanalytic psychotherapist working with children and adults, she is especially interested in the "present moment". She has been greatly helped in life by both psychoanalysis and Buddhism. Since contributing to this book, she has become a practitioner of Soto Zen.

Myra Berg is a child and adolescent psychotherapist currently working and teaching at the Tavistock Clinic. She treats children and parents in both clinical and educational settings and enjoys the variety this brings. Her interest in Buddhism has been with her for a long time, and provides a great opportunity for her to attempt to integrate all the things she learns in every life setting she encounters. She continues working on this total integration/inter-connectedness on her journey through life.

Nicholas Carroll is a relationship and psychosexual therapist in private practice in London, trained in EMDR and Sensorimotor Psychotherapy for trauma. He has studied and practised Buddhism for over forty years and was instrumental in developing the lay community ALBA at Amaravati Buddhist Monastery, Hertfordshire, UK. Interested in the interface between psychotherapy and Buddhist teachings and practice, he has organised and facilitated residential conferences for psychotherapists around the theme of *anatta* (the Buddhist teaching on "non-self" or "emptiness") and the use of self in the therapeutic encounter. He gives talks, leads workshops and retreats, and facilitates an ongoing meditative enquiry group. He is married with two grown-up children.

Deirdre Dowling is a child and adolescent psychotherapist. She is now joint organising tutor at the independent child and adolescent psychoanalytic psychotherapy training at the British Psychotherapy Foundation, after working for many years as head child psychotherapist at the Cassel Hospital. She has also set up the Lantern Family Centre in Bookham, Surrey, with a colleague, an independent therapeutic service for parents and children that also provides training for professionals. Previously, she worked as a social worker, manager, and trainer in child care. She has a particular interest in parent–infant psychotherapy, working with families with complex needs, and teaching and consulting to other professions who are interested in applying psychoanalytic ideas to their work with families.

Ricky Emanuel is a consultant child, adolescent, and adult psychotherapist who trained at the Tavistock Clinic. He works as head of child psychotherapy services at the Royal Free Hospital. He teaches at the Tavistock Clinic, the Birmingham Trust for Psychoanalytic Psychotherapy, and in Florence for Centro Studi Martha Harris. He has published many peer-reviewed papers and book chapters, and has published a book on anxiety. His special interests are in trauma, bereavement, neuropsychoanalysis, and the application of mindfulness to psychotherapy.

Dorette Engi qualified as a child and adolescent psychotherapist in 2006, having worked as a teacher of the Alexander Technique for the previous twenty years. She also practises meditation and studies Buddhist teachings. She spent two years on a Buddhist retreat, where she also worked as a psychotherapist. Being a meditation instructor, one of her interests is to explore the connections between psychotherapy and Buddhism.

Claudia Goulder is a former journalist and now child psychotherapy trainee at the Tavistock Clinic. She has a regular yoga and meditation practice based on Buddhist principles and rooted in its tradition, which helps take herself out of her body and mind (temporarily, at least).

Caroline Helm studied for an Open University degree while at home with her two young sons before training as a child psychotherapist. She worked in community settings including Brixton Child Guidance Clinic and the Child and Family Consultation Service in Richmond. The last ten years of her professional life were spent as consultant child psychotherapist on the regional burns unit at Chelsea and Westminster Hospital, London. She is now retired.

Monica Lanyado was the founding course organiser of the child and adolescent psychotherapy training at the Scottish Institute of Human Relations, Edinburgh. She is a training supervisor at the British Psychotherapy Foundation and is joint series editor, with Ann Horne, of the Independent Psychoanalytic Approaches with Children and Adolescents Series. Her publications include *The Presence of the Therapist: Treating Childhood Trauma* (2004) and, co-edited with Ann Horne, *The Handbook of Child and Adolescent Psychotherapy: Psychoanalytic Approaches* (1999, 2009), *A Question of Technique* (2006), *Through Assessment to Consultation* (2009), and *Winnicott's Children* (2012). She

xii ABOUT THE AUTHOR AND CONTRIBUTORS

has retired from clinical practice but continues to supervise colleagues and trainees, to teach and write.

Sara Leon is a child and adolescent psychotherapist who works for the East London NHS Trust. She has a special interest in early trauma, particularly in children who have learning difficulties and in children who have been adopted. She is also interested in the impact of such trauma on the parental couple and the sibling group. She is training to be a psychoanalytic couple psychotherapist at the Tavistock Centre for Couple Relationships. She practises meditation on a daily basis and regularly attends a Buddhist meditation group. Whenever possible, week-long silent retreats have become an important part of her life.

Steven Mendoza took a degree in psychology and an M.Phil. in human learning. He worked as a consultant in qualitative market research with children and as a generic social worker and mental health welfare officer. He trained as a psychoanalytic psychotherapist and has since remained in full-time practice and teaching. So much that he hears in the consulting room he hears in the binaural audience of metapsychology and Buddhadharma. They do not contradict one another.

Stephen Malloch helps people discover what is important for them, through his work as a workshop facilitator, executive and career coach, and counsellor, based in Mosman, Sydney (see www.heartmind.com. au). He has practised and taught meditation and mindfulness for over twenty years. Originally training as a musician, gaining an M.Mus. in music theory and analysis from the University of London and a PhD in music and psychoacoustics from the University of Edinburgh, he has worked at the University of Edinburgh and University of Western Sydney in research psychology, and in addition to his other work currently holds a research role in the Westmead Psychotherapy Program, University of Sydney. His theory of *communicative musicality*, based in his research on caregiver–infant communication, is now used by a wide variety of authors and researchers in areas as diverse as developmental psychology, psychotherapy, and music therapy.

Graham Music, PhD, is consultant child and adolescent psychotherapist at the Tavistock and Portman Clinics and an adult psychotherapist in private practice. Formerly associate clinical director, he has also worked in the Tavistock fostering, adoption, and kinship care team for over twelve years, managed a range of services concerned with the aftermath of child maltreatment and neglect, and organised community-based therapy services, particularly in schools. He has recently been working at the Portman Clinic with forensic cases. He organises trainings for therapists in CAMHS, leads teaching on attachment, the brain, and child development, and teaches and supervises on the Tavistock child psychotherapy training and other psychotherapy trainings in the UK and abroad. Publications include *Nurturing Natures: Attachment and Children's Emotional, Socio-Cultural and Brain Development* (2010) and *Affect and Emotion*, and he has a particular interest in exploring the interface between developmental findings and clinical work.

Rosalind Powrie is an infant, child, and family psychiatrist and head of the perinatal and infant mental health team at the Women and Children's Hospital, Women and Children Health Network, Adelaide, South Australia. She is a senior lecturer in the Department of Paediatrics and Psychiatry at the University of Adelaide. She has been co-running and researching mindfulness-based cognitive therapy classes for pregnant women for some years and has an interest in integrating secular Buddhist psychology and ideas into mainstream mental health and psychotherapeutic work.

Maria Pozzi Monzo is a child, adolescent, and adult psychotherapist in the National Health Service and privately. She is a visiting tutor at the Tavistock Clinic, the BAP, and teaches and lectures in Italy and Switzerland. She has a professional doctorate in psychoanalytic research in the process of change in brief work with families of children under five. Her publications include the books *Psychic Hooks and Bolts* (2003) and *Innovations in Parent–Infant Psychotherapy* (2007), as well as papers and book chapters on various topics. She was the winner of the Frances Tustin Memorial Prize in 1990.

Jackie Van Roosmalen trained as a drama and movement therapist before doing her analytical psychotherapy training at the SAP. She has worked in the NHS with children, adolescents, and their families since 1997. Jackie's main areas of interest are parent–infant psychotherapy and adolescence. Spiritual experience and awareness in the present moment are integral components of her practice of psychotherapy.

FOREWORD

This is a remarkable book in a number of ways. What Maria Pozzi Monzo has done is to persuade a number of colleagues, mostly child psychotherapists, to reveal in their interviews with her, their experiences of an important element in their lives; namely, the practices of meditation and contemplation. As psychotherapists, these practitioners will have had their own experience of psychoanalysis as an essential part of their training. Many will have sought and continued in analysis for their own purposes of self-exploration, self-discovery, and further personal development. But unusually, those who have spoken so freely and so eloquently to Maria Pozzi Monzo have sought out other pathways, sometimes describing these as having a spiritual dimension, but not always. All connect their various meditational practices with an enhanced sense of self which can then be put at the service of the clients or patients they treat in their work. The overall claim, that such practices engender a sense of calm, which in and of itself then contributes to the establishing of the facilitating environment they then offer to their patients, is a convincing one. Equally convincing are the accounts, so moving and nuanced, of the practitioners` encounters with severely disturbed children.

xvi FOREWORD

While Buddhism and the pursuit of enlightenment is intrinsic to the practice of some contributors, it is not the path followed by all. However, the adoption of a Buddhist position has its forerunners in the psychoanalytic community, not all of whom were as ready as those speaking here to reveal their beliefs. One who was, Nina Coltart, an eminent psychoanalyst, wrote a thoughtful and informative chapter in her book *The Baby and the Bathwater* (Karnac, 1996). The chapter entitled "Buddhism and Psychoanalysis Revisited" gave her own deeply convinced exposition of Buddhism and its practices, and this is coupled with an equally original way of linking her beliefs with her psychoanalytic stance. As she says, "It is my contention that the practice of psychoanalysis in harness with the practice of Buddhism is not only harmonious, but mutually enlightening and potentiating. There does not seem to me to be any area of absolutely radical disagreement or clash between the two … ." (p. 128).

And so to those who come to this book with a fresh eye and with no particular experience of the meditative practices which are so vividly revealed and explored here, there is much to learn. We are indebted to Maria Pozzi Monzo for the patient dedication and subtle sensitivity she has brought to her task of interviewing her colleagues. She and they show us the care that is needed in fully preparing themselves to embark on the psychoanalytic therapeutic encounter with the patients they treat. We can be impressed by such preparation and their consistent efforts to be able to offer themselves to the work, fortified by the further element of their meditative practices. We can also be grateful to them for their generosity in sharing often profound and moving insights with the reader.

Mary Twyman
British Psycho-Analytical Society,
British Psycho-Analytic Association

PROLOGUE

Reflections on Buddhism and child psychoanalytic psychotherapy

Life is a good teacher and a good friend.
Things are always in transition, if we could only realise it.

—Pema Chōdrōn

Introduction

Mattthieu Ricard has remarked that "in a study of children recovering from trauma following a catastrophe, they found that there was a significant difference in the recovery time of children in Bangladesh who were from Buddhist communities. Children who were raised with Buddhist values recovered significantly faster from the calamity and had much less trauma than children from other cultural backgrounds. It seems due to the way they are educated, with the idea of cultivating gentleness" (the Dalai Lama in a talk with Daniel Goleman, 2003a, p. 218).

This study stresses the relevance of the external environment and of social values in child-rearing and in the resolution of trauma. It is also in line with recent neuropsychological discoveries on the developing and functioning of the brain, which is affected by the environment, by the type of early attachment and by repeated traumatic experiences.

xviii   PROLOGUE

The Dalai Lama's thinking—as reported by Goleman—is very relevant to the themes of this book. He writes: "In some cases, even though you may experience powerful destructive emotions, if you feel a deep sense of regret afterwards with the realisation that this was inappropriate and destructive, then you might be able to cultivate a new determination to change. This is a way of learning from the experience of this emotion" (Goleman, 2003b, p. 169).

This means that the full awareness of the destructive aspects of some actions, when accompanied by a reparative stance, can modify their original power and negative effect. Hopefully one can learn from, and integrate within oneself, that experience of negativity and destructiveness. Powerful negative as well as sweepingly exciting emotions are experienced by practically all human beings—by adults, children, and babies. What matters is the transformation and reparation that can take place afterwards, which implies an emotional awareness, a desire to change, and to learn from experience. The Dalai Lama, quoted above, expresses something quite in line with Bion's theoretical and clinical findings on container, contained, reverie, and transformation (Bion, 1962), which I will explore further in this book.

Psychoanalysis is a fairly young tradition—not yet one century old—although it is embedded in centuries of Western cultures and philosophies. Buddhism goes back five centuries before Christianity: an ancient tradition indeed! Both psychoanalysis and Buddhism have been interested in the understanding of the nature and functioning of the human mind, of mental states, and emotions. Both have been concerned with social and emotional learning. Both are concerned with the alleviating of suffering. Emotional learning starts very early on: babies in the West are studied in their emotional interactions and social responses with their mothers and, depending on the quality of such relationship, the baby will be able to develop and grow in a healthy way. Children in Buddhist countries are raised—from very early on—to respect life, to be gentle and compassionate, as the Dalai Lama reported (Goleman, 2003b).

Different techniques are used in psychoanalysis and Buddhism to provide transformative experiences. In psychoanalysis, free association in the context of the analytic relationship offers a path to understand the unconscious mind of the patient and eventually to a mastery over conflicts and anxieties. The practice of Buddhist meditation is the main path that allows the unconscious to become conscious under the guidance of the teacher—called differently in different Buddhist traditions: Roshi, Ajhan, Sayagyi etc.—leading to the awareness, and ultimately to an acceptance, of the emotions and hindrances that have caused suffering, mental diseases, and unhappiness.

Meditative aspects of psychoanalytic psychotherapy and therapeutic applications of the practice of Buddhism

The question whether Buddhist meditation is another form of psychotherapy and psychotherapy another form of religion is often asked. Here is a short description of what meditation consists of. Meditation requires one to sit in a quiet place with closed or half-closed eyes and to become aware of one's physical sensations and states of mind in the present moment: a relaxed and soft state, which will at some point give rise to physical discomforts in the body; where calmness and pleasant quietness may precipitate anxieties, emotional turbulence, and restlessness (Welwood, 1983). The practice of meditation, as described by Welwood, clinical psychologist and Buddhist practitioner, is to observe, to name, to stay with the awareness, without doing anything. These anxious, turbulent, or restless states, with practice, determination, and perseverance, will eventually become shorter-lived and less intense, leading—during meditation—to an experience of greater spaciousness in the mind. Coltart, a British psychoanalyst, and a practising Buddhist, has synthesised Buddhist thinking and ideas in a most clear way and compared them with psychoanalysis in their similarities and incompatible differences. Coltart explains, in an almost scientific way, what happens during meditation. She writes that "during meditation there is a lowering of the threshold of consciousness, and in the steady inward looking that accompanies conscious focusing on the breath, the energy withdrawn from our usual centre of consciousness, the ego or I, activates the contents of the unconscious, and the way is prepared for samadhi or deep concentration" (Coltart, 1996, p. 92).

There are different views amongst Buddhists and psychotherapists whether Buddhist meditation is another form of psychotherapy and psychotherapy another form of religion. Psychotherapy, on the whole, addresses mental disorders and symptoms of emotional disturbance, writes Goleman (Goleman, 2003). Buddhism addresses the human suffering that affects all of us: we all have destructive emotions

PROLOGUE

because that is inherent in the commonality of our human nature. Both psychotherapy and Buddhism have been preoccupied with the transformation of unhappiness and negative or destructive emotions into more wholesome states of mind.

Meditation transcends the merely therapeutic, writes American psychiatrist Paul Fleischman: it is "most therapeutic when it is not looked upon for therapeutic effect, but is put into practice as an end in itself, an expression of an aspect of human nature. [...] So meditation expresses something about the integrated process of a person, rather than being merely a means to ends in other spheres of life" (1986, p. 17). The psychoanalytic method is "psychological-empirical" writes psychoanalyst Eric Fromm (1960, p. 69), who distinguishes it from the Zen method, which consists of a "frontal attack on the alienated way of perception by means of the 'sitting', the koan, and the authority of the master".

The above authors clearly state that the practice of Buddhist meditation is not another form of psychotherapy even though it can be therapeutic in itself.

However, Thich Nhat Hanh (1991, p. 46), a Vietnamese Buddhist Zen monk, says that Buddhism is also a form of psychotherapy and those Buddhists who are not ill practise not to get ill; while those who are ill practise to recover. He believes that Buddhism can heal deep wounds because it studies the functioning of the mind and also has a deep knowledge of the unconscious mind. The unconscious mind is a deep level of conscious which is called store consciousness, which is called tank conscience (*alaya-vijnana* in Sanskrit). It is through the practice of meditation with its different techniques that the unconscious emerges into consciousness. In Buddhism, these unconscious seeds are neither analysed nor linked with the person's life, experience, and situation. They are just observed from a third position, not identified with but accepted fully at an emotional level until they naturally go away. This is one major difference with psychoanalysis, where the unconscious mind becomes manifested through free associations and dreams, which are analysed and linked by the analyst to other mental manifestations, anxieties, fears and conflicts in the patient as well as brought back to the transference relationship.

Psychoanalyst and Buddhist practitioner Epstein—quoted in Molino (1998, p. 124)—clarifies this point eloquently as he writes:

> Buddhist meditation is not some Eastern variant of psychoanalysis; while its method bears some profound similarities, there is an inexorable shift away from unconscious content once sufficient attentional skills are developed. Whereas pursuit of free associations leads to identification of unconscious conflict and of intrapsychic constellations such as the Oedipus, pursuit of mindfulness uncovers unconscious material but "analyzes" it only insofar as "insight" into the transitory nature of thoughts, feelings, and the identifications which form the self-concept can be achieved.

Buddhist teachers do not encourage the analysis of what bubbles up during meditation, nor the links with one's past experience and childhood. They encourage not to become identified with the emotions, the dramas, and the churning of the mind but to observe them from a third position and to see them passing.

Coltart practised Buddhism without ever feeling any conflict in her many years of combining a career as a psychoanalyst with the practice of Buddhism. She wrote: "Of course there are differences, and it is important to know what they are, and to maintain certain distinctions clearly in one's mind. But there are many more extensive and subtle ways in which they flow in and out of each other and are mutually strengthening" (Coltart, 1987, p. 91). In an interview with Anthony Molino, she said clearly that working with the unconscious is specific of psychoanalysis (Molino, 1997, p. 168). Coltart is also very clear that dynamic psychotherapy is non-religious; it does not aim at self-transcendence but at the establishment of a strong ego-identity and it must not be confused with a form of religion. However, she writes that the discipline of meditation practice has enhanced her own contribution to the analytic session, "which sometimes is almost indistinguishable from a form of meditation" (Coltart, 1987, p. 95). In another interview with Molino, she talked about "bare attention", a Buddhist phrase, which "has a sort of purity about it. It's not a clattered concept. It's that you simply become better, as any good analyst knows, at concentrating more and more directly, more purely, on what's going on in a session. You come to concentrate more fully on this person who is with you, here and now, and on what it is they experience with you: to the point that many sessions become similar to meditations. (Molino, 1998, pp. 176–177)

Psychoanalyst Eigen agrees with this view, as he writes: "For me there is a moment when psychoanalysis is a form of prayer. There is, too, a meditative dimension in psychoanalytic work" (1998, p. 11).

To go back to the question of whether meditation is a form of therapy, there is another form of meditation, Kundalini yoga, which is still based on concentration and breathing and has been extremely therapeutic. Shannahoff-Khalsa, scientist and yogic therapist, has used it and has written extensively on specific yogic meditation techniques, which he used to treat complex psychiatric disorders successfully, even in cases where intensive, traditional psychiatric therapies had failed (Shannahoff-Khalsa, 2010). The patients he treated had come to the end of the road with traditional psychiatric treatments and were interested in exploring and committing themselves to these other forms of therapy, namely Kundalini yoga, which proved resolutory for them.

Powrie, Australian child psychiatrist and psychotherapist, has used Buddhist ideas, such as mindfulness, awareness of breathing, and meditation practice, in her work with groups of pregnant mothers, depressed, anxious, and traumatised (2010, 2012; presentations given at the World Association of Infant Mental Health in Leipzig and Cape Town). They were all at risk of developing an insecure attachment to their newborn babies. This has proved to be beneficial and to have reduced depression, anxiety as well as relapse rates. This has been systematically studied by research and has provided evidence of the value of combining psychotherapy and Buddhism (Chapter Two in this book).

Vipassana meditation, which has the breath and the body sensations as objects of observation and awareness, leads to the liberation of mind and to the realisation of the ultimate truth. It is one of India's most ancient techniques of Buddhist meditation and has been taught for the past twenty-five years in Indian prisons. It has proved very successful in reducing the rate of recidivism in the most callous offenders and in transforming their mind, their thinking and feelings by providing them awareness and insight into their actions and crimes. Following such positive experience, Vipassana training has been extended to many other countries not just in the East, including Israel, New Zealand, UK, and the United States (1997, Vipassana Research Institute).

The experiences described above show the practice of Buddhism and its meditation techniques can have a very therapeutic and reparative effect even for people with serious mental disorders and with severe delinquent and criminal backgrounds.

In conclusion, there can be meditative aspects in the stance of the therapist and therapeutic results in the practice of Buddhism. Both practices heal suffering by increasing awareness of unconscious experiences but in different ways. Psychotherapy relies on the analysis of the unconscious and of the transference relationship. Buddhism relies on achieving insight into the true nature of things by the deep practice of meditation.

Attachment, suffering, and the way out of it

One of the tenets of Buddhism is about the reality of human suffering, which affects all of us. Suffering and the cause of suffering constitute the first and second of The Four Noble Truths. These are four simple but fundamental principles that underlie the Buddhist tradition and have been taught since its origins. Suffering in the Buddhist sense is not the neurotic suffering that Freud was hoping to liberate people from, by increasing self-awareness through psychoanalysis or psychotherapy. Freud was addressing anxieties, inhibitions and neurotic symptoms to which nowadays, we could add borderline and psychotic suffering, which can be contained and reduced by appropriate psychotherapies. The ordinary human unhappiness that Freud refers to, would be considered by the Buddhists as suffering.

Suffering, according to Buddhism, is any mental process that disrupts the equilibrium of the mind and disquiets it. Buddhism refers to the Five Hindrances as "unwholesome mental formations". These hindrances are: hatred and ill-will, sensual desire, doubt and confusion, torpor, restlessness and anxiety and their derivatives. They afflict and obscure the mind from seeing reality as it is. They are quite similar to what we all have to deal with and what patients bring to, and have to work through in their therapy.

Many schools of Buddhism say that the primary cause of human suffering (Second Noble Truth) is our human propensity to grasp, to cling to our misconceptions, and to attach to conditions such as the permanence of external objects, possessions, people, and so on, as well as internal states of mind and emotions. We attach to conditions as if they lasted for ever. For example, often when we are happy we want that happiness to continue for ever and when it stops we suffer. Equally, if we are in pain, we may feel it will never cease. We often attach to the idea that our identity, our moods, and reality will not change, despite the evidence that everything is always in a state of constant flux. The Buddhist concept of *anatta* or non-self is linked with this ever-changing reality (*anicca*). Buddhism talks about the condition of being born, growing old and dying as basic commonalities, which, if accepted deeply and truly, will become the source of great contentment and only be experienced as transient suffering.

This starting point of suffering (First Noble Truth), which is considered to be at the core of our human predicament, has often led to the misrepresentation of Buddhism as a negative and nihilistic philosophy of life. However, the third Noble Truth in Buddhism states that it is possible for suffering to cease, whilst the fourth Noble Truth points to the path that leads to the end of suffering. This path is referred to as the "Middle Path" or the "Middle Way", because it wants to avoid extremes; one extreme being the search for happiness through sensual pleasures: a very common aim in people's lives. The other extreme is the search of happiness through renunciation and asceticism. The Buddha himself experienced both extremes in his life; he had started as a prince in a rich Indian family with a lifestyle that had sheltered him from unpleasant and ugly aspects of human life. However, when he accidentally walked out of his palace enclosure and met a beggar, a sick man and a dying one, he realised that he had not known the reality of human life and suffering. He also met a monk and such view inspired him to look for a possible way to overcome suffering. He left his palace life, his wife, and newborn son and took on total self-renunciation and asceticism to the point of nearly dying by starvation. But he did not find the Truth he was looking for. He eventually realised that the Truth resided in the Middle Way. Then he could see and was enlightened into the reality of life, death, and how things really are. The Middle Way consists of the Noble Eightfold Path, which—when it is understood and practised—leads to the cessation of suffering. The eight categories forming the Noble Path are: right understanding, *samma ditthi*; right thought, *samma sankappa*; right speech, *samma vaca*; right action, *samma kammanta*; right livelihood, *samma ajiva*; right effort, *samma vajama*; right mindfulness, *samma sati*; right concentration, *samma samadhi*.

By practising this Path, it is possible to diminish or end suffering and to realise a more refined and more spacious level of consciousness, where one can go beyond mental constructs and emotions. This is sometimes called the pure mind or the luminous mind, and it refers to a state of pure awareness (not to some "thing" glowing somewhere). "It is a path leading to the realisation of Ultimate Reality, to complete freedom, happiness and peace through moral, spiritual and intellectual perfection" (Rahula, 1959, p. 50). This may sound somewhat religious and idealistic, but this path emphasises morality and ethics and has nothing to do with worship or prayers. I agree with Coltart's view (1996, p. 130) that it is the "spirit" that counts not what sounds "extreme and pious" about the traditional way the steps in the Eightfold Noble Path are set. Buddhism is far from being a negative philosophy of life as it proposes the possibility of radical transformation. Living from this place, the person is more deeply in touch with life, with others and with their environment than if they were embroiled in their own particular concerns. However, there are also obstacles, the five Hindrances, which make it difficult to tread the Path; they are quite similar to what patients bring to therapy.

Psychotherapy offers tools to modify states of unhappiness, conflicts, anxieties and mental discomfort in the patient as they emerge in the here and now of each session. Close attention of the patient— and of the therapist too—may lead to a moment of "O" or "ultimate reality", as Bion called (1970, p. 26) what seems to be something impalpable and beyond thoughts. Something which can only "be", i.e. experienced and apprehended through an "act of faith" and as an intuitive understanding of the "other person's evolving truth" and not just through thinking, as Coltart said (Molino, 1998, p. 177). This state cannot be comprehended through the intellect alone. This requires the therapist to become the patient temporarily, that is, to be at one with him in order to get to "know" the patient at a place below thought and before the therapist re-finds himself. This is called being in projective identification with the patient. True understanding of, and compassion for the patient can flow out of such identification. Coltart describes this as the therapist's capacity to fade out of the picture temporarily (ibid.). We find resonances of this state of union in the Christian mystical tradition. The soul reaches, through love, a state of union with God which is based on pure contemplation and not-yet thinking (Hautmann, 2002).

Emotional thinking as a body–mind experience

The psychodynamic thinking, that inspires many contributors to this book, centres on Bion's ideas and clinical practice. Bion was born in Muttra, India, in 1897 and brought up there for the first eight years of his life. Indian culture, which includes spirituality and mysticism, is likely to have contributed to the knitting of the grid of his thinking. There are some aspects of his thinking, which appear to be closely linked with Buddhism. Although Bion is not known as a mystical analyst, he has many ideas that come close to mysticism and Coltart thought that he was an analyst who "understood about faith and mystical experience" (Molino, 1997, p. 175); Grotstein, writes that Bion "was well informed in religious and spiritual matters" (Grotstein, 2009, p. 312).

When Bion wrote about the mind and thinking, he did not refer purely to cognitive and intellectual concepts, rather to something akin to the Eastern notion of thinking, which includes in its definition of mind and thought the notion of heart and emotions. Thinking, for Bion, implies an "emotional thinking", which is the result of a complex relational and developmental process rooted in the interaction between two people, usually in Bion's thinking a mother and a baby, referred to as the container and the contained (Bion, 1962). Thinking evolves as a process where the mind and body of two people are involved in their totality as they interact. When the infant, having had repeated good experiences of satisfying maternal care, can tolerate the mother's absence temporarily, the infant can have the thought of a satisfying mother even in her absence. By proposing a model of thinking as "emotional thinking" and not as an intellectual function split from the emotional one, Bion overcame the Cartesian, dualistic, Western philosophical tradition and approach to existence, which states that we are because we think, the Latin *Cogito ergo sum*. The Zen Master D. T. Suzuki talks of *kufu*, which he describes as the process "of placing a question in the abdomen and waiting for an answer to come from there" (1959, p. 104). This is "not just thinking with the head, but the state when the whole body is involved in, and applied to the solving of a problem". In this respect, there is a similarity between Bion's and the Buddhist concept of thinking, although the process of thinking evolves in different forms. For the former, the presence of another person to be in relationship with is essential, while the latter does not require nor emphasise such presence.

Mindfulness, suspended attention, and free associations

It seems that what Buddhists call "mindfulness" is similar to what analysts would call "suspended attention". Mindfulness practice, through meditation, is the awareness of the flow of thoughts, feelings, sensations and intuitions as they arise and cease without stopping them or judging them. Observing what goes on in one's sensations and reflecting on one's emotions is a meditative, observing, contemplative state. For example, when we perceive a colour, a sound an image, or any tangible object, we become aware of that object at that moment in time. We see the colour or hear the sound just as it is in its "is-ness", and not for its qualities, uses or functions. Venerable Kusalcitto, quoted by Goleman, writes that: "whatever comes into one's awareness is perceived as just 'a form and a name' where the mind stays neutral no matter what arises in it. You simply recognise whatever comes up for the mind as a natural process, arising and passing, that stays with you for some period of time and then goes away—as it does not stay for ever. And then you can enjoy a state of peace and calm." (Goleman, 2003, pp. 170–171).

Freud encouraged the patient to let their mind wander freely and to report back his free associations and the psychoanalyst to listen to the patient with "evenly suspended attention" (Freud, 1912e, pp. 111–112) during which the critical faculty is suspended, allowing for "impartial attention to everything there is to observe. He should simply listen, and not bother about whether he is keeping anything in mind." Psychoanalyst Sarah Weber writes: "Freud's goal may have had something in common with those of mindfulness meditation: a cultivation of the moment-to-moment awareness of changing perceptions in a neutral, impartial way." Neutrality, she continues: "means seeing things as they are, fully aware of one's perceptions, from a foundation of equanimity and deep acceptance, including physical and emotional pain and even evil" (Weber, 2003, pp. 173–174).

The therapist, too, embraces the patient fully in all his aspects pertaining mind and body and psychoanalyst Joseph Bobrow (2003, p. 214) links the two traditions as he writes: "a profoundly accepting, inclusive attitude towards all our internal experience, a non-judgemental approach, is a hallmark both of the analyst's free-floating attention and of Buddhist mindfulness". In addition, Freud, by encouraging the patient to free associate, fostered mindfulness and a capacity to observe one's internal processes.

xxviii PROLOGUE

Reverie, containment, and transformation

The practice of meditation, as described above, leads to a widening of one's awareness via the observation of one's breath, body sensations and mind activities—such as feeling, thinking, remembering etc. During this practice, which is a life-long project or, as Buddhists might say, a project for many lifetimes, a continuous transformation of bodily sensations, emotions and mental activities occurs and this limits and eventually brings to an end the unhappiness they bring to the self and to others. Depending on one's level of meditation practice, emotions can be observed after they have arisen and been expressed, and the consequences they give rise to can be seen and evaluated. If one becomes aware of them as they arise, and allows them just to come and go, then they need not trigger a subsequent chain of thoughts or actions, they simply come and go. "The Tibetan word for meditation means in fact 'familiarisation'. One becomes familiar through practice of seeing thoughts come and go" (Ricard, 2003, p. 84). Matthieu Ricard in his dialogue with the Dalai Lama says: "then, when you are quite experienced, the final state comes. Even before an emotion might arise, you are ready in such a way that it will not arise with the same compelling, enslaving power. This step is linked to realisation, a state of achieved transformation, where the destructive emotions don't arise with nearly the same strength" (ibid.). This does not mean that we repress our emotions, far from it, but it means meeting them or pre-empting them with a reflective inner dialogue that helps us understand their true nature, their insubstantial nature.

A mother, who is going to give birth to a baby, and the baby, who is being born, have an experience of pain and suffering, along with the mother's joy at bringing her child into the world. Suffering is a component of what is the most common and natural life event that we all experience. The environment usually brings relief to the experience of birth, which is often referred to as the first trauma. The baby can be helped in the transition from uterine life to being born. The mother, too, can be helped in her experience of giving life. In other words, transformation and reparation occur for them both. In these most ordinary circumstances of birth-giving, both parties recover and their suffering is contained and transformed. In normal circumstances, calmness is re-established. However, new and inevitable tensions and needs soon arise in the baby—even when all goes well between mother and child—hunger, cold, bodily and emotional discomforts so closely linked together, stir up the baby. The mother, when well supported by the environment, partner, family and friends, attends to the baby's needs, by satisfying and soothing them and bringing joy to her baby. She can thus modify her baby's needs and tensions, help transform them and restore a state of calmness and happiness in her baby and in herself. A new cycle of ordinary suffering, containment, and transformation into a need-free and happy state, has occurred. The mother performs reverie with her infant. Something similar happens in the psychotherapeutic process. The nature of the setting facilitates the emergence of the patient's difficulties, for which he has originally sought help. The therapist offers himself to the process, that is, as a whole person with mind and body, which is aware, thinks, feels and perceives conscious and unconscious communications from the patient. The therapist performs a function of reverie and transformation similar to that of the mother.

A very comprehensive definition of reverie is by psychoanalyst Joseph Bobrow (2003, p. 211) in a chapter where he explores the complementarities between Buddhism and psychoanalysis. "Reverie is a resonating process. The mother, using all channels, knows the infant's state within the matrix of her entire being. Her intuitive responses, co-arise with, and are not separate from this knowledge. A living, vibrating emotional field takes place." This field of "emotional interconnectiveness stimulates the growth of neuronal connections in the brain essential for affective life and creative thinking. Body and mind work seamlessly together." Grotstein, in his commentary to the above chapter, elaborates as follows: "The mother, in a state of reverie, which is tantamount to meditation, is enabled to use her 'dream-work alpha' (alpha function) to understand her infant" (2003, p. 225). Bion suggests that—continues Grotstein—"for the mother and the analyst to obtain reverie, they must abandon memory, desire, understanding, preconceptions and all the other forms of sensuous attachment to objects". Grotstein explores how, according to Bion, the mother employs her alpha function with her infant. "The mother both (a) meditatively attunes, matches, symmetrises with, and 'becomes' the distressed infant (transformation in 'O') and (b) translates, (transduces, reflects upon) this experience as to impart meaning to it so it becomes a pragmatic realisation in regard to the caretaking of her infant" (ibid., p. 226). Thus, one could say that Bion implied that the mother must employ the functioning of both cerebral hemispheres while attending to her infant with her reverie.

The mother and the therapist in a state of reverie are indeed separate, respectively from the baby and the patient and continue to think. However, there is a moment in the session, Grotstein says it clearly, when the therapist is temporarily taken over by the stories told by the patient, by the projections and the atmosphere of the here-and-now. This moment of "becoming" the other, of being in union or at unison with the patient and before thinking is resumed, is akin to a mystical moment and the process leading to it is akin to the process of meditation There is a link between reverie, projective identification and mystical union at that particular moment in the therapeutic encounter.

In Buddhism, a lot of the work of transformation is done by the individual within oneself and in the context of a training practice, in addition to the work done within the spiritual community, called Sangha. This usually includes a master or a teacher, who performs a similar function to that of the mother with her baby or of the therapist with a patient. They all assist and guide the individual in their developmental path, their emotional, existential, and spiritual journey. However, one difference from psychoanalysis is that in Buddhism the transference is neither taken into consideration, nor analysed nor thought about.

The four attitudes, called *Brama-vihara*, foster the process of reverie, containment and transformation of negative or unwholesome states of mind. These attitudes or personal dispositions that become the object of meditation and daily practice are: loving kindness (*metta*) or unconditional love like the love of a mother for her only child; compassion (*karuna*) for even the most disturbing and repelling aspects of oneself, others and life; sympathetic joy (*mudita*) in others' success and happiness; equanimity (*upekkha*) in one's disposition towards oneself, others and life's vicissitudes. These are qualities that are also part of the therapist's tool-kit and broaden the capacity to embrace the whole patient and optimise clinical work.

In the dialogues to follow in this book, a particular emphasis will be placed on the work of infant, child, and adolescent psychotherapists as they are exposed to very primitive states of being in their patients, that is, to developmentally early stages in the forming of the mind–body whole. Body and mind are closely interconnected in the baby and within the relationship with the mother. By attending to the physical needs of the baby, the mother also nourishes the emotions in her baby and in their relationship, similarly to what the therapist does with the patient in the practice of psychotherapy. Buddhism notices the "stark aspects" of the person and the sensations, primitive emotions, and thoughts presenting during the practice of meditation. In this respect, too, there is a close link between the two practices.

References

Bion, W. R. (1962). A theory of thinking. In: *Second Thoughts* (pp. 110–119). London: Maresfield Reprints.

Bion, W. R. (1970). *Attention and Interpretation*. London: Tavistock.

Bobrow, J. (2003). Moments of truth—truths of moment. In: J. D. Safran (Ed.), *Psychoanalysis and Buddhism* (pp. 199–249). Boston: Wisdom.

Chödrön, P. (1997). *When Things Fall Apart*. London: Element.

Coltart, N. (1987). The practice of Buddhism and psycho-analysis. *The Middle Way, 62(2)*: 91–96.

Coltart, N. (1996). *The Baby and the Bathwater*. London: Karnac.

Eigen, M. (1998). *The Psychoanalytic Mystic*. London, New York: Free Association Books.

Epstein, M. (1998). Beyond the oceanic feeling: psychoanalytic study of Buddhist meditation. In: A. Molino (Ed.), *The Couch and the Tree* (pp. 119–130). London: Constable.

Fleischman, P. R. (1986). The therapeutic action of Vipassana: why I sit. N. 329/330: 1–45. Sri Lanka: The Wheel Publication.

Freud, S. (1912e). *Recommendations to physicians practising psycho-analysis*. SE, 12, pp. 109–120. London: Hogarth.

Fromm, E. (1960). Psychoanalysis and Zen Buddhism. In: A. Molino (Ed.), *The Couch and the Tree* (pp. 65–71). London: Constable, 1998.

Goleman, D. (2003a). Our potential for change. In: D. Goleman (narrator), *Destructive Emotions and How Can We Overcome Them: A Dialogue with the Dalai Lama* (pp. 205–234). London: Bloomsbury.

Goleman, D. (2003b). Cultivating emotional balance. In: D. Goleman (narrator), *Destructive Emotions and How Can We Overcome Them: A Dialogue with the Dalai Lama* (pp. 157–176). London: Bloomsbury.

Grotstein, J. S. (2003). East is East and West is West and ne'er the twain shall meet (or shall they?). In: J. D. Safran (Ed.), *Psychoanalysis and Buddhism* (pp. 221–229). Boston: Wisdom.

Grotstein, J. S. (2009). The clinical instruments of Dr Bion's treatment bag. In: *But at the Same Time and on Another Level* (pp. 327–338). London: Karnac.

Hautman, G. (2002). Sviluppi bioniani ed alcune forme religiose della Mente. In: *Funzione analitica e mente primitiva* (pp. 343–350). Pisa: Edizione ETS.

Molino, A. (1997). Nina Coltart. In: *Freely Associated* (pp. 165–211). London/New York: Free Association Books.

Molino, A. (1998). Slouching towards Buddhism: a conversation with Nina Coltart In: *The Couch and the Tree* (pp. 170–179). London: Constable.

Powrie, R. (2010, 2012). Presentation given at the World Association of Infant Mental Health in Leipzig and Cape Town.

Rahula, W. (1959). The Fourth Noble Truth. In: *What the Buddha Taught* (pp. 45–50). London, Bedford: The Gordon Fraser Gallery.

Ricard, M. (2003). A Buddhist psychology. In: D. Goleman (narrator), *Destructive Emotions and How Can We Overcome Them: A Dialogue with the Dalai Lama* (pp. 72–86). London: Bloomsbury.

Shannahoff-Khalsa, D. S. (2010). *Kundalini Yoga Meditation for Complex Psychiatric Disorders*. New York, London: W. W. Norton.

Suzuki, D. T. (1959). Zen and swordsmanship. In: *Zen and Japanese Culture* (pp. 87–136). New York: Pantheon.

Thich Nhat Hanh (1991). Seminando nell'inconscio. *Paramita, 37(1)*: 45–52.

Vipassana Research Institute (1997). *Doing Time, Doing Vipassana*. www.prison.dhamma.org. DVD available at email address: bookstore@pariyatti.org.

Weber, S. L. (2003). An analyst's surrender. In: J. Safran (Ed.), *Psychoanalysis and Buddhism* (pp. 169–197). Boston: Wisdom.

Welwood, J. (1983). On psychotherapy and meditation. In: *Awakening the Heart* (pp. 43–54). Boston, MA, and London: New Science Library.

INTRODUCTION

The seed of *The Buddha and the Baby* started to take shape when, in the late eighties having finished my training as a child and adolescent psychotherapist, I discovered meditation in the Theravada Buddhist tradition and noticed the many similarities, complementarities and also differences between psychoanalytic psychotherapy and Buddhism. Antony Molino's book *The Couch and the Tree* has inspired me in the choice of both the format and the title for this book, which, then, began.

In interviewing the contributors, I have noticed a common line of thinking over questions such as attachment, no self, emptiness, and so on, a thread that runs along people's ideas and clinical practices. However, each interview will reveal specific vertices and unique aspects, which make these dialogues so deep, interesting, and enlightening.

My gratitude goes to these fellow travellers for having given their time and heart to share their professional, personal and spiritual path by talking with me. Buddhism and psychotherapy, when harmoniously combined, seem to have informed the professional stance of quite a few people, indeed like a guiding parental couple offering the backdrop to one's existence.

xxxiv   INTRODUCTION

I feel privileged, enriched and more knowledgeable for having actualised the vision of compiling this book.

The issue of confidentiality has been explored in depth with the interviewees, who are happy about the clinical vignettes, disguised and not identifiable, as well as with the few personal details revealed in the book.

CHAPTER ONE

A baby is born

Dialogue with Claudia Goulder

Live the questions now. Perhaps you will then gradually, without even noticing it, live along some distant day into the answers.

—Rainer Maria Rilke, 1903

MP: Claudia, I am delighted that this first interview for this collection of dialogues entitled *The Buddha and the Baby* takes place with a five-day-old baby in your arms: she is your first baby peacefully cradled in your body just like the Buddha, who was the first child in his family. I am grateful that you have agreed to this conversation at such short notice and so soon after the birth of Imogen. This is the first dialogue for this newly born project of a book. I have read the paper you have written and kindly sent me on "Cultivating the observer within: a meditation on the links between yoga and psychoanalytic thinking", and I was very interested on the concept of bodily countertransference and how you apply it in your work with children. You are clearly very tuned in with what the body expresses, having practised yoga for twelve years.

CG: Yes, I have taught yoga as an amateur way to children in a primary school and adolescents in a special unit. I did breathing exercises with them. You know, I'm using it more and more, and during my pregnancy there was a strong body countertransference; I've noticed that my body talked first to the children patients. There were so many patients who picked up on my pregnancy before it was at all visible.

MP: Perhaps also before you knew?

CG: I knew very early on, within a week. There is this metallic flavour in your mouth, and quite a number of pregnant women had that, and it is not something that Western doctors can explain what that is. My patients picked up and, that's the thing, you don't know whether they pick up on you knowing and acting differently, but I felt it was a bodily thing as well. They are very perceptive, more perceptive than adults, and may have noticed the fullness of my face, I don't quite know.

MP: How mysteriously interesting! I once heard of a borderline patient being discussed in a seminar with John Steiner, who said that such patients usually know even before the therapist does know she is pregnant. That particular patient was already acting out something about the therapist's pregnancy, which she could not make sense of, as she did not know she was pregnant then! It is the hypersensitivity that psychotic patients have and animals still have just like little children do; they somehow sniff it!

CG: It's such a mysterious thing!

MP: I am thinking of how they find the reincarnation of a new Dalai Lama, by showing some of his objects to small children, whom they have cues may be the reincarnation of the deceased Dalai Lama. It's uncanny and fascinating to see how the next lama relates to these objects or even to physical places, as if they knew them or had been there already, don't they?

CG: I don't know what to make of this idea of reincarnation, but in my family there are a few examples of members dying just before a new baby is born, and so it happened with my baby too, born a few hours before a great auntie died.

MP: Life and death are so mysteriously interconnected!

CG: I am just thinking of a sort of dream I had last week after coming home with the baby, I woke up feeling "I am the baby" and my hormones told me, of course, that I had to breastfeed, but I also felt "where is my feed?". There is something about feeling like a baby and feeling the baby as well as feeling a mother; and I feel, it's very hard to explain, but I am even moving like the baby at times; then I remember I need to feed the baby.

MP: Perhaps you are in touch with you when you were a baby, as well as being in a fusional state of unity with your baby? You feel so identified with your baby in Winnicott's description of "maternal pre-occupation" that you become the baby temporarily, don't you?

CG: That's absolutely as it feels. Even in pregnancy, my husband said he'd never seen that face before; it was completely, yes there is fear and helplessness, but it was also, I think I really did, even though I was about to become a mother, I was a child. It's like a bubble now, but it was something, part regression, but it was something, I don't know what to make of it; I definitely felt very identified with baby parts.

MP: We see it in parent–infant psychotherapy: when parents have a baby they re-live their babyhood and childhood and that's where the unresolved issues of those early times pop up in the present time. That's where I see a link with meditation, which brings up very primitive issues as well as bodily stuff. It brings up the most primitive unconscious, which is made of bodily sensations as well as protomental elements.

CG: When things bubble up in meditation and yoga, you observe them with awareness but do not try to do anything with it, and that's quite different with what you do with the unconscious as a psychotherapist, when you see it expressed by the child in play, drawings, movements, etc. We verbalise the unconscious that emerges in the child's play activities or dreams, when they do tell us dreams, don't we?

MP: Yes, now look at your baby, sucking blissfully at your breast and also absorbing your peace of mind at this moment! The Buddha and the baby seem to connect: the Buddha being a wise, old sage with great wisdom but also perhaps looking like a baby, with the

4   THE BUDDHA AND THE BABY

simplicity and naturalness of the baby as well as the connection with the instincts and the primitive aspects of life. Also the blissful state of some images of the Buddha is so often compared with that of a baby at his best moments. He's happy as a Buddha—you often hear people say about babies with a full, round belly, satisfied after a good feed!

CG: Yes, breastfeeding feels like an absolute connection, a life support for the baby.

MP: Well, I'd like to ask you about these two choices in your life, that of being a Buddhist and a child psychotherapist, and whether either has a link with your family of origin.

CG: I have found Buddhism by practising yoga at the same time when I started my own psychotherapy, yes, before I started to train. I did not come from a family of Buddhists or psychotherapists but from a family where there was always a lot of doing and not much time just to be. When I left home, I did not know how to just be with myself really, or be in life without something to do. I am thinking of D. H. Lawrence, who wrote quite a lot about people who live in their body and people who live in their head and implied that the people were happier or lived truly when guided by their animal instinct. So that idea was interesting to me. Then I started to do yoga and went to a yoga centre and they did T'ai Chi and meditation, so a bit of everything. I really enjoyed it, and it helped me to be with other people who could sit in silence and I did not feel guilty for it. Perhaps a year later, I started my own psychotherapy and felt guilty about that and what did I get from it, and, was I wasting time? But my therapist sanctioned that. I was coming from journalism, which is very much working with deadlines, and was very much in line with my family style. My mother fostered children, so as well as my other three sisters, there were always a lot of people in the house: it was a very happy and loving childhood, but we were always doing things. I learnt from going to therapy that you get a lot of different things. It has been ten years of slowing down, and yoga again is like a sanctioned time out of all of that; there is something about stepping onto the yoga mat; suddenly, you are in a zone where you just are.

MP: It's like stepping onto the cushion, the meditation cushion, I imagine.

CG: I hesitate to say that I am a Buddhist because I have found the Buddhist philosophy through practising yoga and through teachers who are deeply rooted in Buddhism, who have thrown out seeds in classes that I have taken and been piecing them together but have not formally studied it.

MP: Do you have an object of meditation in your practice?

CG: Not really, just the breath. I don't know if what I said explains how I got there: therapy, yoga, meditation, yes, they were born more or less at the same time.

MP: Similarly to today's multiple births: the very recent birth of your baby, this conversation and the birth of this book. But … listen … the baby is now making herself heard: she's breathing and we were talking about breathing, just now.

CG: The baby forces you to live in the present: there's nothing in my diary now; the baby is in the present, has no mind about yesterday or tomorrow.

MP: It's very Buddhist: only the now exists, no past, no present, they are just in the mind but only the now exists and it is now.

CG: The Buddha and the baby again, I assume the Buddha—of all beings—was able to be in the present. He probably went full circle. The baby starts in the present and then gradually becomes like the rest of us, worried about time, past and present.

MP: Yes, that is another interesting link between the Buddha and the baby! Now, what about your practice of yoga and meditation, how do you think they are influencing and affecting your practice as a child psychotherapist and vice versa?

CG: I think it's in the attitude. Breathing is quite important and I obviously have to keep notice of my countertransference: some patients make you tighten your breath or shorten it or make you feel headachy, you know, a physical kind of reaction and transference. My practice of yoga, Buddhist-oriented, is based on listening to the inner observer, which helped me think about patients in the

6   THE BUDDHA AND THE BABY

session and metabolise what's gone on and go back to the next session with a kind of clearer mind.

MP: Nina Coltart talks about "bare attention" and how the meditation helped her to be focused in the here and now of the session and of the moment (Coltart, 1996).

CG: Yes, it's almost like the practice that takes practice; it's the same thing that you do when you do breathing meditation, that is, tune into the breath and practice that over and over. The same with psychotherapy: it's a practice and you do it over and over.

MP: Do you use any of your yoga and meditation technique with your patients as yet?

CG: No, not really, but I would like to, at some point, integrate the two somehow.

MP: Psychiatrist Ros Powrie from Australia (Chapter Two in this book) has been running groups for perinatally depressed mothers using mindfulness and has achieved amazing results in reducing maternal perinatal mental disturbances. She talks about that in a later conversation in this book. Also in India, they have tried to teach Vipassana meditation in prison (*Doing Time, Doing Vipassana*, 1997) and have achieved unimaginable changes in callous prisoners, who have been able to take responsibility for their actions, to grieve for their crimes and the damaged caused and to truly repair. In Kleinian terms, they have moved from a paranoid and persecuted state of mind into a more depressive and reparatory one (Klein, 1926–1961).

MP: Moving onto another question, how do you reconcile the ideas of ego development, the Buddhist non-ego, and attachment and non-attachment?

CG: I suppose I reconcile these key Buddhist ideas with psychoanalytic concepts by interpreting them in a certain non-literal way. To me, although Buddhism rejects the notion of a permanent self, I am not sure it rejects the notion of an empirical self composed of constantly changing feelings, thoughts, and sensations. One can have thoughts and observe those thoughts, and even let them

A BABY IS BORN 7

pass, without being defined by them. I read the idea of "no-self" as an ideal, a state of being that is free from the heaviness or burden of being one thing, defined wholly by one's thoughts or actions. I also see all individuals as more than just a self or an ego, but a small part of a greater sphere, in which we are all rooted and through which we all connect. So while we have individual selves, we are also ever-changing vessels within a wider and more powerful context. I do not think this jars or clashes with psychoanalytic concepts of ego; in fact, I think it helps by thinking about individuals as all connected on another level by a force greater than the individual ego or mind.

MP: This is interesting and links with the Buddhist idea of interconnectedness. Do you think it does relate to your work as a child psychotherapist?

CG: As therapists, we arrive to our work with the whole of ourselves and with the backdrop of how we are on that day, let alone arriving with no memory or desires! (Bion, 1967). If our suffering is too close to the surface, then we cannot help patients much. Hence our analysis and training help us keep a right balance of suffering. In the past few weeks, I have started back to work after one year of being on maternity leave (this is the revised version of our dialogue started about a year earlier), and I have been in touch with my vulnerability at going back but that was helpful as I did not feel too porous. The mother–baby relationship is at the forefront of my mind: and I compare this to the therapist–patient relationship. What is important is to take in the child's projections without being pulled and pushed too much: just allow oneself to suffer to some degree then you need to have your protection or you won't be any longer helpful but flooded with projections. Thinking of attachment, that is a difficult one as the two ideas seem quite contrasting, don't they? We do attach, for example, to my yoga teacher repeating a mantra or some interesting thought: the unconscious does attach. If you say: "Stay calm, don't attach", it doesn't mean that you can do it. The wish to do it doesn't necessary lead to success.

MP: We do want our child patients to attach to us as therapists and to develop an attachment, which—if that child suffers from a

8   THE BUDDHA AND THE BABY

particular dysfunctional attachment—can then be hopefully modified into a healthier one.

CG: I do struggle with that notion as Buddhism doesn't say: "Do not attach", it says "Let go", but that's not easy either. It is important for patients to jump into life and the relationship with the therapist, but then it's necessary to step back, to be separate. That's how I would conceptualise this idea in my work with children: to help them attach and then dis-attach and let go of the therapist.

MP: Well, perhaps this is a good moment to dis-attach from this conversation and to end, with many thanks, Claudia, for sharing with me and the reader some intimate moments of your life as a mother and therapist.

References

Bion, W. R. (1967). Notes on memory and desire. *Psycho-Analytic Forum, 2*: 272–273; 279–280.

Coltart, N. (1996). Buddhism and psychoanalysis revisited. *The Baby and the Bathwater*. London: Karnac.

Goulder, C. (2012). Cultivating the observer within: A meditation on the links between yoga and psychoanalytic thinking. Unpublished paper.

Klein, M. (1926–1961). *The Writings of Melanie Klein, Vol. 1–4*. London: Hogarth and the Institute of Psycho-Analysis.

Rilke, R. M. (1903). *Letters to a Young Poet*. Letter n. 4. London: W. W. Norton, 2004.

Vipassana Research Institute (1997). *Doing Time, Doing Vipassana*. www. prison.dhamma.org. DVD available at email address: bookstore@ pariyatti.org.

CHAPTER TWO

Let us allow to arrive: bringing into being

Dialogue with Rosalind Powrie

You can be normal without being alive.

—D. W. Winnicott

MP: It's a real privilege that you have agreed to talk with me about Buddhism and psychotherapy here, on the top of Table Mountain in Cape Town, which is at this moment surrounded by mist but, still, it's an extraordinary meeting point between Australia and England. We are both here for the World Association of Infant Mental Health biannual Congress, where we have run a workshop on our therapeutic work with mothers and babies, a work informed also by a Buddhist, meditative stance. It seems to me the right place and the right time to talk about this.

RP: Yes, and the mist will clear up. After all, it is impermanent!

MP: This is a good start to our conversation, indeed, and I would like to begin by asking you about these two choices in your life: one, to be a child and adolescent psychiatrist, who treats pregnant mothers with depression or at risk of mental health problems, and the other is to practise meditation and be interested in Buddhism.

10   THE BUDDHA AND THE BABY

How did you come to Buddhism in your life, and do you come from a religious, perhaps a Buddhist, family yourself?

RP: No, my family weren't religious at all; in fact, my father was a professed atheist, but I believe that was probably a reaction to being the eldest child of five and been brought up Seventh Day Adventist. So, I remember in my childhood getting a lot of messages from my paternal grandparents about God and their particular beliefs, you know, which even as a child, I thought were unkind and rather harsh. Well, not unkind, but I thought there was a lot more of punishment than kindness in the teaching, you know. I received a lot of stories in the form of children's books about morality and what was good behaviour. There was not much else in it, and so I never took it particularly seriously. But, on the other hand, my paternal grandparents were very, very kind people just by their manner and demeanour, and I loved them deeply. So, maybe that made more of an impression on me than their belief system. I remember as a child my father saying to us: "You don't have to believe in anything, you make up your mind when you grow up, about what you want to believe." So he wasn't saying: "Don't believe in anything", but "You make up your mind." I thought it was incredibly liberating.

MP: What about your mother?

RP: My mother was raised an Anglican, I think, and we went to church a few times as children to Sunday School, but that was entirely boring for me and I did not get anything at all from it. Then my father died when I was quite young, eleven, and that was a very difficult time in my life all through adolescence, so by the time I got to my early twenties, when I started university, I was looking for something that would hold me and get me through difficult moments. I believe I was looking for something that would make sense of what was happening to me in my dark moods, my feelings of isolation, my terrible fits of anxiety, about not succeeding, the struggle about what I was doing, whether I was happy doing what I was doing, you know, I was quite torn at times.

MP: Was that linked with the death of your father?

LET US ALLOW TO ARRIVE   11

RP: Probably linked with that and the struggle of growing up without a father, in a large family with my mother also struggling very much.

MP: Do you have any brother or sister?

RP: I have two older brothers and a younger brother and sister, so a family of five, and I am in the middle: the seesaw, I am the fulcrum.

MP: Hence your choice of profession!

RP: Well, my personality and position in the family, in the sibling group, somehow, I came to see myself in this way, as needing to balance things and be the listener, I think, because I was more the listener than I was the talker. Also, because I was the older daughter, my mother, in her grief, somewhat relied on me, and that influenced me. Then in my early twenties, I became interested in transcendental meditation. By the way, my brothers by this stage, in their adolescence—they were three and four years older than me—got involved with a young Indian guru, who had quite a big following. It was during that time, that Western youth were interested in Eastern religions. Anyway, my brothers couldn't convince me to follow their guru, I felt they were pushing something onto me which I resisted, so I didn't go along with what they were inviting me to do, which was very difficult because they were very devoted. It was quite frightening to me at that time—I think I was about sixteen—to think that my brothers were so intensely involved in this. It was too foreign for me. But when I was about twenty or twenty-one, I did some meditation with a transcendental meditation teacher in Adelaide and, when you've been meditating for a particular period you come with gifts to the teacher and are given your mantra and then off you go, practise for the rest of your life.

MP: Is that the meditation you are still practising, using the mantra?

RP: No, I've actually forgotten the mantra, but during my twenties and thirties, I would go back to this at times of extreme distress. It was like my safety net I would go to at times, but I would not practise regularly.

12   THE BUDDHA AND THE BABY

MP: So your interest goes back quite early on in your adolescence with your brothers also being interested in this type of spirituality.

RP: Yes, I guess so, I haven't thought of it like that but I think there was that influence. Also, I was very interested in existentialism—typical adolescent—and I started reading the French existentialists and became very enamoured with Simone de Beauvoir and Jean-Paul Sartre and asking that question: What is the meaning of life? And how did I get involved with Buddhism? I've always been very interested in the body and when I got very ill with a neurological condition about twelve years ago—where your breathing can be totally affected in the most serious cases—I started more intensely taking up yoga and also going to Buddha House, which was a Tibetan Buddhist temple in my city, and did a few retreats, and started reading a lot more about Tibetan Buddhism. By the way, my brothers had also been interested in Buddhism, in their early adulthood and I had read a bit of *The Tibetan Book of the Dead* (1927) and things like that, so it was at the back of my head. But as a way of trying to recover and think about why I got so ill and what was happening in my life, I started reading more. It was not until my illness that I think I began to more seriously take it up; then I started doing retreats with a particular teacher some five years ago, and at the same time I started learning about this particular incorporation of mindfulness teaching in mental health settings.

MP: Yes, would you please say more about this joint enterprise, which I have heard you talking about in our joint workshops at WAIMH congresses.

RP: I did the mindfulness-based cognitive therapy (MBCT) classes as a participant, and then further training in order to teach these classes.

MP: How long did that training last?

RP: It was for eight weeks, two hours a week. So here was an interesting integration of a traditional mental health intervention: cognitive therapy and bringing mindfulness to this. I had done some training in dialectical behaviour therapy, which is also an integration between Eastern spiritual ideas with behavioural

LET US ALLOW TO ARRIVE   13

techniques. This was originated by Marsha Linehan (1993) and part of this training teaches something called "radical acceptance of suffering", of what is happening in the here and now.

MP: Quite different from your grandparents' strict religious background, by the sound of it.

RP: DBT is a therapy for borderline personality disorder and it teaches distress tolerance through mindful practice, body work, acceptance of what is, and some behavioural self-soothing and regulation techniques. Acceptance and commitment therapy (ACT), is another therapy incorporating mindfulness. These therapies are known as the "third wave" of mental health therapies.

MP: This differentiation is interesting and new to me.

RP: So these three therapies: DBT (Linehan, 1993), MBCT (Segal et al., 2012), and ACT (Hayes et al., 2003) all have similar kind of focus on this idea of being present in the here and now, using mindfulness techniques to reduce psychological symptoms of suffering and distress.

MP: When you teach mindfulness, what do you exactly mean by mindfulness?

RP: Well, it's one of the foundational teachings of Buddhist psychology and philosophy; it's a form of mind training, where through meditation and mindfulness practices, for instance, mindful walking, eating, and so on, one learns to more fully be aware and pay attention to the present with non-judgement and kindness towards our experiences, whatever they are.

MP: It's awareness, isn't it?

RP: It's a form of training of one's attention to certain objects, it's being present and focusing on one thing at a time with gentleness and compassion towards our experience, and through that training we are able to develop greater awareness of what's happening in our thoughts, feelings, and body.

MP: Being full of mind versus mind-less, I suppose.

RP: Yes, being aware of where we are, who we are with, and what is happening; this is Thich Nhat Hanh (Vietnamese Buddhist monk

14   THE BUDDHA AND THE BABY

and writer) definition, which I like, because mindfulness has a relational component not just an intrapersonal one; it's not just about looking into ourselves and being aware of what's happening in us. It also has a component of being aware of our relationships with other people, the environment, and the rest of the world.

MP: This is very important as one of the criticisms of Buddhism is that it is too individualistic, too intra-directed.

RP: Perhaps that idea that it is very individual comes from the archetype of retreat and the monk or nun in the cave meditating for years and years and years to understand the nature of reality. But in most cases monks did not stay in caves but came out and lived in the world in a different way. Even the English nun, Tenzin Palmo, who spent many years in a cave in the Himalaya, had a book written on her experience, and now she has established a nunnery. She is also very focused on changing the gender inequality in Buddhist teaching (McKenzie, 2008). The interpretation of Dharma has been so influenced over the years by cultural systems and the original teaching sometimes gets obscured by layers of other stuff, I mean traditionally, I think, it's been the men who passed down the knowledge and the teaching. The women in Buddhist monasteries have not been given the same access to the teaching nor the power.

MP: Yes, they had serious difficulties recently over this issue in some Theravada monasteries in England and many nuns have now disrobed due to this inequality. But to go back to your work: I find your application of mindfulness to your practice as a psychiatrist very interesting and fascinating. Can you tell me more?

RP: There is so much cross-over between some of the ideas and concepts in Buddhist philosophy and what we know of being with someone else and intersubjective experience and psychoanalytic concepts. There are so many similarities, say, between the way we pay attention in therapy, the "bare attention" Nina Coltart refers to (Coltart, 1992) and meditative experiences. The groups I am running with my colleagues are for pregnant mothers who are at risk of anxiety, depression, and psychological distress in general. They are screened at the first maternity visit as having risk factors for depression or currently having symptoms. We invite them to

LET US ALLOW TO ARRIVE   15

join the classes after an interview and discussion about what the classes aim to do and what the benefits may be but also that there may be some risks.

MP: How do these first classes work?

RP: The class goes for two hours; people are welcomed, are given a handout each class in terms of the teaching we are doing and CDs of the meditations so they get guided meditations, which we also teach in classes. We clarify that it is not group therapy, but at the same time we need to apply group therapy principles of course, about the dynamic of the group, and make sure that things don't get out of hand, and one person does not begin to dominate. This is all discussed in the pre-class interview and in the beginning of the course. But really the core of it is teaching meditation, it's experiential and also teaching about the links between thoughts, feelings, and bodily sensations as in cognitive behaviour therapy.

MP: You mean they become aware of their thoughts and sensations as one does during meditation?

RP: Yes, and how they are linked, how a certain thought may lead to an immediate tummy reaction, a feeling in the body or an emotion, and in this way the women begin to discover what their own habits of mind are; what they continually seem to go round and round with.

MP: Is it that, for example, the thought that their baby may be damaged may lead to a state of anxiety and fear?

RP: Yes, and that can then be associated with other kinds of anxieties if, for example, they will be ready in time for the baby or will their partner support them; it might go back even further to earlier anxieties, the previous "ghosts in the nursery" (Fraiberg, Adelson & Shapiro, 1975). We don't interpret these; we just really help them to be aware of their own mental phenomena which arise during the meditations. And if women choose to make insightful statements, that's fine, and we will accept them and congratulate them for having made those links; we congratulate people for just being aware of what's going on, not for changes. These women are so keen to get rid of unpleasant feelings and solve problems before

16   THE BUDDHA AND THE BABY

the baby arrives, but we say this is not what the class is about. And that's a great challenge for anyone, let alone for a woman who's about to have a baby!

MP: And also we know that changes occur once we accept fully the reality of our anxiety, stress, etc., which then pass and changes can occur, rather than us fighting against reality.

RP: Yes, and getting into a struggle about how things should be or how they are and this is the subject of a lot of discussions in the group, this idea of stopping the struggle in themselves, stopping the judgement, and the proliferation of thoughts that come from such struggle.

MP: Yes, the monkey minds, as the Buddhists call the mind that cannot stay still for any length of time!

RP: Yes, and also we've woven in more components around teaching about self-compassion, as women often are the first to criticise themselves and judge and feel ridden with guilt. In this society, people are striving to be better and are constantly conditioned to evaluate themselves against other people; in this individual-based culture, we are more prone to self-hatred than possibly in an Eastern, community-based society.

MP: You told me that there is a high success rate in reduction of anxiety, and depression with these groups; can you say a bit more?

RP: So far, in the small evaluation we have done, it is so, but we haven't compared the results in women doing these classes with other brief interventions (currently underway) known to reduce depression and anxiety. So far, we have done evaluations up to six weeks postnatally and we have done qualitative evaluations. The women also found benefits a few months down the track after they've had their baby. This is their reporting of their subjective changes. But there are many other studies in other adult populations, showing that mindfulness-based cognitive therapy and like therapies and teachings are mental-health promoting. They have kept people well, even people with serious mental illnesses: it's about their attitude towards their illnesses and an improved sense of balance in life; perhaps learning about equanimity.

LET US ALLOW TO ARRIVE   17

MP: Do they help with non-identification with their illnesses, I mean: I am me and have this condition but it is not the whole of me?

RP: Yes, I am not, for example, a depressed person in my totality. This is something I struggle with from time to time, just like suffering from a physical condition: asthma, diabetes, bad back, etc., but it's not the whole of the experience.

MP: Can we link this attitude to the concept or experience of no-self, I mean, if I don't identify with my illness, and there is something more than me having an illness or being cold now, for example?

RP: I can only give an explanation of how I understand this and not a scholarly explanation as I very much struggle with this idea of no-self. I think it is related to the Buddhist idea that I construct my world, we construct our experiences, which are all, in a sense, illusory, which is a bit mind-blowing and mind-shattering: once I understand that actually, what I see, hear, and feel is illusionary in some sense, so is this idea of a self, this idea of me.

MP: Illusory?

RP: It's ephemeral, it changes, it's not static, it's not solid, it's not what it seems.

MP: It comes and goes, in this sense it's an illusion, perhaps?

RP: Yes, and this is the basis of dependent arising: it's the idea that if you watch and observe your experience long enough in meditation practice, you find that all experiences are in a state of dynamism and change. So nothing is the same from moment to moment, and that is a very hard concept for a human brain to grasp because we live as if things are the same, we want them to be the same and not to change.

MP: It gives us a sense of security we feel so lost, otherwise!

RP: We have to live in a world where we, in a sense, can lean on the fact that things are solid for a moment, to work in it but in other ways it is illusory.

MP: Back to babies and mothers, you help them to have a better start in life. You spoke of bringing into being in your presentation here at the WAIMH Congress, what do you exactly mean?

18   THE BUDDHA AND THE BABY

RP: There are two parts to that: bringing into being as being a parent bringing a child to life, to have a being and to be in a relationship, but there is also the parallel meaning of meditation, which in its derivation from the ancient Pali language (the language in which the original Buddhist texts were written) means: bringing into being or cultivating. It's bringing awareness into being. Bringing into being is about becoming aware. Buddhist practice and mindfulness helps us to move beyond the solid world: this is a rock, this is you and me. There are various levels of experience of reality we might work with in psychotherapy, from the concrete world and external reality to the representational world and then the capacity to reflect on these: a reflective position towards one's experience. Mindfulness developed through meditation can take us one step further. We go from the representational world and reflective self to a mindful self that can be aware of being aware, meta-awareness. And that is where the idea of no-self comes in, who is being aware of being aware?

MP: Yes, who is that? Is it awareness?

RP: It's not-me.

MP: Have you ever had an experience of no-self of being aware of no-self?

RP: Rare glimpses sometimes during meditation retreats; it's like a flash, a momentary stillness and spaciousness that I sort of sensed but it was so elusive. It's a sense of not being my body, my physical boundaries; dissolving and being part of something else. People have described this as a sense of dissolving, of becoming that wall, for example, or that tree.

MP: A kind of union with the other?

RP: Something like that. That's my interest, if you like, about this area, because that, I think, provides such a sense of containment and security.

MP: In our existential struggle, doesn't it?

RP: Yes, it does and it's beyond reifying something, it's beyond beliefs; it's getting to know what you are experiencing. "I" is real in that sense, it's not a cognitive or intellectual belief or something you worship.

LET US ALLOW TO ARRIVE   19

MP: Thinking about no-self, how do you reconcile the idea and practice of letting go of the ego and the self and the experience of emptiness or *suniata*?

RP: Isn't it linked with who's the one who's doing the thinking, who's the one who's doing the perceiving? Can you say a bit more about *suniata*?

MP: Well, as far as I understand it, emptiness in the Buddhist sense is not: nothing, the void, a black hole; it's more linked with spaciousness, perhaps.

RP: I think it may go back to the idea that nothing is solid and that we can only see things or perceive things in impressions. What we think is solid and what we name as an object, a tree, and a chair, is influenced by causes and conditions and these are ever-changing. I think the idea of emptiness harks back to the idea that we see things as we want to see them, not as they are. But I truly do not understand it much at all!

MP: How does that relate to your work, and how does that help you in your life and, in particular, in your work with mothers and babies?

RP: Well, it helps me to know that the work is a process; it provides me with a framework to know that I can trust more my senses and trust my experience rather than an idea and to watch and to observe processes and interactions more closely rather than have some preconceived idea of where I should be going with this person that I meet or where they are in that moment. I try attending to that as best as I can; what happens moment to moment is in the frame rather than something I am striving to achieve or them striving to achieve. We meet in the moment. It's something Daniel Stern talks about in a book he wrote about psychotherapy, *The Present Moment in Psychotherapy and Everyday Life* (2004). He talks about momentary experience and this is very much related to Buddhist philosophy and ideas, I think. If we can attend to this process, we can help others observe their experience of patterns of thought and feelings. This can help to de-identify from their thoughts, feelings, and ideas and perhaps attend to process rather than content. This allows psychological flexibility and the ability to take on multiple perspectives rather than one rigid perspective

20 THE BUDDHA AND THE BABY

and identify with that. It releases them from the constraints of a solid idea or attitude or a rigid reaction to other people's ideas as well as to their own thoughts and feelings. It allows more choice and flexibility and in that then they can accept more readily the challenges and the struggles of life.

MP: You seem to say that it fosters an observational stance as the person de-identifies and then can observe and there is a space between the observer and the observed.

RP: There is a space and that's where change occurs and it's in the intersubjective space. We are much more complex and multifaceted; there isn't one me, for instance, there are many mes. We have to understand that we don't have to be one me, there are many sides to us and that can change from time to time. We don't have to be bound by a fixed view of how things should be.

MP: And that is helped by the realisation of emptiness, isn't it?

RP: Yes, I think so, but again I am out of my depth with such profound concepts!

MP: Here we are surrounded by mist on this Table Mountain, and this could be a metaphor.

RP: Well, a metaphor for our limited capacity as humans to see. We only see what our structure, our human body, and our mind will allow us to see, and that is the limiting factor: we cannot see things as they are, you know, unless we go through a process of very rigorous learning because of how we are structured physically and how our brain works and everything else. They (Buddhist teaching) thought that thousands of years ago and the neurosciences are now beginning to confirm that.

MP: The mist surrounding us at this moment is almost synonymous of our journey across the mist caused by delusions and a beam of sun now appearing amongst clouds is like a small enlightenment in our conversation!

RP: Yes, the fog we are experiencing is a bit like delusions and anxieties. Meditation helps people to see that there's more that's going on in their mind than they think there is and to pay more attention to that.

MP: Now regarding attachment, in psychotherapy and psychology, it is essential to foster a healthy attachment to the maternal figure for a sound ego to develop in the infant; yet Buddhism talks of non-attachment. Can you tell me your thoughts with regard to this point?

RP: I think there are different levels, though, and there are different kinds of attachment or non-attachment experiences. I think you have to experience attachment to then move beyond it and know what detachment is; detachment in the Buddhist sense isn't not to feel; it's not being detached from feelings.

MP: Do you see detachment and non-attachment as the same?

RP: Ahh, I see them as the same but that might not be right, maybe they are terms that are used interchangeably, but perhaps detachment gets mixed up with psychological coldness. Non-attachment, I think, is more linked to that notion that you experience things as fluid and ever-changing, and so therefore there's nothing to attach to, because you cannot attach to things that are always changing.

MP: I had attached a lot to this interview with you on this Mount Table and expected an ideal situation of warmth, sun, and the spectacular view you can have from here, but instead it's windy, cold, and grey mist is moving fast and bringing drizzles, plus noisy crowds around us: far from the ideal picture I had attached to.

RP: And you may have attached to this interview being clear and simple while it feels clouded and confused!

MP: To the contrary, your theoretical approach is quite interesting, clear and inspiring.

RP: But, maybe I need to have a bit of the opposite approach as well and need to balance it out because I get attached to ideas and theories and that obscures what they are actually trying to convey: the experience. That's the scarier part, I guess. So, I do think non-attachment is different from the attachment we talk about in attachment theory. This is just another level and they should not be confused. Back to your question about how to reconcile ideas with experience in mothers' group, well, I think what we're

22 THE BUDDHA AND THE BABY

trying to provide is a secure place for them to explore, you know, challenging experiences and ideas by not trying to be an attachment figure but being someone who is accepting of whatever they give us, whether it's confusion, whether it's frustration or it's something else, we try as best as we can, as the teachers in the group, to convey a sense of acceptance of them in whatever way they present themselves to us.

MP: I'm trying to link this with the idea of non-attachment: do you help them not to attach, for example, to their anxieties, fears, and phantasies?

RP: Exactly that, to help them see that if they really watch through mindfulness practice and they are able to observe and describe, in a way somewhat removed as a third person, removed from what they watch, then they can become a little less identified, which is a way towards non-attachment.

MP: Ros, that's a very clear link you've just made.

RP: Yes, we help them to become non-attached to their states of mind, fears, anxieties of what will happen during birth etc., and we do that by outlining, I guess, a sort of framework for them to observe these phenomena and to actually teach them that mental phenomena, feelings, bodily sensations are not static; they come and go, they rise and fall, but they are linked and influence each other.

MP: Do you have any story or experience you can tell about helping these mothers to get in touch with the baby inside them, or telling you something about their discovery of something to do with the baby inside them?

RP: Usually the discovery comes through one of the meditation practices, whether it's the body scan or meditation on the breath, on sounds or whatever. They come to discover things they may have not noticed: "Oh my baby is sleeping, oh my baby is active, or I'm filled with joy and happiness in being with my baby now." I think because we do ask them in the meditation practice to focus—when we get to the belly—to focus on their baby and imagine their baby and how they bring life-nutrients to their baby by every breath. As we invite them to observe and think about their baby, they begin, then, to expand into the relationship they're forging with their baby and their future baby and a lot of them do express feelings of bliss and gratitude and care, and sometimes fear about the responsibility of bringing this life into the world. They have moments of very moving feelings towards their baby: some of them just suddenly recognise the importance of this phase they are going through and that all of their petty worries and all the other stuff that's in their mind, that they focus on, is inconsequential compared with the fact of bringing a baby into the world.

MP: This is lovely, Ros, it's clear to me that you help them to de-attach from their worries, anxieties, and negative thoughts and to attach to the real baby growing inside them, don't you?

RP: This is what some mothers tell us, and I think that is certainly another aim of the mindfulness classes: not only to reduce distress and prevent depression, if we can possibly do that, but it is also asking them to start to experience their baby, to think about their baby, to reflect around their baby's life.

MP: To bond with their baby, perhaps?

RP: Yes, to bond, to attach: we try to help them be in a relationship with their baby already and think about that relationship that it's already started in the womb, and then it will continue and what are their hopes, dreams, and wishes for their baby are and how they can start to actualise that in the here and now.

MP: I heard of a very ill mother who had denied being pregnant up to the moment she began having contractions. It sounds just the opposite of what you are doing in your mindfulness groups.

RP: Yes, from research instruments such as the Adult Attachment Interview (George, Kaplan & Main, 1996) used in pregnancy, one can predict the infant's attachment at one year of age meaning a mother's representations of her baby before birth are very important to the subsequent "real" attachment relationship. So one of my notions, and it may be far too ambitious, is to start to change that already in pregnancy. Say, if a mother is avoidant or preoccupied, we can start to loosen that up a bit and help her to develop a more secure relationship with her baby in the womb, then, hopefully that will carry on postnatally to a more secure attachment.

MP: Yes, it's very interesting and exciting because, as you know that happens also at a physiological level: mothers whose stress or depression are reduced during pregnancy produce less cortisol, the hormone that counteracts stress to keep a hormonal homeostasis in the womb. This already affects the forming baby *in utero*.

RP: That's right. Vivette Glover's work in London (Glover et al., 2002) and many other people have researched the impact of stress, not only on pregnancy outcomes but also on the baby's developing brain and physiology, and it's not looking good if the stress is high in pregnancy.

MP: Your mindfulness therapeutic intervention has an effect on the mental health of the mother and on the forming baby-in-the-womb at the very early stage of forming the body–mind of the baby.

RP: Yes, that would be a hope: reducing the impact of stress on the baby's developing brain and that will have an effect on the emotional-cognitive development of the child as well as fostering the attachment relationship.

MP: The title for this interview, "Let us allow to arrive and bringing into being", seems to me a very good synopsis for this conversation: the mother arrives at a mindful state that brings the physical and emotional baby into being.

RP: Yes, allowing the arrival of the baby and of the woman to be a mother.

MP: Do you recollect mothers being able to transform negative feelings about the baby, not thinking about the baby in the womb and later being able to talk about the baby and change their view?

RP: Mothers say: "I'm no longer afraid of what might be; I'm much more content with just allowing things to be as they are and meeting them in the moment", or something like that. There are lots of anxieties whether the baby will be normal, whether they'll be able to cope with the pregnancy; actually there's a wonderful story from a woman who used meditation during labour. She was very worried about having panic attacks and postnatal depression, but she used some of the affirmations that we gave women in little postcards during the sessions. She put these up around her labour room to remind her and used that learning from the class to get her through the labour.

MP: An example of these cards' affirmations?

RP: Hmm, I think there were cards about being kind to yourself; taking one moment at a time; using the breath to focus your attention, and so on. People have used things in different ways. Quite transformative experiences these were for some women. One woman was able not to attach to her intrusive thoughts but just see them as thoughts; a lot of women who get postnatal and antenatal depression start having thoughts of harming the baby; that they'll lose control; they have, you know, these horrific thoughts of smashing their baby against walls, murderous thoughts, and learning not to be spooked by those things, to detach from those thoughts, to stop the whole struggle with it, the suffering and usually these thoughts go away or lose their impact.

MP: What did that woman say after transforming such negativity?

RP: She said: "It changed my life!" And another woman—you know, there are lots of women who have crying babies—so-called colicky babies, another woman said something like: "In the middle of the night when I was up for the tenth time and my baby was crying and I was feeling helpless and overpowered, I just remembered that this was just a moment of suffering and would pass!"

MP: Indeed, it's impermanence!

RP: Impermanence and it will change. "What I need to do is to be kind and compassionate to myself, go and make a cup of tea, let it pass, not attach to the idea that it is going to last forever or that something awful is going to happen.

MP: This is very moving and exciting to think of the value and relief brought by this intervention. This is a moment of enlightenment and clarity about the real essence of your work. Look the sky above us is also clearing up. The transformation of anxiety, fear, depression, fantasies for these mothers about the baby inside

26   THE BUDDHA AND THE BABY

them is very beautiful and also how they can use the Buddhist ideas that you teach them at an emotional level.

RP: There are all sort of metaphors we use for women to think about their thoughts, for instance, we have a thought-stream: we can jump into the stream and get washed away with it; or there is a train we're waiting for, so we can get into the carriage and get taken to a destination we don't want to go to; or we can wait and not hop on the train and not go somewhere we don't want to go to, which is where our thoughts take us.

MP: It's how to master negative, fearful thoughts, the real task, isn't it, Ros?

RP: Well, any thoughts we might get attached to, it could be pleasant ones, too, because we crave only to have pleasant experiences. So we emphasise that attaching too much to thoughts or sensations or experiences is causing suffering, too. Attaching too much or identifying too much to either good or bad experiences causes suffering. We also use the metaphor of the movie i.e. life is like a movie and we can be sitting in the audience watching it and sometimes we feel what the characters feel but we still know it's just a movie, but some of us think we're actually in the movie and we start to dramatise and all of that. So there are several ways that help bring awareness to becoming caught up in experiences which lead to more distress.

MP: That's probably where emptiness and spaciousness are created, when you don't identify with the movie or become the characters but you stay as the observer knowing that it will pass.

RP: And to open the space and to reflect; and this is where I'm hoping that increasing mindfulness will also increase the ability to reflect because it does give us space in the mind to watch and observe. There's no space when you're just following things like the white rabbit in *Alice in Wonderland* by Lewis Carroll. You know, talking with you also helps me to reflect on what we're doing, what we're trying to help these women with; you don't appreciate that unless you stand back a bit and discuss with someone else. So thank you for asking me to do this.

MP: Well, mutual thanks, as I feel we got to a moment of real creativity and connection in our dialogue: it's been very exciting to hear about your application of Buddhist practice to your work, which is what is usually done only tangentially as we will see in the dialogues with other contributors to this book. The physical sky above us is now also clearing, just like our minds!

References

Carroll, L. (1865). *Alice in Wonderland*. London: Usborne.

Coltart, N. (1992). *Slouching Towards Bethlehem*. New York: Guilford.

Fraiberg, S., Adelson, E., & Shapiro, V. (1975). Ghosts in the nursery. *Journal of the American Academy of Child Psychiatry, 14*: 387–421.

George, C., Kaplan, N., & Main, M. (1996). Adult Attachment Interview protocol (3rd edn.). Unpublished manuscript, University of California at Berkeley.

Glover, V. (2002). In: O'Connor, T. G., Heron, J., Golding, J., Beveridge, M., & Glover, V. (2002). Maternal antenatal anxiety and behavioural problems in early childhood. *British Journal of Psychiatry, 180*: 502–508.

Hayes, S. C., Strosahl, K. D., & Wilson, K. D. (2003). *Acceptance and Commitment Therapy: An Experiential Approach to Behaviour Change*. New York: Guilford.

Linehan, M. M. (1993). *Skills Training Manual for Treating Borderline Personality Disorder*. New York: Guilford.

McKenzie, V. (2008). *Cave in the Snow*. New York: Bloomsbury.

Segal, Z. V., Williams, M. G., Teasdale, J. D. (2012). *Mindfulness-Based Cognitive Therapy for Depression (Second Edition)*. New York: Guilford.

Stern, D. (2004). *The Present Moment in Psychotherapy and Everyday Life*. New York and London: W. W. Norton.

The Tibetan Book of the Dead (1927). Oxford: Oxford University Press.

CHAPTER THREE

The Buddha in the sky

Dialogue with Stephen Malloch

Power without love is reckless and abusive, and love without power is sentimental and anaemic.

—Martin Luther King, Jr.

MP: Well, this is really extraordinary for me: to have this dialogue across oceans and continents via Skype! Yes, Stephen, I can see you in your house in Sydney while I am based in the room you used when you stayed with us in London some years ago on the occasion of your book launch. Well, I would like to focus on the aspect of your working life related to your research in musicality in mother/father–baby communication and ask you how you integrate your Buddhist self into such research. To begin with, could you tell me when you first became interested in Buddhism and in researching the musicality in mother baby interactions?

SM: I came upon Buddhism first of all when I was living in Cambridge and I was studying for my Master's in music theory and analysis at the University of London. I was living in Cambridge with my first wife and she started going along to a group called Friends of

29

30   THE BUDDHA AND THE BABY

the Western Buddhist Order; she had been there a few times and I went along with her and I remember the first walking meditation I did. In Cambridge, the shrine room they had was below street level, down in the basement of the house, and I remember saying to the person who was leading the meditation: "It feels like I was walking around my own psyche".

MP: That's interesting and what an immediate impact that had.

SM: Yes, I still remember that and it was about twenty-three years ago. So, the walking meditation, in particular, made a profound impact on me. Yes, it was interesting as it was like walking around my own psychic landscape, as I've said. I remember another time, walking down the main street in Cambridge and suddenly coming to a halt and realising that the sound of the traffic was nothing compared to the sound of all my thinking inside my own head. And thinking, my God, it's so loud out there and it's so noisy inside my head! These are my two early memories of me beginning my journey into meditation. The Friends of the Western Buddhist Order teach meditation very well: they're very structured in their teaching: they teach basically breath awareness and loving kindness and so I stayed in that tradition for about two yeas, the time I was living in Cambridge. After that I moved to Edinburgh, which is where I subsequently did my doctorate. It was in Edinburgh that I started to explore the Tibetan tradition and I went along to some meetings of the New Kadampa Tradition. I didn't quite fit there any longer or with the Friends of the Western Order, and then I came across some of the books by Thich Nhat Hanh and one had a card in it which advertised a group that met in Glasgow. I went across to Glasgow, met with Ian, the person who ran that group and they showed a video of Thich Nhat Hanh; as I saw him, tears came to my eyes and I was ever so moved by this man, just by his presence and his being. I don't remember what the video was about, but I remember feeling there was something quite special and precious about Thich Nhat Hanh.

MP: I went to listen to Thich Nhat Hanh for my first time, when he came to London last May. He came with his Sangha of thirty or more nuns and monks, who were all on stage at the Royal Albert

THE BUDDHA IN THE SKY   31

Hall: they chanted then he spoke non-stop for two hours (the translation appeared on the little screen they now use in theatres) and it was amazing. He covered the whole of Buddhism starting from the human condition of life, suffering, up to the way out of suffering and his view on life, existence, death, and all. It was a very organic, simple and very deep way of dishing out his enlightened mind to us ordinary people in the audience. An extraordinary experience indeed! But I've never been to Plum Village: I remember you going there when you last came to London.

SM: Yes, I've been to Plum Village twice and spent three weeks there the first time I went. So having seen Thich Nhat Hanh on that video, I then moved to that tradition and met a woman who played quite a big part in informing me about Buddhism; her name is Ani Lodro. She was a Tibetan Buddhist nun when I met her and she still lives in Edinburgh. She had been living in Samye Ling [a Tibetan Buddhist Monastery in Scotland], where they conduct closed retreats that last three years, three months and three days, and she had done two of these retreats back to back, so she was very committed to her practice. When I met her she was starting to leave the Tibetan tradition and was discovering Thich Nhat Hanh. There was this little group in Glasgow with this amazing Tibetan nun, and we became very good friends and we would share car rides and have long conversations. In the three weeks I spent in Plum Village—she and I went there together—she was a great pillar of strength at that time and she was always extraordinarily supportive, a wonderful woman.

MP: How important to have such people around one's life!

SM: After I left my first wife, I was back in Edinburgh and I went to visit her; I'd been talking about the separation and my feelings about it. As I was leaving she said "Stephen, I've got a hook on the back of my door", and I said: "I don't understand, what do you mean you have a hook on the back of your door?" She said: "You might like to leave your whip there!"—meaning that I was giving myself a very hard time and blaming myself harshly for the ending of my marriage. It was the beautiful way she put it and the metaphor that struck me.

MP: And did you?

32   THE BUDDHA AND THE BABY

SM: Well, I'm not sure that I left it there and then, but I went through a process of leaving it behind, yes; I probably left bits scattered around the world.

MP: As it often happens.

SM: So, during the time in Edinburgh I started to lead meditations and to take more of a leadership role in the *sangha* and all this was highly informative to my early exploration of meditation as well as exploring my own psyche. Probably in the past four to five years the tradition of Thich Nhat Hanh has played less of a central role in my life and indeed Buddhism has played less of a central role for me.

MP: Is that because you feel more settled in your life, with your second wife etc.?

SM: I think my interest in therapy actually has played a part; but I think I now have more of a broad view of what a spiritual life means and what a therapeutic life means. I have also become more interested in the teaching of Ram Dass, who lives in Hawaii. So I suppose my viewpoint on spirituality as I get older has got broader.

MP: Ah, Ram Dass lives in Hawaii now; he's is in a wheel chair isn't he?

SM: Yes, he cannot leave, he cannot fly any more and I'm not quite sure why he's chosen Hawaii, but he's got a support group around him and he teaches via the internet.

MP: Is he the main influence for you at this moment?

SM: He and Thich Nhat Hanh form the joint influences; they complement each other: Thich Nhat Hanh, I feel, is more about being precise and present, I suppose; while I feel Ram Dass is more about the heart and is broader, in some ways.

MP: I see, and are you saying that your interest in psychotherapy is taking over your interest in Buddhism now?

SM: They're very much lying alongside each other and very much complementing each other and I can see how they support each other.

MP: You've also moved to being a counsellor, I understand, haven't you?

SM: Yes, I've been doing that for about five years; that, plus my own therapeutic journey have both been highly informative of my view on life and myself. Buddhism and psychotherapy are for me a dual way of understanding the psyche, a dual way to understand my own psyche; so, I suppose I see psychotherapy as coming to the psyche from the level of my own personal history, the way I behave in the world, the way I relate to other people, how I resolve my own conflicts, how I integrate my personality, and so on. I see spirituality as coming at who I am from a different direction, which puts the emphasis on the holistic nature of life and the universe and there's a way of being, that is beyond the individual ego. Meditation is a way of contacting that non-individual aspect of being human. So, that's how I see the two of them complementing each other: psychotherapy is for me about how I understand and deal with my own personal history; and spirituality, in particular Buddhism and meditation, is about how it demonstrates for me and gives me entry into the part of me that's not about my individual history but that is about interconnection with everyone and everything else and with the part of me that isn't just about Stephen.

MP: It's about human nature at large, would you say?

SM: It's about human nature and Truth with a capital T: it's about the Dharma. In that way, I feel that spirituality and psychotherapy are like two pillars in my life but they're entering from different doors.

MP: This is somehow linked with the two apparently conflicting ideas of ego and non-ego.

SM: Hmm, and the paradox of that, which can be seen as a conflict or can be experienced as two, I suppose, incompatible truths, pointing to something larger than either of them; and sitting into that paradox and the richness of that. The psychological trauma and history impacting on the present life of one of my clients I am thinking of, I see also as something bigger than that: my client is

34　THE BUDDHA AND THE BABY

more than just her psychological history; she's someone who has a 'soul', who has a spiritual dimension as well, and I see that as part of the strength of my own way as I work with my clients. But also, even if I never talk about that with clients, I still hold that other way of looking as I sit with my clients. So, I never see the person as inevitably trapped by their own psychological history, there's always a part that is beyond that.

MP: What do you mean by the part that is beyond that? Do you mean that she represents human suffering in general?

SM: There is part of her that is also free, which in Buddhism you'd call Buddha nature; in other spiritual traditions they may call it the soul, you may think of a soul taking this particular incarnation—whatever words you want to use. There's an aspect to her that isn't limited by her own personal history.

MP: How can this be linked with mothers and babies and your research into mothers and babies?

SM: What a very good question! In terms of my therapeutic practice, my research into mothers and babies informs me in terms of an attunement to the mutuality of the therapist and client. When I first started studying mothers and babies I was, and still am struck by the behaviour which is about the mother saying to that baby and the baby saying to the mother: "I see you, I recognise you and through my behaviour I'm demonstrating that I see you and that I'm being affected by you even though I can't have words to say it". It is through the mutual dance that's occurring, through the affect attunement that's occurring, that that message is being heard loud and clear when the communication is going well. There are two beings who are witnessing each other and they're informing each other that they're seeing each other and are being touched through each other's presence. So, I suppose that realisation has formed the central aspect of the way that I've researched mother–baby communication; that has also, I suppose, made me very sensitive to that mutual recognition that also occurs in therapy. It can be about words but it's also about the way that the body is held through all the gestural narratives, as I call them, that are occurring in the therapeutic relationship and how that is informing both people that they're being witnessed by someone who is being sensitive to them.

MP: The body narrative, you are talking about now?

SM: Yes, the narrative of the body and also the way the voice moves: the pitch movement of the voice, the volume of the voice, all the gestural narratives of the voice along with the gestural narratives of the body. That's certainly one way that the mother–baby research has influenced my therapeutic interactions.

MP: I just had an inspiration: you've been talking a lot about the communication through the body, the voice etc., I wonder whether meditation contributes to refine your understanding of the body communication, because as we know, meditation is a lot about the body: it focuses on the various parts of the body and on the breath. It's not an intellectual or cognitive practice, as some people may mistakenly believe. Meditation is a lot about becoming aware of the body states, of the breathing, the passing thoughts, and so on.

SM: Yes, it has certainly given me a much greater ability to focus, and meditation has certainly given me a quieter mind so I can pay greater attention to my clients with greater awareness. I can put aside my own inner dialogue to be more with what the client is saying. More recently I've been playing with how to split my attention between the gestural narrative of the client and the verbal content of what is being said, which I'm finding is taking a certain degree of practice because, I know, at times, I will be very aware of the movements of the hands and the up and down of the voice and the way the head is moving and then realise I have no idea of what has just been said! I'm getting better at splitting my attention between those two things but also at remembering both whilst they are all occurring.

MP: Does that also include the awareness of the baby and mother's gestural and vocal communication?

SM: Yes, that then became the focus of my research of looking at those gestural narratives of voice and body between mother and baby. The sensitivity around the body interactions and the timing between myself and the client, as we work together, has been influenced, as I've said, by this fine-tuned research on mothers and babies.

MP: I remember the fascinating video you showed at the Tavistock when you came to London, of a prem baby on his father's

36   THE BUDDHA AND THE BABY

chest: the baby produced almost inaudible sounds and the father responded to those sounds with extraordinary sensitivity.

SM: I'm now interested in how that gets played out between the adult therapist and the adult client.

MP: My other question is about attachment and its different meaning in Buddhism and in psychotherapy: you have a lot of experience in witnessing the attachment between mothers and babies that is manifested through the gestural and vocal holding you've so eloquently described.

SM: Your question is about the necessity for a healthy attachment as opposed to non-attachment in Buddhism. I suppose the way that I see them fit together is again a paradox: in this incarnation we need healthy attachment: it's the way our ego develops, it's the way we function well in the world with other people and it starts with secure attachment with our mothers. Whereas Buddhism is talking about something very different: Buddhism is talking about this ego's or this incarnation's wish to attach to things and ways of being, as well as seeing that it's all impermanent. It's the holding of the two in a way that we see it is important to form attachments and that it is also important at the same time to see that attachment is ephemeral and impermanent. It's also about, as an adult, having the courage to love knowing that the object to which the love is directed, the person, will eventually leave or die. There is riskiness in all of that. If we don't embrace that risk, we would never love.

MP: This is very clearly put. How can you link that to the mother and baby or the father and the baby?

SM: If Buddhism were misunderstood by a mother, then she would say: "Well, I won't get too attached to my baby; I won't get too involved with my baby because of non-attachment, because of impermanence. I will always know that it's pointless to attach too strongly because it will all pass." That would be a gross misuse of the teaching on non-attachment in Buddhism. It's about recognising the strong necessity for healthy attachment and the paradox of that with non-attachment. Attachment is very important in parent–infant relationship, and this can be coupled with acknowledging the reality of the impermanent nature of it all and how the practice of non-attachment can help to bring the realisation of the impermanent nature of it all.

MP: While you were talking a new thought has come to my mind, and this is the beauty of these dialogues: it's a mutual creative process. I was thinking that a form of non-attachment in the parent–baby relationship could be in the ideal separateness: the parent has an attachment and a bond to the baby but also has to admit that there's separateness and this means they have to let go, for example, of the desire to possess the baby; they have to let go and to accept that there's a baby there, acting and behaving in a way which is different from how they would expect or how they would want that baby to behave. So the idea and the realisation of non-attachment also comes into the intimate, close and very early relationship between parent and baby.

SM: I think that's a lovely idea, because it's love with space.

MP: Exactly and it's done for the baby in his or her own right and not because of, say the parent who wants to sleep through the night and is fed up if the baby is waking up ten times in the night and having many needs. The parent may no longer act for the baby's welfare etc., but for his or her own interest. So it's really love for the baby, the way the baby is, the way the baby needs to be loved.

SM: Yes, and acknowledging, as you say, that the other person is never going to be the perfect object of love because they're going to have their own mind.

MP: So we see non-attachment to a phantasy of a baby, if we think of parent–infant relationship. One may have a fantasy of a perfect baby and it's the non-attachment to that fantasy that I'm thinking about.

SM: Yes, and it's also non-attachment to the thought that this baby is mine.

MP: Yes, because the baby is not mine.

SM: And yet it is my baby. So that's the paradox again.

38 THE BUDDHA AND THE BABY

MP: So, whose baby is it? Who's the owner of the baby?

SM: Perhaps this is a question that can never be answered.

MP: The baby is not the owner of himself; or maybe the universe owns the baby.

SM: Perhaps it's a bit like when Christ said: "I am"; similarly the baby just "is".

MP: The baby doesn't have to be owned; perhaps the baby is owned by life.

SM: Yet there are responsibilities but, yes, the baby is owned by life and by death. But I like the original idea on non-attachment in terms of allowing separateness.

MP: Now, to move on to another question: the idea of emptiness, how does that inform your research with parents and babies? Emptiness and fullness, because the parent–baby relationship is a full-on relationship, isn't it?

SM: I'm reminded of Thich Nhat Hanh, when he writes that when we're talking of emptiness we need to ask ourselves: empty of what? He means empty of a separate self and we've already touched on this in a way. As the mother and the baby are one, literally they're one in terms of growing inside the mother, and yet the baby also, from the immediate moment of growing, is also a separate entity, a separate person. So, the teaching on emptiness would be that, yes, the mother and the baby are one, both are empty of a separate self. Just like you and I are both here, talking with each other, and there's an apparent separateness between you and me, but the teaching on emptiness says to see that we aren't separate beings—we are both empty of a separate self. But, we are also separate; we both have our own wants and dislikes. So, similarly with mothers and babies, as you've already said quite eloquently yourself, the mother is responsible for the infant and yet the infant is also a separate being. The mother and the baby are empty of separate selves, they are interdependent on each other, yet it is also important to see they are separate beings; so we're pivoting back to the paradox of it.

MP: The last question, when you run your groups and teach meditation, is there something about the baby self or the infantile self that is addressed in your teaching, for example?

SM: The short answer is: "no".

MP: Well, do you have a longer answer to the last question i.e. whether you've ever had any mystical or extra-ordinary experience, something impalpable for example?

SM: Well, I'm just thinking about it; in meditation I've certainly experienced great, great stillness and there's great spaciousness in that for me; a spaciousness that is not about normal everyday going about my business. I suppose that experience of great spaciousness informs me that this sense is lying behind my everyday experiences and I'm mostly out of contact with it; so that sense of spacious awareness, which I touch on occasionally in meditation and the love that is inside that, reminds me of that, which I forget as I go about my everyday life and its business and I forget that loving, spacious awareness is sitting behind it all. To think about your question again, sometimes I will have a sense of an answer to something. As a child, I would stare at the sky and—if there were a few clouds around that was better—I would put a question and the answers that I would get back have been very useful at times. I think what I'm doing is I'm opening myself to something bigger than me and therefore opening myself to a wisdom that is greater than my everyday psychology.

MP: This is a beautiful way of being and do you still do that?

SM: I do, yes, I do. I used to do it as a child and I've done it more or less, depending on life circumstances and I've been remembering it more recently, when I looked up at the sky and there were some clouds there and I was worried about something; I also became aware of a huge amount of joy. It just reminded me of the joyfulness of being alive and the joy of existence and the joy that lies behind it all.

MP: This is beautiful. Someone, whom I've recently interviewed for this book, has sent me something about Thich Nhat Hanh: it was about the joy of being alive and it's exactly what you're saying

40 THE BUDDHA AND THE BABY

now, Stephen. Life is the best thing we have and any moment of our life is good. To be open to the universe and see what the universe brings, how this dialogue with you will pan out, and how this book will take shape, it's all up to the universe to inform the work put into this book.

SM: And maybe we're back to emptiness again: it's about letting go of outcomes and trusting, just Trust with a capital T.

MP: The outcome, yes, this is one of the most valued and favourite word in our media and psychological world: everything has to have an outcome, measured and demonstrated as being of value; and it comes down to an economic value, in the end, let alone the value of spirituality!

SM: What I've just told you about looking at the sky and opening to the universe, I've told very few people about that and I'm quite happy I've told you.

MP: And are you happy to have this precious childhood memory and later experience to be in the book?

SM: Yes, I'll be quite happy for it to appear in this book because it feels like something very close to me and I'm very pleased to have shared it with you. It feels very lovely to have shared it with you.

MP: And I do feel privileged of this true emotional connection; it feels a soul to soul communication and it's beautiful because I often think or talk of, or thank the universe for all that it provides, for all that it leads to. It's all stuff that goes beyond me, the small individual me.

SM: As you were talking, I was thinking that talking of the universe could sound quite far from me, but it actually feels extraordinarily personal and close. So, it's me looking at the sky and having a sense of joyfulness of being alive and also seeking some personal reassurance or some answers to a question I have. It's both impersonal but also highly personal; it's an interesting juxtaposition.

MP: Yes, it's another paradox and with this lovely thought, we should perhaps let go of this dialogue, Stephen.

SM: Yes, it feels a nice place to conclude.

MP: And thanks for doing it on Skype, daunting as it was at first!

SM: We, too, can be high-tech people sometimes! It was a lot of fun, thank you to you, too.

Reference

King, Martin Luther, Jr. (1967). *Where Do We Go From Here?* Annual Report Delivered at the Eleventh Convention of the Southern Christian Leadership Conference, 16 August, Atlanta, GA.

CHAPTER FOUR

Serendipity in the magic garden

Dialogue with Deirdre Dowling

When you touch one thing with deep awareness, you touch everything. The same is true of time. When you touch one moment with deep awareness, you touch all moments.

—Thich Nhat Hahn

MP: Thank you, Deirdre, for agreeing to talk with me in your beautiful garden on this topic, which is dear to me. As I may have mentioned already, the title of this book is going to be: *The Buddha and the Baby*, hence we need to focus on your work with children and parents.

DD: Oh, it's a lovely title.

MP: Oh good, I'm so glad you approve as I value you opinion as a writer. I'd like to start with the two choices in your life, of being Buddhist and a child psychotherapist, and how they came about for you.

DD: They're linked in a way. As you know, I was born and brought up in a Jewish family but I have been interested in Buddhism since my late teens. I was first introduced to Mahayana Buddhism through a close friend from Sri Lanka when I was at university in 1969, and I enjoyed finding out about the Buddhist way of life from his family, therefore I joined them going to the temple in Chiswick. I then trained and worked as a social worker, only taking up the training in child psychotherapy fifteen years later. However, it was on a visit to California in 1980 that I first found out about Zen in a book *Zen Mind, Beginner's Mind* by Shunru Suzuki (1970), a monk who taught in San Francisco and started a Buddhist community there. When I came back, I started to teach myself meditation and I became involved with Rigpa, a Tibetan Buddhist centre led by Sogyal Rinpoche, a fascinating but rather charismatic leader. I went on a few retreats with them and learned more about meditation. After this, it was many years later when I returned to Buddhism and meditation, with a community based in Surrey called New Buddha Way, where they were practising meditation and trying to express Buddhist ideas in a simpler, modern English form. There I discovered the work of a Vietnamese monk Thich Nhat Hanh, who has influenced me enormously. He's probably the person I regard as being my teacher, by reading his books. I often listen to his talks when I do gardening and I'd like to go to Plum Village, the community he has set up in France He's the person I've been inspired by mostly. I find his approach to therapeutic issues very interesting. When he talks about anger, he would say you have to get to know and understand the feeling, a bit like in therapy, and then stand back from it and he would talk about transforming it. He also has the whole idea that there's no happiness without suffering. So, I just find his approach very accessible, you know.

MP: In psychoanalysis, we also have the concept of transformation of states of mind into something more benign and acceptable, as Bion describes so aptly with his idea about the container–contained process (Bion, 1962).

DD: I'm not sure I use that sort of language. I suppose the difference is that therapy is in a relationship with someone, while meditation is in a relationship with yourself.

SERENDIPITY IN THE MAGIC GARDEN   45

MP: Yes, but also with the teacher, guru, roshi, Rinpoche etc., however you want to call him or her.

DD: I suppose that's true, to some extent, although a lot of mediation time is spent on your own, but yes, there's always a teacher.

MP: But also therapy has to do with yourself and the relationship within yourself, doesn't it?

DD: In meditation, I don't think much; while therapy is more of an intellectual approach with feelings, at least with more adult patients, perhaps not so much with mothers and babies. That work is more intuitive and perhaps it's a different part of me at work then.

MP: But therapy is not just intellectual, it has to be an emotional experience doesn't it?

DD: Absolutely, I agree with that. I love Wordsworth's phrase on poetry being "the spontaneous overflow of powerful feelings: it takes its origin from emotion recollected in tranquillity" (Preface to *Lyrical Ballads*, 1978, p. 151). This is about poetry, but people often quote it to describe psychotherapy. But I can't quite say that meditation and psychotherapy are the same.

MP: They are not of course, but there are many overlapping aspects, aren't there? But to return to your history: how did you move from social work to child psychotherapy?

DD: When I was a social worker, I was struggling to decide whether to take a young girl into care and I wanted good advice. So I telephoned the Anna Freud Centre and they said why don't you come and discuss your case here? Anna Freud was still alive then. So I presented her situation and my dilemmas at a clinic meeting and Anna Freud said, in her imposing way,: "If you take this child into care, you will have to get her psychotherapy". So that's what happened, the girl went into care and into therapy and became an intensive training case for a trainee therapist and I used to drive her up to the Anna Freud clinic three times a week. I became intrigued by the therapeutic work and decided to apply for training myself. I trained with the BAP, which had just started

46   THE BUDDHA AND THE BABY

its child psychotherapy then and I've now been working as a child therapist for twenty-three years.

MP: An interesting evolution, indeed. Now, how do you think the practice of Buddhism has influenced your work as a child psychotherapist?

DD: It helps me calm down and centre myself. I know how to use it so that I can be quiet at the beginning of a session, when I'm just settling myself down after doing other things, you know. Sometimes when I'm listening to some of the Buddhist talks or I'm mediating, something comes up from one of my patients unexpectedly and I'll think about it. Another child psychotherapist I know says that he uses deep breathing to help a child to calm down. I wouldn't but what I have done is bargain with an over-excited child to have three quiet minutes in the chair while we think together. That's using a technique to find some stillness.

MP: I try to do something similar with violent, acting out kids to try calm them down.

DD: So that's where the two worlds meet for me: it is about finding that quiet place inside, isn't it? I have some very angry, depressed, and sadistic children at the moment. This idea of helping these children change their state of mind by observing it and then without interpreting, just being there with them through it, I find helpful. You know, in the chapter I wrote about parent–infant work, "The capacity to be alone" (Dowling, 2006), I talked about the importance of finding oneself by "being alone in the presence of another". I was using Winnicott's ideas from his chapter "The capacity to be alone" (Winnicott, 1965). In the final sessions with mothers and infants, when they were ready to end therapeutic work, I would just be there while parents were playing with their child and interacting, and I would try and create a calm atmosphere, provide a secure base for this development to happen. If the baby was very agitated, I tried to find some calm inside me and support the mother to calm, too, and encourage her to make contact with the baby and use a quiet voice. I don't think that's so different from meditation: finding that "still point" inside you that you can use. So that's how I use it and that's as far as I can get, I think. The idea of "being in the moment" is also very useful with adult patients.

MP: That's where there is a good marriage between psychotherapy and Buddhism, isn't there?

DD: I think that something of our meditation practice, the readings we do, must get through to our patients unconsciously. The other thing just to tell you as it's interesting. A couple of years ago, I went to Sri Lanka to teach therapeutic approaches to work with children to teachers, community workers, priests, and the army officer in charge of the child soldiers at rehabilitation centres. In Sri Lanka; they have a Buddhist culture and what I taught was child development from the cognitive, social, and emotional point of view, just like I used to do here as a social worker teacher. We looked at those different aspects of the child at different stages of development and the participants said: "What is missing is the child's spiritual development." It was such a new idea for me. In Sri Lanka, the spiritual aspect is part of your daily life, of your conversations, of how people recover from trauma and so on. And it made me think that we don't talk about that aspect of child development in England as they would expect in Sri Lanka. I was so excited when I came back thinking about how the community works there in helping each other. There is no money, but everybody helps. The army officer, after hearing about Winnicott and the transitional object, asked for a collection so he could go back and buy each of the child soldiers a teddy bear.

MP: How very moving, and I believe that the Dalai Lama has similar thoughts about the spiritual development in children.

DD: Yes, it was very touching.

MP: Thinking of some the Buddhist theoretical ideas such as no-self, emptiness etc., how do you reconcile them with our psychological work in which we help children to develop a secure sense of themselves and their ego?

DD: I've always struggled with that, but what Thich Nhat Hanh suggests is that you've got to discover a sense of self before you can give it up (2006). I would agree; for me, my analysis was about discovering a sense of self. I can only understand the idea of "interconnectedness" as described by Thich Nhat Hanh. His idea that the flower, the rain that made it, the cloud that made the rain, the earth the plant grew in, the person who grew it are all interconnected; you can't separate them. It's like saying that there is no baby without a mother. That's the only way I can understand the idea of self and no-self: you can't take the self without the other. I can think of interconnectedness not so much of no-self. I will never be able to give up my sense of self but I can see myself as part of a whole, interconnected, and therefore not separate.

MP: In that sense, you feel you let go of your individual self, perhaps?

DD: Partly. I like the idea of ecology, that if you move something, for example like a pebble on the beach, you're affecting everything else. But I think I will never stop being individualistic. Regarding the question about emptiness, I see it more as a still point: that sense of stillness inside, that is common to all religions, isn't it? So I don't really worry about the concept of emptiness.

MP: It's interesting because I think the still point is what creates spaciousness, which is really what is translated into emptiness, from what I understand. It's not empty equal: nothingness; on the contrary, there is a whole new dimension that emerges there.

DD: Yes, I do understand spaciousness and the loss of ego if you meditate for a long time. When you go to retreats you can get very calm, don't you? And I really like that sense of being very quiet within myself. Perhaps that's what they call emptiness?

MP: Perhaps, but what about attachment and the different meanings attributed to this word by the two traditions? How do you think of attachment?

DD: When I first heard that you're not supposed to be attached to wealth or happiness etc. I used to think it was absolute nonsense. I was 21 and I was desperate to have a decent house, to be happy and all those things, you know, that you want when you're young: so I was very dismissive of the idea. Now, I actually think that things that matter are not material things. I can see that chasing wealth is a game that doesn't lead anywhere. I think Buddhism

SERENDIPITY IN THE MAGIC GARDEN   49

for me is about the Middle Way and I don't go any further than that in terms of attachment. I think you need good relationships. I don't think there is a conflict. I think they're talking at different levels, don't you?

MP: Yes, and I think they mean: don't grasp for things.

DD: You can't have permanency; I think I've learnt that, don't you? You can't make things stay, can you? Of course one wants stability and a secure base. So I take the aspects of Buddhism that help me.

MP: In your work with mothers and babies, you would encourage attachment, wouldn't you?

DD: Of course, and the compassion meditation where you have to develop the loving kindness towards your loved ones. I try to practise that to get less irritated and to remind myself that getting angry is a waste of time. Buddhism is about making good, loving relationships and being tolerant of oneself and others, isn't it? So non-attachment is really not holding the moment: I may work all the summer to make a flower like that and then … it's gone; but I know it will go and it's accepting it, isn't it?

MP: It's an interesting link between being attached, for example to a relationship but not to hold on to it and to accept its impermanence. In this sense, Buddhism means non-attachment. That's why I think many people turn to Buddhism or to religions, at a time of being ill or getting old, having to face death, etc.

DD: To find something to get their head round things. Meditation somehow sorts your head out, like writing does for some of us: it focuses the mind.

MP: Would meditation, writing etc. be like a transitional space for you?

DD: Hmmm, yes, that's right, you create a space where things emerge and that's true of therapy, of writing and of meditation as well, don't you think?

MP: Well, yes, it feels like that. Does any thing come to mind about your work with children or parents and meditation?

DD: When one child plays and you try to make sense of what's

50 THE BUDDHA AND THE BABY

being communicated, week after week, there is a similar sense of trying to give shape to something in your mind. I think when you're meditating you keep going back, don't you, to the breath, but things take shape and emerge in your mind That's what you do when you watch a child playing, don't you? When you're just watching, when you don't know what to say or when you're waiting for a parent struggling with something, or a teenager is in a mood, and you're thinking "what might I say" but you wait. Well, I wait and hope that something comes up. I do believe in the unconscious. That's a similarity and then I suppose the other thing is that meditating helps one to be a bit more patient with oneself in that waiting process. It's about allowing uncertainties and doubt, isn't it, and the unknown. The other thing is that meditation works best when you do it over time, like in a retreat, it accumulates, doesn't it? You begin to develop a clearer sense and something unfolds. And I think that is the same overtime in sessions with people, that things emerge, like in writing, too, it's the same waiting game, isn't it? Things you don't know that evolve and change and anything can happen and I like that, that sense of ... serendipity, where anything can happen and you don't know what's going to happen; you do have to have a certain path, but you don't know how you're going to get there. Serendipity: here is the Google dictionary definition: "The facility of making fortuitous or beneficial discoveries by accident; discovered by chance or lack; a former name for Sri Lanka." It also comes from a fairy tale, *The Three Princes of Serendip*, discovered by Horace Walpole (1754). It's a happy accident or happy surprise by chance. Your writing of this book, you don't know where the interviews are going to take you, do you? That's serendipity, isn't it? It's just trusting that it will take you somewhere and take shape.

MP: Yes, but now I'm at a point of uncertainty and anxiety about this project.

DD: It's an interesting project as there's quite a lot of orthodoxy around. Spirituality is unfortunately not part of our discourse and I think it should be much more. So you're opening things up.

MP: I heard Allan Wallace talking at an international conference on mental health and meditation and saying that after the person has done all the psychiatric things necessary such as medication and talking therapy, to regain his or her mental stability, then meditation is a very good tool to maintain the achieved mental stability: it's a maintenance tool. I found that very useful and inspiring.

MP: A last question, now, Deirdre: did you ever have any particular, mystical or similar experience?

DD: Not really, but you're drawn to certain things and people and you don't know how they will connect up, do you? Serendipity is a good word for me because I like what pops up; I like the fact that I've found a very interesting flower that I haven't planted because the seeds have flown. This garden is fun I like to play around and see what happens, I'm not very ordered.

MP: It's a fantastic and amazing garden, magical is the right word to describe it, or perhaps serendipity; and with this we have come to end of this peaceful, summer afternoon full of surprises.

References

Bion, W. R. (1962). *Learning from Experience*. London: Tavistock.

Dowling, D. (2006). *The Capacity To Be Alone: A Question of Technique*. London: Routledge.

Suzuki, S. (1970). *Zen Mind, Beginner's Mind*. New York, Tokyo: Weatherhill.

Thich Nhat Hahn (1992). *Touching Peace, The Art of Mindful Living*, p. 123. Berkeley, CA: Parallaz Press.

Thich Nhat Hanh (2006). *Mindfulness and Psychotherapy*, Sounds Tru CD.

Walpole, H. (1754). *The Three Princes of Serendip*, quoted in a letter written by him to Horace Mann, January 1754.

Winnicott, D. W. (1965). The capacity to be alone. In: *Maturational Processes and the Facilitating Environment*. London: Hogarth.

Wordsworth, W. (1978). Preface to *Lyrical Ballads* (p. 151).

CHAPTER FIVE

The presence of the therapist

Dialogue with Monica Lanyado

A good traveller has no fixed plans
and is not intent upon arriving.
A good artist lets his intuition
lead him wherever it wants.
A good scientist has freed himself of concepts
and keeps his mind open to what is.

—Tao Te Ching

MP: Monica, thanks for agreeing to this project of talking about your long-standing experience of using your meditative approach in your work as a child and adolescent psychotherapist. I'd like to start by asking you about these two choices in your life and how they came about: that of becoming a child psychotherapist and also a meditator, perhaps not quite a strictly speaking Buddhist meditator, but surely greatly influenced by its ideas, if I am correct.

ML: I'm not a Buddhist but meditation really matters to me. I have had various, different teachers, including Buddhists depending

54 THE BUDDHA AND THE BABY

on where I was in my life. That's been so from when I was a teenager.

MP: You come from a Jewish background, so you were probably brought up as a Jewish girl?

ML: Yes, but not orthodox, not observant, but the Jewish beliefs, ethics, and morality were central in my life; so observance was not so much important; we were not *kosher*, and followed few of the rituals. My father was more interested in an inner life, really, and in studying and understanding. He was learned and he knew a lot but it was his manner that was very decent, good-hearted, and gentle; I always feel that this was greatly informed by his understanding of Judaism which was part of him; they were inter-linked. When I was about thirteen, the Rabbi of our newly formed community was Lionel Blue. He was such an important influence on me and my Batmitzvah ceremony was with Lionel. He is still there in my life.

MP: Yes, that's very fortunate indeed, and I do enjoy his radio pro-gramme *Thoughts for the Day* when I can listen to them. Do you still see him?

ML: Occasionally; but he's not that well now and he struggles with his health, but he's still wonderful in spirit, in humour and wisdom. His autobiography *Hitchhiking to Heaven* I find just wonderful, as it charts his own spiritual development in a very human and open way. You know, he was very important when my parents were elderly. When they died, he lead the prayers and buried them. So Lionel has been there throughout my life. I started with a Jewish influence, but then I left that for many years.

MP: What about your mother: did she have a spiritual influence on you?

ML: Not a spiritual influence on me: she sadly lost her mother and many of her family in the Holocaust and she really never recov-ered from that. Like many people who suffered these losses, she rejected religion. But she and Lionel got on very well together. She would listen to Lionel give a wonderful talk or sermon, but then she would say to him: "Lionel, you don't really believe in all of that do you?" He loved her, but she didn't have any religious spirit and

THE PRESENCE OF THE THERAPIST   55

was determinedly irreverent, if anything. So, as you can see, I'm not a Buddhist, but there was a period when I lived in Edinburgh, when I was very close to a lovely colleague and her family, who were Buddhists. We worked in an EBD school (emotionally behaviourally disturbed) and she was just wonderful. Her name was Seija Burstall and she was a teacher who had individual time with the children. She had a very strong sense of the soul or essence of the children she taught and never rejected them even when they were awful with her. They felt that she loved them and they could safely love her. When I tried to supervise her in "Seija's room", it was an extraordinary experience. Every ten minutes or so, a child would knock on the door, pop their head round the door of her room which was in the centre of the school, and would simply say: "Hallo, Seija" to her, and she would respond to them simply by saying: "Hallo darling, how are you?". That was all, even if they'd just been utterly foul to her, with such warmth that it felt as if she was a lodestone for them, drawing them to her warmth. The child would then go off again feeling "better" in some way. She never rejected them and truly took them to heart. From observing these interchanges, which puzzled me a lot at first, I realised that the fact that she loved them and also that their love was welcomed by her, was very powerful and therapeutic for them. They felt that they could not destroy her love despite their behaviour at other times. I was meant to be supervising her but I learned a fortune from her. She and her family were very serious and committed Buddhists, and I used to go along and meditate with them at the Dharma Centre they set up in Edinburgh. They taught me a great deal about Buddhism and Buddhist meditation. Seija was an extraordinary mix of vitality and energy, together with deep capacity for contemplation and stillness. She was also an exceptional teacher, vivacious and therapeutic with the children. But the way she was as a person, had been refined by her Buddhism and her meditation practice. She's been a great influence in my life.

MP: So these are the origins of your spiritual interest.

ML: Yes, and Margaret Sampson, too, who was a Sufi teacher. I met Margaret before going to Edinburgh and she was probably the most important influence, someone whom I think of as a

56   THE BUDDHA AND THE BABY

spiritual guide in my life. I met her when I was about thirty-four or thirty-five, and she helped to reconnect me with the spiritual path that had started with Lionel. During my twenties, with the busy-ness of raising a family and doing the child psychotherapy training, I had lost that connection. Margaret was a very active member of Mrs Irina Tweedy's group, a well-known Sufi group based in London, and had all sorts of psychoanalytic experiences. She had been in analysis, worked at the Cassel Hospital as a psychiatric nurse and taught autistic children. Frances Tustin had come across her and quoted her in one of her books. She had had a very lengthy analysis, with an eminent analyst (amazingly at no cost), so she could really understand what analysis could do, and what meditation could do, and how they seemed to work within different aspects of the human beings' inner life. So there are all these interconnections, and now the other important person in my spiritual life is the Rabbi at the synagogue I've become a member of in the last few years, Jonathan Wittenberg. He's inspirational and seems to bring out the best in people, helping them to really try to live up to the very best of their abilities. Through his sermons and study groups, I've become more able to understand Jewish thoughts about ethics, theology, and my Jewish roots. Having spent most of my life fascinated by Eastern religions—I also had a very good teacher of chanting, meditation, yoga, and the Bhagavad Ghita in particular—I have now found much that interests and moves me in this way, from within Judaism. It's a "return". I have been very fortunate to have such a varied experience of spiritual teachings and teachers.

MP: Can you tell me how you integrate your spiritual approach with your work and if you do use some specific meditation techniques with your patients?

ML: I am not in clinical practice any more but supervise many colleagues and trainees. This is why it now feels ok to talk in such a personal way about the impact of meditation on my ways of being, working, thinking and teaching. I was more cautious and private about sharing all of this in the past. When I was seeing patients, if there was a crisis and the patient was going through a terrible period in his or her life and suffering a great deal, or if there was a patient who was very aggressive and violent,

THE PRESENCE OF THE THERAPIST   57

and I would feel frightened before seeing them, I found it very helpful to make a point of trying to get to a calmer place within myself for even just a few minutes before the start of the session. So sometimes, if I could, I would meditate for a few minutes in the consulting room. This seemed to help me to clear my mind and to be there calmly in the room before the patient entered it. I think this helped both because of something within myself but also because of something that I think was then there in the room, before the patient came in—a kind of atmosphere or potentially calming energy. It's like in a concert hall: the music needs to sort of begin to fill the auditorium, so sometimes the first part of the music doesn't quite set up the same vibrations as by the end of the concert. It's as if the vibration needs to fill and inhabit the space, I don't know how to describe it. Similarly, I think sometimes it's got to do with what you bring to the session and with the presence of the therapist. You can try to establish in the room a calmer space both within yourself but also literally by you having been in the room meditating a bit beforehand, particularly with very agitated patients. I think they enter a different space. How much that helps them and how long that helps them, I don't know, but it just gives them a little bit of a chance to get to a calmer place. Of course there are other ways of trying to bring that peace into the room as well. The same thing at the end of session, and I say this to supervisees as well. If at all possible, try and take just a brief period of time to recover a bit after a particularly demanding patient—as well as to prepare themselves as much as possible before seeing such a patient. As well as this being potentially better for the patient, I think it's quite dangerous for the therapists' emotional and physical wellbeing to go straight from one very difficult session to another without some recovery time and preparation time.

MP: Because we put it onto the next patients?

ML: It's not even that; our training helps us to try hard not to let this happen. I'm not sure that we put it onto the next patient, I think it's what goes on within ourselves, that's the burn-out, you know, that it accumulates and accumulates. I certainly would find that I would reach the end of the day almost giddy with all the stuff that had been put into me. There had been no opportunity to process

58   THE BUDDHA AND THE BABY

what I had experienced. I know that it's not always possible, but sometimes if you know that a particular patient is really demanding, it can help to shift session times, literally just five minutes this way, five minutes that way to get some breathing space, some recovery time. If you really regard that kind of recovery time as a central contribution to your way of being in a session, it gives you a fighting chance to hold onto some calm within the storms that patients need to bring to therapy. We know we've got to calm patients who are in these very agitated and distressed states, before we can do anything. We've got to calm them and if our own anxieties are shooting up together with them, it makes it much more difficult. Whereas if we can start from a steadier base, and that's where for some people, regular, if possible daily meditation comes into it, then there's a better chance for us to be able to know the patient's state of agitation, to attune to the affect and understand it more. I felt that with certain patients I could feel my anxiety rising as the session time approached and that's why I started to meditate in the morning. Through the regular meditation practice, I set my "anxiety thermostat" to a lower, calmer level. I found I was more able to stay calm within myself and be open to whatever the patient brought. So that was the way in which meditation helped me to do work: I would be more grounded and genuinely calmer. So meditation became an ongoing, regular practice, a daily routine, as much as I could. For many years, I started the day, and I still do, with something meditative and contemplative. I think that has accumulated and it become very much a part of me.

MP: Apparently even just twenty minutes' meditation a day changes the brain.

ML: Yes, I can well believe that. Yoga also really helps to steady and calm one. The two together for me are very important.

MP: So you think it does have an effect on the patient, don't you?

ML: I think so, in the ways I have just described. At first, before I "came out" and started to talk about the importance of meditation to me, I felt this was something that I had to keep in a separate part of my life, even though I knew it greatly affected the way I was when with my patients—my "presence" when with them. I talked

THE PRESENCE OF THE THERAPIST   59

about it a lot with Margaret Sampson, but I didn't think I could talk to colleagues.

MP: When I did some visualisation and breathing exercises with a very disabled adolescent boy, in a state of excruciating physical pain, and whom I had presented at an ACP conference and then written about, I felt very unsure and scared about coming out with other colleagues. I remember finding your response and comments at that time extremely encouraging and supportive (Pozzi, 2005).

ML: I remember and what a wise and helpful thing you did then with your patient.

MP: It's necessary to adapt to these situations in ways which may be un-orthodox but necessary and helpful. Then years later, we find out that they become much more acceptable and other people also work like that. But as you said, one has to prepare oneself, one's own internal self, just as much as one prepares the therapy room and the atmosphere of the room before patients who are taxing and challenging emotionally. So the techniques need to change and adapt to the needs of these patients.

ML: The patient comes into a certain atmosphere, and a certain space, which is thoughtful, emotional, and also spiritual, and I think is influenced by that. Meditation is, as I said, a very fundamental way to prepare myself for the work. It's very hard to work in the NHS nowadays because of the pressure, and that steady state of mind is very much needed.

MP: Can you say something about the Buddhist ideas of no-self, emptiness, and attachment versus non-attachment, and how they relate to your work?

ML: The idea of egoless-ness totally puzzled me to begin with and I couldn't make sense of it. Now, I understand it quite differently, and I think it refers to a quality in people, which I really value and recognise, where the power-driven ego is not to the fore, you know, and doesn't have to be constantly fed. The idea of "I must express myself, me, me, me", I don't think leads to happiness in the self or in the people around us. I value the writings of the Dalai Lama on the importance of happiness; strangely, we don't talk much about happiness or love in psychoanalysis, and yet they are vital to how

60 THE BUDDHA AND THE BABY

people live (Dalai Lama, p. 19). Buddhist wisdom in the *Tao Te Ching* by Lao Tzu (1997) is an important companion to me, full of wisdom, very useful. The philosophy of Buddhism appeals a lot to Jewish people who can't find spirituality in Judaism. There are lots of Jewish Buddhists who are searching for a spiritual core which had been lost, particularly after the concentration camps of the Second World War. The translation I love of the *Tao Te Ching* by Stephen Mitchell (1999) uses very ordinary language and the beautiful wisdom it expresses often comes into my mind. For me, it captures the idea of egoless-ness in a Buddhist sense, which is very different from how we use this idea in the West. Perhaps we idealise the Eastern philosophies to some extent, I don't know. I find it particularly interesting when writers and teachers translate Eastern ideas for the Western mind—like Matthew Ricard, who wrote *The Philosopher and the Monk* (1993) and *Happiness* (2003), combining Buddhist ideas with his neuroscientific knowledge.

MP: How does that relate with emptiness?

ML: Well, I don't know. But another idea, which I find very helpful and comes from Buddhist meditation, is the idea of this interesting balance between something within you that you still, but then something else that arises from the depths. I like this idea that through the stillness something else can arise to the surface, and it took me a long while to understand what that was about. I do think that from the stillness you can find in meditation or from the guiding principles in your life, the possibility of contentment, simplicity and compassion (part of what the the *Tao Te Ching* teaches) can arise. But that's not the same as the "emptiness" that I think you are referring to. So I have much I don't understand here. In meditation, you try to let go of the "monkey mind" (as I think Buddhists call it) which is "all over the place". And you may briefly have a moment that is truly quiet or maybe "empty" in the sense that you are referring to. Or you might just have got a bit closer to this "empty" state of mind, and then other things begin to "arise" from the depths. I think that the point about meditation is that repeating and repeating the practice may lead to that productive emptiness and then other things begin to arise. So I find that can be very helpful—but I am not sure that I have done more than scratch the surface of this idea.

THE PRESENCE OF THE THERAPIST   61

MP: Something arises from emptiness: it's how to understand the terminology, isn't it?

ML: Yes, but may be also related to the particular translation of the original text, that's why you've got to be very careful which translation you read because some of them are not that clear. The *Bhagavad Gita* (translated by Christopher Isherwood) and the *Tao Te Ching* (translated by Stephen Little) are books I come back to, over and over again. Also *The Prophet* by Kalil Gibran (1926) is very present in my life—such beautiful poetry and wisdom about human relationships. But the translation is always very important to help understand the thinking and access the wisdom of the text.

MP: Did you ever have any particularly mystical experience for example of no-self or no-time, through your meditation practice?

ML: Sometimes there are those times in meditation where time really ceases to have meaning, when you suddenly find that you've meditated much longer than you thought and you think: where have I been? You've not been asleep; you've not been thinking and yet the time has gone. Where to?

MP: Is it like losing oneself in time or the time is no longer there, somehow?

ML: Perhaps; I find time is a bit like an elastic band; sometimes time stretches itself out and so what is a short time could feel as if it's so much longer than it is and you think: "Oh was it only last week? So much has happened since the event." What is actually physically short in time, feels as if it's extended over such a long period of time. Time can also compact somehow. Some periods of time feel quite impoverished in my life; other times feel to have been a rather rich experience of time; so much has happened in a short period of time.

MP: Do you experience the same with children patients?

ML: You can feel that in sessions, of course. At some point, the session will fly past and other times it's just unbearable and so hard to stay in the present moment. That's again where meditation can help you to be focused and to keep coming back to the present

62   THE BUDDHA AND THE BABY

moment. I think it's very hard to do that. I think it's Nina Coltart (1993, 1996) who talks about that: returning to the present moment with determination—to come back again and again and again. We learn that through meditation. We have to do that with patients, you know, keep catching ourselves when our minds go off somewhere else with a patient. We have to keep coming back. That's what we know from the neuroscience that we have to do. To un-learn destructive old patterns of the brain and give a new pattern a chance to grow; to do this, you've got to keep repeating the new. Repeating is so very important. Keeping on trying (and therapeutically repeating new efforts to change) and the quality of determination are a central part of the experience of meditation— and very central to ideas about the therapeutic process.

MP: Can you say a bit more about the neurosciences?

ML: Well, I'll try. It's moving at such a pace, and my understanding is limited, but this is what I make of it at the moment—clinically. When there's a destructive pattern that has been burnt into the brain since early infancy due to external or relational trauma, it becomes the "natural" or default pathway. These pathways go directly from the limbic system (the animal/reptilian reactive brain) to action without bringing in the cortex and the thinking part of the brain; they are what we often encounter in the consulting room. The established neural pathway within the brain, in such a case, is of flight, fight, and frozen fear. That's the natural way it flows and you've got to create a new flow and you've got to un-learn the old pattern of reaction. Un-learning is so difficult but, alongside that, there's the beginning of new pathways. It's as if the neural flow is used to going down the old destructive pathway and you want to encourage it to go down this new less destructive and hopefully developmentally more sound pathway. You've got to both try to diminish the flow in the old destructive direction and at the same time to coax things in the new direction that's going to be more positive, and that takes lots of repetition and time.

MP: That's what the practice consists of: repeating over and over again, and this creates a new pattern.

ML: That's right and to modify that flow it's, of course, going to take a long time. It's not just a moment of insight, although that can

THE PRESENCE OF THE THERAPIST   63

be a powerful, final step after a lot of trickling like that has gone before. This reminds me of a Buddhist teacher in Edinburgh, who said about meditation: "Just do it. Just sit there, sit on the cushion and just do it! When you notice that your mind has gone off, just do it, just return to the object of your focus." In Judaism, the idea of return, of going back and trying to repair, is also very important. So this is an interesting link for me with Judaism.

MP: That's also part of therapy with children: to go back over and over again on issues the child brings to sessions and revisits all the time and we try and give them a different response and experience from their known patterns of behaviour and responses.

ML: Yes, and the two reinforce each others, I mean the spiritual and the relationship in therapy. We don't talk enough about ethics and morality: where do they sit within psychoanalytic practice? They come from the philosophical and religious tradition.

MP: How can this issue of ethics and morality apply to child work?

ML: That's interesting. I remember when I was doing a research project at Great Ormond Street with young adolescent sexual offenders. I remember strikingly, a child whose father had abused him, but the boy never the less had a strong, strong sense of knowing all along that what his father was doing was wrong. Even when he was a young child and the abuse was happening, he knew the wrongness—but it was his father! But how did he know it was wrong? Where does the sense of what's right and wrong come from? In this instance, from when he was a very young child, the boy knew his father was "wrong".

MP: That's interesting, and presumably he was one of the kids who did not go on to abuse others?

ML: I don't think he did; I don't remember clearly, but what I do remember is that this boy who came from this ghastly, dreadful abusive life was never the less able to say something like: "My dad didn't teach me right from wrong but he is still the only dad I had." He knew that, and it was very painful. The great religions and philosophies address these questions about how do we come to know as an ordinary individual, what's right and what's wrong? It's society, it's sociology, it's anthropology, and it's also religion and philosophy laying down what is the ethical,

64   THE BUDDHA AND THE BABY

moral way of living this life; it's very much what they're about. These ideas are to some extent conveyed through our earliest relationships, but they are not only conveyed in this way. They are in the culture. And they are complex systems of thoughts and arguments, you know, within the Buddhist tradition, and they often resonate with Jewish philosophy.

MP: Would you say that they're engrained in human nature so that some kids have it and others have it less, for reasons we are not sure about?

ML: I don't know; I' m very idealistic about this, so I'd like to think that we all have it but then it can get hammered out of us, according to our life experiences. You know, I'd like to think that as human beings we have that natural potential and capacity—as appropriate at different stages in our lives.

MP: Winnicott said something along these lines, didn't he?

ML: In a way, yes, but I don't think he wrote specifically about a spiritual dimension of experience as such, although I think it is very evident in his ideas. I'd like to think that we all come with that capacity to be creative and ethical but that life experiences obviously shape and affect this natural ability.

MP: You spoke beautifully about preparing yourself, the room, the atmosphere, the environment etc. with the presence of the therapist and something is transmitted to the child in the session.

ML: I do think that the non verbal communication is so important. I remember a little boy who'd been adopted; he was a highly intelligent little boy, who'd been very attached to his foster carers, and his adoptive parents had been very attuned and tried to help him deal with this loss of his foster carers; so they worked well with this. He also had a failed adoption prior to the foster care. It was so painful to be with him: he had such a pained expression, which may have been in connection with the failed adoption, which it seems he had deliberately broken down. He had a strong intuition as to who was "right" for him, and who wasn't, and I was so intrigued that I said: "You mean you can say straight off who is for you and who isn't for you?" "Yes" he said. It was as if he had developed these antennae to know immediately if somebody was

THE PRESENCE OF THE THERAPIST 65

really open to him or not and who was on his wavelength and who wasn't. I don't know what we make of that; but it could well be that in years to come we will have suitable technology and be able to understand this.

MP: He felt that the right thing for him to do was not to be with the first adoptive parents, wasn't it?

ML: Yes, he just felt that.

MP: Perhaps the work with you and your meditative way of being helped him to develop these antennae?

ML: No, it happened long before he was in therapy. It was his survival mechanism.

MP: Would you say it was a spiritual intuition for him?

ML: No, I don't think so in this instance. It's more about the non verbal communication that goes on between people, what we mean by this and how it actually takes place.

MP: Yes, indeed, Monica, and perhaps with this aura of mystery we can end this most interesting communication and with many thanks.

References

Blue, L. (2005). *Hitchhiking to Heaven*. London: Hodder and Stoughton.

Coltart, N. (1993). *How to Survive as a Psychotherapist*. London: Sheldon Press.

Coltart, N. (1996). *The Baby and the Bathwater*. London: Karnac.

Gibran, K. (1926). *The Prophet*. Melbourne, Auckland, and London: Heinemann.

Lao Tzu (1997). *Tao Te Ching: An Illustrated Journey*. Tr. Stephen Mitchell. London: Frances Lincoln.

Pozzi, M. (2005). Love at first sight: psychoanalytic psychotherapy with an adolescent boy with severe physical disabilities. *Journal of Child Psychotherapy, 31(3)*: 203–316.

Ricard, M. (2003). *Happiness: A Guide to Developing Life's Most Important Skill*. Tr. Jesse Browner. New York: Atlantic Books, Little Brown, 2006.

Ricard, M., & Revel, J. -F. (1993). *The Philosopher and the Monk: A Father and Son Discuss the Meaning of Life*. New York: Shocken Books.

CHAPTER SIX

The moon allows the sun to shine on it

Dialogue with Dorette Engi

There are only two ways to live your life. One is as though nothing is a miracle. The other is as if everything is.

—Albert Einstein

MP: I am rather excited about this interview, Dorette, as I know you have a lot of experience in Buddhist meditation, having spent two years in retreat in the south of France. You are also a child psychotherapist. I understand that you practise psychotherapy within a Buddhist community, that's very interesting and unique. Do tell me how you first became involved with Buddhism.

DE: In 1978, I met Sogyal Rinpoche, a young Tibetan lama, who was the translator for His Holiness the Dalai Lama during his first visit in the West. I became very interested in Tibetan Buddhism and started meditation on and off. But since 1995, I have been practising regularly and it has seen me through difficult times in my life. What I loved about receiving teaching from these many Tibetan Lamas, whom I met during this time, was that their teaching was very experiential, personal, and not heady or intellectual. Being in their presence often leads to a clarity of mind and peacefulness.

68 THE BUDDHA AND THE BABY

MP: If therapy works well it may lead to a state of clear and enlightened mind; doesn't it? Does this relate to working with children in your experience?

DE: Yes, but I often puzzle over the differences between the two. There is something about the relationship and the personal one-to-one connection, which is very important in the work with patients and also for our often neglected and abused child patients, whilst meditation is more about settling the mind. Here we do not enter emotional states, whereas in therapy you work through emotional states to get to a more settled mind. The danger of therapy is that you may get stuck in the emotional intensity and the danger of meditation is that you may get detached from your emotions.

MP: Do you have any experience of meditation and psychotherapy coming together?

DE: Yes, one example comes to mind of an eight-year-old child with autism with whom I had struggled for a year and a half without much contact growing between us two; he used to walk up and down the room pulling at his trousers' string in his attempt to avoid making contact with me. In the autumn, coming back from a Dzogchen retreat (Teaching of Great Perfection), I had felt very transformed and things had opened up for me. I think it was in the second session, as always he walked up and down, when he suddenly stopped beside me and looked at me intently and seemed to be interested and curious about something in me. He said: "The moon allows the sun to shine on it". Ahh, it still really moves me. It was a complete and real connection for the first time with him. I often wondered what that was about and all I can think is that I was clearly very open and very much in love with life at that particular point and perhaps that was what he saw and was curious about. What was interesting was that I was not trying to make contact with him but I was just present and open to him. Perhaps this allowed him to drop his autistic barrier for a moment.

MP: I was thinking of a good combined object inside you, the two parents in a constructive intercourse, the moon and the sun being together in a creative and lively way and he was being created and born out of his autistic shell.

THE MOON ALLOWS THE SUN TO SHINE ON IT   69

DE: Well, the work kept going on for two more years with ups and downs, but that moment held the hope that this boy had potential and could come out of the autism. By the time we stopped his mother gave me his first coloured drawing that he had done just as the end of therapy approached. In it there were two trees connected by a row of flowers with a sun and a little cloud. I thought that the two trees connected by a row of flowers symbolised two people connecting in a benign way.

MP: Perhaps the expression by your patient about the moon allowing the sun to shine on it was like a moment of enlightenment for both of you presumably; enlightenment within a relationship, which is a miracle for a child with autism.

DE: Yes, I have no idea how he came to say that; but he was very intuitive and it was very poignant.

MP: Once I was seeing in therapy an extremely abused, intellectually delayed and neglected adolescent girl, who saw me "not being there". I was preoccupied, unwell and cloud-minded somehow and she repeated: "Miss Pozzi wakey, wakey". She was absolutely right: my mind was not spacious and empty to receive her stuff but clattered by my own stuff. Her intuition was amazing despite her cognitive disability. This is similar to psychotic patients, who can be ahead of therapists on some occasions.

DE: You must be familiar with the mirror neurons. In 2009, Daniel Goleman, the author of *Emotional Intelligence* (1995) and a member of the Mind and Life Institute, spoke to Rinpoche about new scientific research in the field of neurology and psychology that has discovered something called "mirror neurons".These neurons get stimulated and activated when we focus our mind onto another person. It was discovered that this particular set of neurons actually "picks up" and matches the brain activity of the person they are focusing on. It has been shown that people who rank high on a scale measuring empathy have particularly active mirror neurons systems—a discovery which led an eminent neuroscientist, Ramachandran, to call these "empathy neurons" or "Dalai Lama neurons" (2007). When one sits with an advanced meditator who is in a peaceful state of mind, and one is focused on that person deliberately as one does in meditation, one mirrors

70 THE BUDDHA AND THE BABY

his state of being. The discovery of mirror neurons is shaking up numerous scientific disciplines and is shifting the understanding of culture, empathy, philosophy, language, imitation, autism, and psychotherapy.

MP: An adolescent boy patient of mine with Asperger's, in his last psychotherapy session became poetic and wrote a lovely poem about him and nature at a point when he clearly felt more separate, less persecuted by possible intrusively perceived closeness with me (Pozzi, 2003). There was more space and he must have felt freer similarly to your boy, who may have felt that your mind was for your new love and spiritual third party. There may have been some jealousy of course, but it's the kind of jealousy that may propel the child with autism to come out of the shell and to relate a little better, as we often see in clinical practice. To return to your Buddhist practice, how does it affect your work as a child psychotherapist?

DE: I have worked within a Buddhist organisation for the last few years. Interestingly, the Buddha seems to become a benign and helpful internal object when you work. I once saw an eleven-year-old child who had bad dreams. During the assessment she told me about a dream in which she was walking down a road, which was like a cutting in a forest. It was very dangerous, there were horrible creatures coming from all sides and she prayed to the Buddha and then the Buddha appeared to her and saved her. So this was quite a powerful dream and a powerful experience for her. I found it very helpful when a tutor, in a seminar group during my training as a child psychotherapist at the Tavistock, emphasised the importance of even encouraging our patients' mind to turn to a good object rather than only focusing on anxieties and negative objects. That little girl turned to her good object, called the Buddha.

MP: Your role as a Buddhist therapist within a long retreat and in the context of the Buddhist Community is very interesting. It reminds me of child psychotherapists working in schools or in therapeutic communities or hospitals: they have to take into account the patient's transference to the institution in a specific way related to that specific institution and to what it means for that specific child.

THE MOON ALLOWS THE SUN TO SHINE ON IT   71

DE: Of course the Lama is very important during a long retreat and has a paternal function. He sometimes sends people to therapy when he thinks there is a psychological issue, not an issue related to the spiritual practice. It becomes a very organic process.

MP: The Lama and the therapist are like two parental figures working together or two institutions: clinic and school working for the benefit of the child and family, don't they?

DE: You also need to be very flexible in this context and to adapt to the retreat schedules and changes.

MP: That's right and is similar to working with children in schools and on hospital wards. Now to go back to the work with a child, what do you find useful in Buddhism in your therapeutic work with children?

DE: In our training, we learn to monitor our thoughts and emotions and to work with our transference. When working with difficult and aggressive children, I can close down or seize up emotionally, and this is when I find the practice of Tonglen very helpful. It is a practice where you take in with your breath pain and suffering and you send out compassion and ease in your out breath. Once, when I was with the boy with autism whom I have mentioned earlier, I felt quite dizzy because of his relentlessness, a mantra came to me, and I recited it silently to myself and that was my healing, good internal object or Buddha. That is bigger than me, and it usually helps or at least it doesn't make it worse, and the boy calmed down because I'd calmed down. A process of containment occurred.

MP: Would you use any Buddhist technique actively in your work with children?

DE: At this stage I have not asked patients explicitly. I try not to jump models and since I am both a meditation instructor and a psychotherapist, I try to stay in roles and I don't mix the two. I don't know in the future, I might change. Some people learn mindfulness techniques and use them with patients. Jon Kabat-Zinn, the creator of the Mindfulness Program and the author of the book *Full Catastrophe Living* (1990), said in his talk at the conference of medicine and Buddhism in October 2010 in Lerab Ling: "Mindfulness-Based Stress Reduction, MBSR, is Buddhism

72   THE BUDDHA AND THE BABY

without the Buddha. It's secular Buddhism." These programmes aim to help with chronic pain and depression, but here the aim is not enlightenment.

MP: So you would not ask a child who is particularly aggressive, punches you, or kicks you, to focus on anything, to breathe, would you?

DE: I would love to experiment with that in a group and to look at children's fears as I now do with adults in the context of the Buddhist retreat. But I don't focus on breathing with them; they're all meditators and are used to practising. We might explore how to apply the meditation practice to their particular issues.

MP: Another question I have is about the ego and the Buddhist idea of no-ego, no-self, what's your thinking about that apparent contradiction?

DE: I think what the Buddhism calls ego and what psychotherapy calls ego, are two different entities. In Buddhism, ego is self-centred and only wants something for the self and doesn't think of others. It is narcissistic, basically. Ego is an organising principle in psychology. I feel there is a parallel between Klein's paranoid-schizoid and depressive positions and the Buddhist ego and the Buddha nature within us. There is a switch into the depressive position and similarly a switch into a compassionate mode of functioning. But I think Buddha nature goes much further, into a joyful state; while depressive position sounds to me to be a bit depressive. Freud spoke of transformation into common unhappiness, whereas a Buddhist would aim for enlightenment or full awakening. This comes from the concluding paragraph of Freud's *Studies on Hysteria* (1895d), which has been translated many times, hence the varying words of the quotation.

MP: Even though there is the creativity that goes along with the depressive state of mind?

DE: Yes, I suppose and the joy of creativity and love, and Klein speaks a lot about love and gratitude (1942).

MP: Could we say in a nut shell that the ego—in Buddhist terms—is of a narcissistic nature, while the non-ego is more compassionate, concerned about the other and the welfare of all beings?

DE: Yes. Chogyam Trungpa was really the first one of the Tibetan lamas to marry the Western psychological and spiritual ideas. He worked in Colorado and wrote a book called *The Sanity We Are Born With* (Trungpa, 2005) which is fascinating in terms of psychoanalysis and Buddhism. Many lamas don't understand the concept of self-hatred and the lack of self-esteem, which is endemic in the West. In his book, Trungpa connects this tendency with the concept of the original sin of the Judaeo-Christian tradition. Buddhism talks of primordial purity or fundamental goodness, which is often meant by Buddha nature as the potential core of our being. All the rest is *kleshas*, that is, negative emotions, concepts, habitual tendencies, and karmic traces; these are the clouds that cover our original state. The concept of original sin is a powerful concept in all religions, and I wonder whether this is related to the difficulty many patients have in believing in their inherent goodness.

MP: This depends a lot on the kind of parents one had and if they saw you as a child, mostly loveable, good, and they accepted you as you were. We may call this unconditional love. Thinking of the idea of no-self (*anatta*) and of emptiness (*suniata*), non-attachment, which are cornerstones in Buddhism, how do you reconcile them with psychoanalytic theory and practice when it comes to working with children?

DE: These three concepts are very deep and interesting; one refers to the absolute, that is, to Bion's "O" (Bion, 1959). This is a mystical concept, while psychoanalytic concepts are, in general, on the relative level. Concerning emptiness, I would attempt to have an attitude of no desire or memory; isn't that similar to being open and in the present, or here and now, when with the child? We don't sort of gallop to a room with all sorts of programmes and ideas of what we need to do with a session. Our aim is just to be there with the child and that attitude is itself quite empty or open, present. In our work, we have a set beginning and an ending, which give a frame to the session, but we don't have any strategies in our work with the child.

MP: The moment of letting go, for example, of hope, when things are desperate with some patients, is for me very difficult to obtain, and yet when I allow it to be, then things happen.

74 THE BUDDHA AND THE BABY

DE: Isn't that interesting: accepting that it's hopeless infuses hope; it's contradictory, isn't it?

MP: Yes, a paradox.

DE: I would think that partly why we can't let the situation be as hopeless as it is, is because we protect ourselves. It's so unbearable to us, as we fear that we might be a bad therapist and fail the patient who is suffering so much.

MP: Yes, it's very hard to accept suffering, especially of children. To go back to babies and interdependence etc., the dummy is such a cherished object for babies and Bowlby's very important ideas on attachment (Bowlby, 1969) seem so much in contrast with the Buddhist aspiration to non-attachment. How do you reconcile the two in your work as a child psychotherapist?

DE: I remember Rinpoche teaching children that the Buddha is their dummy. The dummy is like the link to mummy or to the Buddha: it makes the child much happier. When you are a baby, you should be attached to mummy, daddy, and the dummy. It's all about the right attachment at the right moment. I think that non-attachment is highly misunderstood.

MP: Tell me more.

DE: Non-attachment can feel like a rejection of enjoyable things and that's due to the Calvinist, puritanical attitude. We need attachment from a psychological, developmental point of view; from a spiritual point of view, our attachment is due to ignorance and fears. Non-attachment is linked with the realisation of *shunyata*. In a nutshell, I think attachment is often misunderstood by us Westerners: we are seeing a lot of children with problems in attachment, and there are issues with attachment as they don't attach healthily; that's on a psychological level. If we attach safely and healthily, then we also become more flexible because when we feel self-confident, we can let go. However, it's hard to let go because when early attachment is not good enough, then all sorts of problems for the child occur. The state of huge need and un-satisfyable hunger is represented by the Hungry Ghosts of the Buddhist Wheel of Life. These Hungry Ghosts never get enough: they are depicted with huge bellies, thin mouths, and tiny throats

THE MOON ALLOWS THE SUN TO SHINE ON IT   75

so they can't take much in; they are always hungry but cannot allow the nourishment in.

MP: I'm thinking of the "no entry" defence so vividly described by Gianna Williams in her book on psychotherapy with youngsters with eating disorders (Williams, 1997). This problem starts in the very early relationship between the mother and the infant, when—due to relational, constitutional issues—the baby cannot take in the good feed and thrive.

DE: And also with love and nourishment: non-attachment has to do with allowing things to be as they are, without an ego attached to them.

MP: So, non-attachment has to do with love for the object: you love, you lose, you mourn and let go, doesn't it? Now, how do you relate this awareness of impermanence and non-attachment to your psychotherapy with children?

DE: There is a chronology, a sense of time and space in the session; there's a beginning and an ending; the therapy itself will come to an end: we are not the child's parents. This defines our role: we can be paternal or maternal but we are aware of our position and don't take over. I think that non-attachment is linked to all this.

MP: Yes, it's essential in our work with children: first we help them to attach to us as therapists, so they can re-work through the traumas and issues, which they come to therapy with. Then we help them to let go of us, to separate, accept ending and keep us inside them in their mind and memory.

DE: This also applies to our attachment, as therapists, to our patients: we work through our attachment to them and let go of them, we dis-attach gradually.

MP: This is very clear, Dorette. Now on a different and more personal level: have you ever had a mystical moment, a moment of enlightment in your many years of practice as a Buddhist?

DE: I think so, it is hard to say for sure. But you have those moments when you are on retreat. But we tend to fixate on a concept of enlightenment. It's a changing experience: things become very clear and light, you almost see things in a different dimension;

76 THE BUDDHA AND THE BABY

they finally make sense and are completely perfect. It's the way things are, without mentally clouding over or delusion. For me it was a most extraordinary sense of beauty. It's not the thinking mind, which is enlightened; it's not even the feeling, it is ... I don't really know!

MP: Hard to put into concepts and words, presumably?

DE: Yes, it is a mystical moment. When I talk about it, it becomes something else. It's a moment of perfection and everything becomes open, vast, clear and profoundly deep. It's a holy experience in the stillness of the sitting with the group of us training during retreats.

MP: It seems to me to be in line with the experience of no-self, I once had during a retreat where I experienced to be beyond Me and to be pure consciousness observing I and others in the meditation hall. It was not a dissociative state but a fleeting sense of a universal awareness and wide spaciousness. It was a blissful moment but it soon went, as it happens! What a good point to end this very enriching conversation. Many thanks, Dorette, for sharing your experience with me and co-guiding this dialogue.

References

Bion, W. R. (1959). *Attention and Interpretation*. London: Tavistock.
Bowlby, J. (1969, 1973). *Attachment and Loss*. Vol 1 and Vol 2. London: Hogarth.
Freud, S. (1895d). *Studies on Hysteria*. SE 2. London: Hogarth.
Goleman, D. (1995). *Emotional Intelligence*. New York: Bantam Books.
Kabat-Zinn, J. (1990). *Full Catastrophe Living*. New York: Dell.
Klein, M. (1942). *Love, Guilt and Reparation*. New York: Delta Books, 1975.
Pozzi, M. (2003). The use of observation in the psychoanalytic treatment of a twelve-year-old boy with Asperger's syndrome. *The International Journal of Psychoanalysis, 84(5)*: 1333–1349.
Ramachandran, V. S. (2007). *The Neurology of Awareness*. California: Brockman & Weinberger.
Trungpa, C. (2005). *The Sanity We Are Born With: A Buddhist Approach to Psychology*. Boston, MA: Shambala Publications.
William, G. (1997). *Internal Landscapes and Foreign Bodies: Eating Disorders and Other Pathologies*. London: Duckworth/Tavistock Clinic Series.

CHAPTER SEVEN

Coming home

Dialogue with Anonymous

There's nothing to do, nowhere to go, no one to be.

MP: I appreciate that you have agreed to talk to me about your experience as an NHS Child and Adolescent Psychiatrist and a Buddhist.

A: Yes, at the moment.

MP: I would love to hear about how you can use—if we can say so—your Buddhist background in that role, but before that I just want to ask you at which point in your life you began this journey, if you come from a family with religious or Buddhist tradition and how this dual interest—the Buddhist choice and the psychiatrist choice—came about for you.

A: The direct antecedents, when I was at medical school and even going further back when I was a teenager, I remember buying a book on yoga and began doing yoga exercises and also read about terms such as *Dharma*, *Dhayani* (wisdom), and I was curious about this. At university, I went to a transcendental meditation class and that made an immediate link for me to the stuff that I had read.

78 THE BUDDHA AND THE BABY

I learned to meditate with that approach with Maharishi Yogi the founder. I found it quite helpful but was not interested in the super structure created there. It helped me to cut through tense or difficult states of mind: it did work for me. I was fairly constant and meditated regularly, daily using the mantra. Then about ten years later, I decided to travel the world and as part of that I spent several months at Dharamsala. It was like a call, just like a call: I had to go to Dharamsala. This was in 1998 or 1999, around the time the Dalai Lama won the Nobel Price for peace, and he was still relatively unknown and was not the hugely international sort of presence that he is now. At that time it was quite small, the hills were still very unspoilt and it was actually possible to meet the Dalai Lama. I used to go to the library where they ran teachings for Westerners every morning six days a week. There would be very traditional lamas talking Tibetan and being translated into English and there would be about fifteen to twenty people. I went there every day for months and months.

MP: Did you read the texts there?

A: It was a traditional formal Buddhist approach: The Lama read the text, and then explained it. I also read very widely. I met briefly and shook the Dalai Lama's hand at the Tibetan New Year celebration. When I was very young, about nine years old, I had found a book at home which described Tibetan iconography, and though it didn't make much sense at the time: I do remember the description of Mount Meru, with a palace on top. So to read and hear about this again while living in Dharamsala all those years later was like coming home. When I came back to Britain I looked for and found a Centre to support me in my practice.

MP: What a real journey of inner discovery!

A: Yes, coming home as the Buddhist just seemed to make sense to offer a context from which to understand myself, other people, the mind. All these Lamas around were living examples of what I had read about. I felt very comfortable with them.

MP: Now, thinking of your role in your position particularly at Trust meetings, how do you link it with your meditation experience. Also in your direct work with kids—I believe you specialise with

COMING HOME 79

adolescents—do you use any Tibetan visualisation technique or other techniques in your activity as a child psychiatrist?

A: I would never use any meditation techniques directly with patients or with colleagues, because that would be entirely inappropriate, because that's not what I'm trained to do, you know, either as a medical manager or clinically, so I wouldn't do that. However it's interesting that mindfulness based meditation is now finding its way into psychiatry but I've never linked to that directly. But I was thinking how the Buddhist view has informed my work. For example, there is an adolescent whom I've known for many years, as an inarticulate boy with ADHD, who recently wanted to talk. So we agreed to a trail of weekly appointments to explore his relationship issues. However, soon after that he got into trouble with the law and was imprisoned. On release he asked to see me again. Still a fairly inarticulate young man, he would come into the room and often say nothing but pull his hoodie over his head. However, he always arrived, never missed appointments and was just there. I would find a way to start a conversation and had to think hopefully of the right questions to ask. He would give minimal information and I would use whatever he gave me as a way to try to understand where he was at. I worked to understand what he was going through, what was important for him at that time. What sustained this work was my sense that he found a space he could be himself with me. I needed to be patient and just be there, and the rather one sided conversation was simply a flow of words that said in effect, I am here, I am aware of you, I am thinking of you. In the end, it seemed clear it was not about cleverly working out what he might be preoccupied with, rather simply being a benign presence. He relaxed into that. Over time, he sat up, looked at me directly, smiled, and then talked about what was on his mind. When I asked what had helped, what had made the difference, he immediately said that he still wanted to come because I listened to him and I make him feel better. I very much thought that simply being present was key, and linked this to my understanding of what it is to meditate, which is settling the mind, being undistracted, simply being present and aware. It struck me that he responded to that rather than anything I said!

80   THE BUDDHA AND THE BABY

MP: Even if he talked very little, it was mostly your listening that was helping him.

A: Yes, he said: "But you try and understand". To link that back to Buddhism, you know, what I would do in those sessions, when he said hardly anything with his head down and elbows on his knees, so I could not even see his face (sometimes he even had his hood on), at those points I was just sitting there with him and I remember sometimes thinking to myself: "How would I explain to a commissioner what I was doing? How could I possibly say sitting here with this young man, who's saying nothing, is actually a useful, worthwhile thing to do?"

MP: And to be paid for it.

A: Exactly and to be paid. I had my own doubts. But what I would do from a Buddhist point of view is recognise these as simply my own doubts about doing anything useful, which could have driven me to end the sessions, or seek a more verbal contact with him. But I had a young man in the room, who had chosen to be there, and he didn't have to come, but he came very regularly. But importantly he changed over time, from inarticulate, possibly depressed, lost and angry to someone who was much happier and able to stay out of trouble. He made some positive decisions about his life as he went along. So I believed that was finding something useful in coming to "sit" with me.

MP: "Sit" is what we say when we meditate and that young boy, too, had somehow "come home" in his sessions with you.

A: Yes, or something like that. What I needed to do was be a presence; I found myself in a meditative state, meditating in the sense that I would just be there, in the room, with him in that state and try not be distracted by any other thoughts or doubts coming to my mind, but stay with it whatever and that made it possible for me to sit with him in a very relaxed way, week after week after week, while actually very little was probably being said. I came to believe that this was a useful thing to do.

MP: Child psychotherapist Monica Lanyado, whose interview is part of this book (Chapter Five), wrote about the presence of the therapist with these types of neglected, inarticulate patients and

COMING HOME   81

describes a very similar experience to yours. It's not possible with these patients to do the traditional psychotherapy based on interpretations; just being with these patients is being therapeutic and provides a containing presence: that is what is needed. Also what I think is being communicated in silence can be more effective and less misleading, at times, than talking can be.

A: You notice things: you know, that's the thing about silence is that, if you're able to be present and not carried off by your own thoughts, then you hear birds, the rain etc., but you also see and you feel, so you can become much more aware of the other, which helps us be grounded in the present moment as opposed to being carried away by thoughts or emotions. In my own psychiatric training of many years ago, the psychoanalytic model had been much used, even to explain things like psychosis and severe mental illnesses. R. D. Laing was pioneering his approach trying to understand the psychotic journey. But around that time, in the late 1980s, with the discovery of the brain's neurotransmitters, there was this immense hope that they would soon be able to discover the biological bases for schizophrenia, depression, and so on. So I was trained in an atmosphere where the scientific method was gaining the ascendancy over the psychoanalytic. We were trained to ask precise questions to delineate symptomathology clearly as the basis of making a diagnosis. While this made sense intellectually, I did not buy into the whole medical model approach, which seemed to be blind to the internal experience. Rather ironically, my last training placement was with Sula Wolff, a well-known child psychiatrist in Edinburgh for her own academic work in the field, yet as a clinician she appeared to be ever interested in the child's lived experience. Her clinical approach and supervision was all about making sense of what the child was going through or had experienced, in order to understand their particular problem. With hindsight, I now realize that her use of theory and application of knowledge were tools to help get at where a child might be, in terms of development and lived experience, not as final explanations in themselves. They were only maps to help orientate to the real territory that is the child's actual experience.

MP: Two fundamental strands.

A: I learned from her to develop a critical mind to understand the child, to consider what they're born with, the genetic aspect, as well as the whole attachment, other experiences, and all that adds up to form the individual.

MP: You tried to integrate the strands you had learned in your university times: the medical, the psychodynamic orientation, and your meditative stance, which clearly helped you offer something valuable to the silent youngster, who would mostly slouch silently.

A: I also read a lot of Bion: his container–contained model made much sense. I remember him describing his observations of psychotic patients from a position of silence, where he remained very silent and observed from there; so something there also made sense for me.

MP: You know that he was born in India, spent the first nine years of his life there, in a philosophical, spiritual, and presumably meditative, environment?

A: Yes, I read his autobiography and if you believe in reincarnation, I thought, you know, he was in the right place to be an Indian reincarnated into a Western body, if you like!!

MP: This is an interesting idea: I think he was one who brought a spiritual side to psychoanalysis—well, there was Jung and Fromm and others, of course—but the way Bion conceptualised the development of thinking, that is, it's the thought out there that comes to the thinker, is similar to the meditative process where things come to you or emerge inside you.

A: That's right, and the you, the real you, is not actually your thoughts, you know; you can see the thoughts as coming and going and your feelings as coming and going, but you, the observer, continues to be, irrespectively of this coming and going.

MP: This leads to another question: how do you reconcile the ideas of self and non-self? In our jobs, we try to help our little patients, the adolescents, the parents, to develop an ego, a strong sense of themselves, but then Buddhism says: no ego, *anatta*?

A: Well, I think it's important to hang on to what the Dalai Lama says, because he makes an important point. While Buddhism

COMING HOME   83

denies the existence of a discrete I or self that is a permanent, unchanging "ego" as real, Buddhism very much affirms the need for a strong sense of self based on the actual nature of things and the nature of mind, which is ever changing, interdependent, and so on. There are two opposing, philosophical standpoints or arguments in Buddhism: everything exists as you perceive them to, you know, things do exist as solid and real, and then there is the other extreme that nothing really exists, nothing at all, nihilism, a bit like existentialism, nothing counts, nothing matters. You could go to the other extreme: the self exists, is permanent and real, and you want to believe that there is a permanency there. However, the reality is things do exist conventionally, they do have forms and functions, you know, it's not that they don't exist, but that they do not exist in the way we believe they exist.

MP: They don't exist for ever, they are not unchangeable, is that what they mean?

A: That's right, they don't exist for ever nor are un-changeable, isolated, which is how conventionally and intuitively we believe things to be: that is, that we will exist for ever. It's how we usually relate to things and people, that they will be there for "us" for ever!

MP: How do you employ this idea in your work with kids?

A: Well, I can use it quite directly, if you've got somebody sitting in front of you absolutely distraught because something has happened, or they're furiously angry or very upset and just feel it's a complete disaster and their life has gone totally wrong, you know, clearly at that point they're identifying very, very strongly with their thoughts and their feelings about this, so they are those thoughts and feelings. If they then make decisions based on that they may make the wrong decision, press the wrong button, you know. Sometimes if I am able to speak to them and say: "Look, ok, I understand you feel that way, and you clearly do feel angry and clearly that's a real, real feeling; it's there and you feel terribly upset and you feel that's such a terrible thing that's happened to you", you know, I don't deny that experience at all, I accept it as that's the way they feel. But you have to try to help them understand that that's just an experience.

MP: Do you do this with kids, too, not just with adult patients?

A: Yes, you can talk to them and say: "Look, the feelings come and go" and you don't deny the fact that they are angry, of course they've every right to be upset, but it's just an experience, it will go.

MP: You validate their emotional reality first of all, don't you?

A: Yes, what you're doing is just pointing out what they already know but at that moment they are not thinking or aware of. They're not always angry, all of the time, or happy, or sad, these feelings come and go. To some kids that makes immediate sense, and that creates just that little bit of a distance and they can then be there in the room instead of totally there in their experience. They are still experiencing, but what they're experiencing is not as solid and fixed as it was; it's a little bit more transient. And that can be a relief, you know. Buddhists practise this over and over again, but even introducing this as an experience to a child, I think, is giving them an important new experience because that's not how we talk most of the time.

MP: So, that's how you marry your profession to your Buddhist practice somehow?

A: Yes, that would be one very conscious kind of link in my therapeutic work with kids; I would never use Buddhist terms, but I would use my knowledge of the Buddhist understanding of experience to help to explain to them what they are experiencing at that moment.

MP: This also links up to my next question on attachment and the apparent contradicting use in psychology and in Buddhism.

A: I think part of the problem here is terminology. Bowlby's work on attachment takes a technical-term describing a set of behaviours, interactions, and types of relationship based on these as he observed interactions between a mother and an infant, which I am pretty certain that any Lama would accept as part of what happens between any mother and child in normal child development.

MP: And you obviously agree with that!

COMING HOME   85

A: Yes, of course and it's an essential part of child development. You can't expect an infant not to seek attachment or a mother not to be attached. I am just thinking in the Buddhist practice of Compassion, one of the traditional ways of trying to remind the practitioners of what empathy and compassion are, is to ask them to remember their mothers, how their mothers treated them, you know, for them to consider all other sentient beings as mothers. So the Buddhist practice uses that experience directly.

MP: What about ambivalence? Has that got any space in this Buddhist practice in your view?

A: Well, that's one of the issues Lamas who were importing Buddhism to the West hit up against; they quickly came to understand this traditional analogy of the loving mother was often not the person's experience; in fact the mother might have become an object of hate. So they learnt to remind people of other experiences in which they felt compassion or empathy, such as looking after a child. They just turned it around.

MP: Or both: loved and hated.

A: Yes, in fact, they could ask you to think how you feel about a child or a pet, to try to get you to develop empathy in another way. The traditional way would be based on the understanding that mothers are naturally empathic and the children feel looked after and cared for.

MP: This also happens in all Western societies, when situations are good enough.

A: Yes, exactly. So Buddhism does not deny or say that attachment is not necessary, infact it says it is necessary. The Dalai Lama would say that the basis for developing compassion in the Buddhist practice is to build on the natural empathy that we all have. You know, Buddhist practice is all about starting with who you happen to be, what you experience and develop from there. So they'd say that, yes, most people probably do have some positive experience of being related to; of receiving some sense of empathy and of gratitude. So they would start from that, then build on that, so they don't deny it or push it away.

86 THE BUDDHA AND THE BABY

MP: Therefore, attachment and building on the ego are essential in Buddhist practice, and then?

A: Going back to the Dalai Lama, he's written so much about this stuff. Most people when they enter Buddhism, they'd be coming with their conventional baggage; some people would turn to Buddhism because they're frightened or worried or had horrible experiences. They're very scared. Other people would be more intellectual but whatever they come with, they'd be coming from an egotistic standpoint: "I'm worried; I'm in a mess or whatever" and the Buddhist practice will slowly, slowly say: "Yes, you do exist but not in the way we think we do" and slowly, slowly will question one's assumption about who we really are and also begin to point out who we really are from the Buddhist point of view.

MP: Are you then saying that Buddhist practice will lead to dis-attach from the image of oneself, which one had when one first started the practice?

A: The way I think about this issue is that you're not asked to adopt a particular view point or are told how to think about yourself, because those are concepts. And one of the messages Buddhism is driving at is that concepts are just that, concepts and not the thing in itself. The practice is to see the reality of the experience of feelings, thoughts coming and going; and see what lies beyond or behind that. What is it that supports these thoughts, feelings and experiences? If you were to let go of all of those things, what is then left?

MP: What Buddhism describes as emptiness, I suppose.

A: Yes, but what is that emptiness experientially? If you get to that point where you let all your thoughts go and you let all your feelings go, clinging onto nothing conceptually or perceptually, whatever, yes, that's emptiness, but actually that's not nothingness. I think it's a Japanese master who said a better word for emptiness is: fullness, yes fullness, because there is an experience there but the experience is different because you've liberated yourself from the solid sense of "I'm angry, I'm upset, I'm this and that" and you are freer from all of that and yet, there's something else arising at that point, which is kind of beyond words, that's when words don't quite convey this: it's a lived experience, but it's not a conceptual fact. It's an experience, which is difficult to describe, to pin down, but it's a real experience one has to have in order to apprehend it.

MP: An experience of space-fullness, perhaps?

A: Yes, spaciousness, you're relaxed, peaceful in that present moment, you're there, you're present; things can come and go. I think that's moving towards what we call the nature of the mind, you know, that's what you really are, if only you could let yourself be that. It's about being able to be, rather than always doing. So that's not nothingness but it's also nothing in particular, it's not a particular thing that I am: I am strong or weak or all those things; it's something else.

MP: May be it's just: I AM?

A: I am yes, in the sense of am-ness rather than existing solidly in one particular way and it's an experience, again, and not a concept.

MP: I think it's important to find words to describe these experiential states.

A: Yes, to communicate we have to find some words but that's where terms such as emptiness, attachment etc. can be confusing.

MP: How would you translate the idea of non-attachment to a kid in pragmatic terms?

A: Buddhism does not deny the fact that people need to relate to each other and it's how we relate to each other that Buddhism is concerned about. If you fall in love with someone, you know, it's unlikely that such a sense of romantic love will last for ever: Western society knows that and Buddhism knows that. So I would try to find a way of saying: don't cling to people; don't cling to a concept of who you think they are because that isn't real and often leads to disappointment. I would encourage paying attention to what the person is really like, behind the words, the behaviours. What is their attitude to things? To do this I would encourage the child to understand themselves first, what do they want, what is

88   THE BUDDHA AND THE BABY

their attitude to things and people. Through this approach they may come to relate from a more open, from a more aware perspective; and perhaps stop hammering things down quite so much.

MP: It is the quality of the relationship that gets emphasised then, isn't it?

A: Yes, so that would be the Buddhist perspective. Even with a kid with ADHD, who's very hyperactive and impulsive; their brain is clearly not working that effectively, you know, you give them Ritalin or something like that; they calm down and that's treated some symptoms and modified their behaviour, OK. But there's still a kid, an individual, they're still living within a family, you know, it's good that they're calmer; it's good that they're less impulsive but that's only going to be of benefit to the child if their relationship with the parents improves, if they're able to access the educational system, to fit in better. Perhaps some of the work that needs to be done is to help parents and teachers relate to their kids when they're calmer. Usually that doesn't have to be very extensive therapeutic work, reminding them what needs doing and if the child can go on and make use of that in an everyday sense, they can relate more positively, they can get better experiences, they can feel they can learn, their self-esteem grows and that's all good. So that's everyday psychiatry. Bringing in a Buddhist perspective, I can go back to the Dalai Lama, who talks about compassion: if I manage to help through the medication, through understanding and talking to people, getting the teacher to give this kid another chance, because he's now on a different place and all that works well, then I've helped them see the child more positively; for me that is enacting Buddhism.

MP: You've helped them to see the child differently and to have more understanding and compassion.

A: Yes, that's right and who knows how things will end up because I only see them for a very short period of time. Then I see them for reviews and try to remind them what it was like a year earlier and things are much better and keep them going. I remind them that the ego or "self" is not fixed and permanent but open to change.

Ego in Tibetan is not a noun like it is in our language, but is a verb "grasping onto" or "grasping at"; it's an act of grasping

COMING HOME   89

or of rejecting. In Buddhism, there are three possible responses to things: grasping onto, rejecting, or ignoring, and all three can lead to problems and disappointment. But conversely, if you stop grasping onto the idea that "I am bad, stupid … etc." then there is room for other experiences.

MP: This can be well applied to children and how to respond to them educationally and therapeutically: for example, clinging to a child's cry or rejecting the cry or ignoring it; none provides a healthy solution.

A: That's right. Beyond everyday experiencing of grasping, rejecting and ignoring, there's this ability to just being aware, if you like, which is not about grasping, not about rejecting; it's just awareness, and out of awareness you can choose to, hopefully, act appropriately, not in an instinctive, grasping, or rejecting way.

MP: These attitudes are always ego-based, aren't they?

A: That's right.

MP: So, in that sense, these concepts or experiences are linked: if you don't grasp, you also don't attach in the unhealthy way described and also you don't affirm a function that strengthens the grasping ego.

A: Yes, that's right. So, grasping, rejecting, and ignoring are all based on self-interest, on maintaining the sense of a solid permanent existent I, and on trying to gain something or to avoid pain and discomfort. But the irony here is that we spend huge effort in maintaining a sense of ourselves that probably is not giving us the happiness we want, and even might perpetuate painful experiences. Whereas the more empathic, compassionate, open style is not to base what you do on what you think you will gain, or to protect yourself, but more on responding appropriately to what is out there. So, you're more able to meet somebody's needs. If somebody's in distress, you're more able to be aware of that, to be available and be there for that person.

MP: Like the kid you mentioned and who got in trouble with the law?

90   THE BUDDHA AND THE BABY

A: Yes, exactly, because in the room when I was sitting there, I was trying not to think about, as I said, "is this a useful thing to do?" and I had to put aside these doubts and just be with him.

MP: I am reminded of a piece of visualisation work which I decided to do with an adolescent boy with severe cerebral palsy, once when there was nothing else that I could do to alleviate his excruciating physical pain. I had lots of doubts and anxieties about going beyond the bounds of traditional therapy at that moment. However, in my conscience, I hoped I could help him a bit with such a visualisation exercise; so I did use it and it did work. This work, despite my anxieties, has been well received by my professional association, despite my doubts!

A: I agree that such integration of techniques is important and this brings me back to another Buddhist term, you know, they talk of skilful means, and I think one of its translations would be: what would appropriately help in a situation? What is skilful in a situation? If it helps, then it's clearly skilful, you know, and there is no manual that says what to do when you are with a cerebral palsied boy in terrible pain.

MP: That's it! On a more personal level, did you ever have any particularly mystical or enlightening experience during your years of practice?

A: When I meditate I can get to a point where I am not thinking of anything or have any strong feeling, and I am present in the moment: I can see, I can feel, I can hear, I'm not distracted by anything, but am just there. I can get to that quite easily nowadays and it feels peaceful, contented and very alive. It's not a kind of nothing; it's not a deadening, the very opposite. There's a sense of openness. Such experiences makes me think that all the descriptions and analogies the Lamas talk about are not just words; they are actually describing a true, living experience that's worthwhile cultivating because it does make a difference to how you see the world and how you experience yourself.

MP: Can you say a bit more about experiencing yourself differently?

A: Well, for example, I was on holiday recently and I was meditating in my hotel room daily in the morning and for the first few

COMING HOME   91

days I noticed my mind was very busy with lots of thoughts about what I had just been doing at work and so on. Then after a few days it was more settled, fairly calm and present; I reminded myself: this state is always there to experience, I can lose it, forget about it, be caught up in things, but this is something I can always rely on—if it gives me the chance to come back to it.

MP: Come back home.

A: Yes, exactly come back home and when you're there, there's nothing to do, nothing to worry about and it just is and yes, you get distracted, a thought, thirst, pain etc., but you can always get back there. If you've learnt how to do this, that would be the answer to anything disturbing that you're experiencing.

MP: Thank you so much for sharing your experience and thoughts so openly and clearly: I really enjoyed this conversation.

A: I appreciate the fact that you wanted to have this conversation and the chance to string these thoughts together that I may not have thought of doing otherwise.

CHAPTER EIGHT

The curative factor

Dialogue with Pamela Bartram

For Bodhi, there really is no tree
Nor any mirror on a stand.
Originally there is not a single thing,
So where could dust be gathering?

—Huineng (seventh century CE)

MP: Pamela, you've already begun to tell me when you started to be interested in Buddhism, it was at university wasn't it?

PB: Yes, I studied Indian philosophy and Indian religion, and as well as the academic studies at that time, in the early seventies, people at university used to talk about and practise transcendental meditation. I didn't ever do it, but an interest in these things, you know, has sort of woven in and out of my life at different times. The time, I think, when I was most committed must have been in my late twenties. I was having a difficult time with lots of personal unhappiness, and somebody I was working with in a children's hospital, who was also having a hard time, just said to me: "You should go to Manjushri." That was the beginning and the end of it, and I just went to Manjushri, which is a place in Cumbria,

94   THE BUDDHA AND THE BABY

a Buddhist centre, and then that's when I really got into Tibetan Buddhism.

MP: It doesn't come as a family tradition then; what about your spiritual drive? Does it come from your family?

PB: No, not at all, but from my own struggles.

MP: That's interesting as quite a lot of people I've met, have turned to Buddhism, for that same reason: suffering and issues of death.

PB: Yes. I was in analysis at that time but I found that seeing my analyst four times a week (this was before I trained as a child psychotherapist) was like a drop in the ocean. So I needed something to fill in those other days and I think that was what such belief system and practice meant to me; I mean something that—really— was there for me, when my analyst wasn't.

MP: Perhaps it was like having two parents there for you?

PB: Hm, yes.

MP: Well, I was very impressed by the paper you read at the British Association of Psychotherapists some months ago, as you are one of the few people who, do integrate your Buddhist ways of thinking with your work as a psychotherapist.

PB: The paper was about disability and became the basis for a recent publication (Bartram, 2013). The first Noble Truth in Buddhism is the existence of suffering or rather the inevitability of suffering. When you work with people who have suffered a disability this is very forcibly brought home. Then, there are two main ways in which one can react to suffering. The first is "Why me?", which can be thought of as a fundamentally narcissistic response. All the energy goes into that and you get stuck. The second response entails the painful process of mourning the loss and moving forward with life. Freud talks about the first response as melancholia as opposed to the work of mourning. I have found that the melancholic response is very common, and perhaps, we could say it is a natural response to suffering. This is like the Buddhist idea that we cherish our selves and have as a main (and misguided) aim, the goal of avoiding suffering. When suffering is accepted and worked through, and loss is mourned, then life can be lived.

THE CURATIVE FACTOR   95

Traditionally in psychotherapy, melancholia and the narcissistic "Why me?" attitude are felt to be pathological responses to loss; whereas in Buddhism, this response is only pathological in the sense that the human condition is pathological. I think this is a gentler, kinder, and more freeing way of looking at things. We start from self-cherishing, and we are devastated when we are afflicted by unexpected difficulties. The Buddhist view takes this for granted and then says "OK, but now what can we do differently to move away from this position?" In disability, you get the human condition in a microcosm, so it offers a really good opportunity to work on letting go of self-cherishing, in the Buddhist sense.

PB: It's so self-evident to me that the two things (Buddhist thinking and psychotherapy) are compatible, that I'm beginning to wonder if actually a lot of people would completely disagree or, well I don't question it in a way, as the two things seem to me to be so much the same.

MP: They seem the same things but presumably they are also quite different?

PB: Well, yes but entirely compatible, you know. I don't think I feel a conflict about that.

MP: It reminds me of Nina Coltart, the British Buddhist psychoanalysts, who also wrote of never having a conflict between her two practices of Buddhism and psychoanalysis (Coltart, 1987).

PB: Oh, that's right.

MP: You were a music therapist before training as a child psychotherapist, weren't you?

PB: Suffering is the thing that connects the two practices for me, because when you are in touch with your own suffering, I think, you feel an affinity with other people who are suffering, with children who are unhappy and the idea of being able to make a difference is where my desire to train came from. With music therapy I started to really question whether I could make much of a difference; I wanted to make more of a difference in children's lives. As a music therapist you only work with the child and working with

96   THE BUDDHA AND THE BABY

families has been tremendously important to me. I don't think you can just take a child and fix the child.

MP: Most parents would like that, though!

PB: Well, we all hope that others will do the work of changing. It's so much easier for us if they do. Then my cherished self can stay untouched!

MP: How do you reconcile ideas such as *anatta*, no-self, and the idea of helping children and families to develop a healthy self?

PB: Well, I suppose you could say that, maybe, psychotic states have something in common with no-self or with meditative states, you could say that, but that's not to say they are the same; so I think that in order to be able to renounce the self, you have to have quite a strong ego and self. You cannot just be psychotic and say: "look, I've renounced the self".

MP: It's intriguing that you see no-self as a psychotic state, somehow.

PB: Not the same, but, you know, it's a kind of sort of association; to lose all boundaries, I suppose. That's what psychosis is. And if you meditate on emptiness and, you know, I think only once, I had a split-second moment of kind of taste of that emptiness. That's probably all I would ever imagine my mind had. And in that state, you're not Pamela Bartram any more, with her boundaries, you know, and that was not a psychotic moment, but I could see that someone might draw a parallel.

MP: I had an experience of no-self, where there was me out there and, what I felt to be consciousness, was aware of me being out there. Again, it was a fleeting moment and I know it was not a dissociated state. Spaciousness was the main feeling then.

PB: No, of course not. I had a patient who had a psychotic breakdown and she was in that state for weeks on end. It was a state of being boundary-less: she could do anything she wanted; she could talk non-stop: she had so many ideas in her mind, she could rise above herself and felt she could do everything. So, I think there are parallels, but the state she was in was a very unhealthy state, she was ill, and I don't think *anatta* is being ill, you know.

THE CURATIVE FACTOR   97

MP: That's very clear. And also, she appeared to be full with herself somehow.

PB: Yes, but boundary-less. She felt a tremendous sense of release because she didn't have to put up with ordinary kind of unhappiness.

MP: This state is very different from meditation although there is a fine line between the mystical experience and the psychotic experience, I believe.

PB: I suppose, I picture the ego as a kind of room and there's a doorway leading out into *anatta* and there is a doorway leading out into psychosis, but it's very important to choose the right door.

MP: It's an interesting angle to look at *anatta* from.

MP: Perhaps children who have developed a strong ego, then they may chose the spiritual path, but I'm not sure how.

PB: Maybe not in this lifetime; but they have to have a good enough ego to not cause a lot of harm, you know, to be kind, to develop compassion; all the sorts of things that we would want our patients to develop and those things would be necessary for a spiritual path, wouldn't they? If you're going round breaking windows, causing suffering, kicking people as some of our patients do, that's not going to go that way.

MP: You just pass on your suffering to others, and don't feel you have to transform it in yourself.

PB: That's right, you project it. I was just starting to debate with myself, and I think I'm a rather conventional person: "It's important to be good", type of thinking. I was wondering if there are more experiential masters who are much more iconoclastic. Perhaps a Zen master, where there is less emphasis on goodness … when a moment of realisation, which comes from something that is not obviously kind and compassionate.

MP: Yes, I think that's more the Zen style, which is very different from Tibetan or Theravada.

PB: I suppose, they would say it's got to do with the motivation and beating them leads the disciple to enlightenment, perhaps.

98   THE BUDDHA AND THE BABY

MP: The Buddha followed the ascetic, tough path at first then realised that it was the middle way that needed to be pursued.

PB: I suppose that is the debate you have in psychotherapy, as well, isn't it? Do you go for the hard line or do you find a way of saying something quite difficult but in the context of the patient feeling authentically cared for? Although, when you hear bad news about yourself, it's almost impossible to feel that it's been given from a good motivation. That's persecution, isn't it?

MP: Yes, it's very hard to believe it's done for your personal and spiritual development and goodness.

PB: So as a therapist, I feel you want to deliver the bad news in a kind way and as a patient I want to hear the bad news in a kind way, as much as possible.

MP: So the question is: what leads to enlightenment or to analytic clarity?

PB: Perhaps, it's not the same recipe for any two people. I suppose for me, I think, there's something about the integration. The Buddhists talk about the need for compassion but also for wisdom which can have an incisive quality, like a sword. If you're endlessly kind, it isn't helpful.

MP: Back to the no-self and emptiness, it seems to me that they're so much linked and I wonder how you translate all this into your work with children.

PB: Most of my children I see, actually never, never talk about what the problem is and yet, they seem to get better. I don't really understand that process well. It's very different with adults who talk to you and you talk back, you know, you make some sort of framework of what you're talking about; it would be linked with what happened yesterday, with what happened in childhood and so on. A child would come in and play football for fifty minutes. In my experience, often, you don't get much of a chance to feedback an understanding of what has been communicated, or if you do, it's highly questionable whether they've heard it or understood it or listened to what you have fed back.

THE CURATIVE FACTOR   99

MP: I find it hard to follow this: surely a lot must have got through these patients of yours, if they got better!

PB: I think they have some sort of experience of being with me, but I'm not sure it's got very much to do with me imparting to them my understanding of what they find difficult in life; I don't think so. I really don't know how to explain this. I feel it may be they're having an experience of being with someone who's not trying to tell them something or not trying to educate them or control them or, you know, and maybe there's something about that experience, which may be a bit related to meditation. But it's hard to understand what psychotherapy does for young children. Of course, that's not to say it's an easy task for the psychotherapist, because offering that kind of space requires a kind of selflessness, a lack of need to satisfy the requirements of your own ego. The other day I watched a friend dealing with a very agitated horse. She was holding him by two lead reins. The horse was rearing and thrashing himself around. First she let go of one lead rein, the horse continued. Then she let go of the other. She stood facing him and talking to him the whole time. After she let go of the second lead rein, he steadied himself and stopped. I had a little patient who was really horrible to me, tricking me, mocking me and boasting when I was successfully beaten. I felt so helpless and angry. I reflected on that, I didn't lash out of course, but I tried to talk to him about how he was treating me and what purpose it served him. I could see it didn't make any difference to him. Then I realised I had to hold the experience of being so badly treated, just hold it. Over time he registered the change and gradually he started to make comments like "Today you can choose", or "I think you should have another turn". The work I had to do was with myself and that freed him to change.

MP: What about your attention to them and interest in them and also your words? In my work with children with selective mutism, I mostly do a guessing game, where I verbalise the very little I can detect in their un-giving presence and on my countertransference. I don't know what I do with them and yet, their parents always report great improvement and the children want to continue coming! Something must be happening then!

100   THE BUDDHA AND THE BABY

PB: However it works, maybe child psychotherapy is a process that allows the child to develop a kind of primary sense of themselves and helps with ego development in a way that wasn't possible before, perhaps?

MP: So the idea of no-self cannot be applied to children, at this point.

PB: I don't think so. I think it's more about helping them to be a self.

MP: Perhaps you find a similar conflict of ideas when it comes to attachment and non-attachment?

PB: That doesn't bother me and they don't seem incompatible to me. I think there's a difference between ordinary, what's good enough attachment and spiritual practice, which is something extra, you know. You have attachments to be able to let go of attachments. If you think of my room image, you know, with the ego in the middle and psychosis there: I would say, you can't go straight from psychosis to the spiritual path, except by going through the middle compartment, through the ego and then you have an ego that is strong enough to let go of attachment. We're helping the people who don't have a foundation, to make a foundation.

MP: How do you help these people with no foundation to develop a bit of an ego with meditation?

PB: Well, I think there's something about the quality of attention that you give a patient, which is a bit like the quality of attention, I think, you would bring to a meditative state, certainly in a Vipassana meditation, where your attention is not single-pointed but you allow yourself to see what's going through your mind and observe all those thoughts but without identifying with them, as being a very rich and powerful experience. I think when a patient is talking to you or a child playing, you give him that kind of attention "evenly suspended attention" as Freud calls it (1912e). So you're kind of listening to everything they've got to say or play and you're also helping them to develop a capacity to observe themselves.

MP: With children also, don't you?

PB: Yes, we do help children to be able to observe themselves, to internalise an "attending mind", and that would link with containment, I think. So if the child feels angry and at first breaks a window, later he can be helped to begin to feel his anger and think about it as: "I've got somebody inside me who can help me not to break it". So I think that the attention and the quality of the attention is very central in both processes of meditation and psychotherapy. There is a paper by Hanna Segal called "The curative factors in psychoanalysis" (1962); even as I read it as a trainee, I felt it didn't express my own understanding of clinical work. She says that the main curative factor in child psychoanalysis is the imparting of insight to the patient by interpretation. I really don't agree with that, it's simply not my experience. Now I think we've moved away from this, but I would pay less importance on getting the interpretation right and more with the quality of the attention. Daniel Stern and the Boston School of Psychotherapy try to capture this in their work. Stern writes about how the centrally important "regulation of the intersubjective field, in therapy, present moment-by-present moment, occurs largely non-verbally, non-consciously, and implicitly" (Stern, 2004, p. 118).

MP: I agree with this wholeheartedly and think of an adolescent girl with a possible diagnosis of conversion hysteria, who does not accept my interpretations at the beginning of sessions. However, if I repeat exactly the same interpretation later in the session, when perhaps enough time has elapsed into the session and she has felt more established there with me, then she is more able to accept the interpretation and to respond and elaborate on it in her own way. I always thought it was a matter of time spent together, but you draw my attention to the idea that it may also be the quality of the attention that the patient has been able to absorb and take, as well as the therapist enduring the rejection of the same interpretation delivered earlier.

PB: Such attention is curative, whether it's in the context of meditation or of psychotherapy or in the context of a mother and a baby, you know.

MP: Do you have experience with mothers and babies?

PB: I said in that paper I gave at the BAP that when mothers are confronted with their babies who look all wrong (because of a handicap), who've got their insides on the outsides, you know, whose

102   THE BUDDHA AND THE BABY

chromosomes are "wrong" through and through, who're very disabled, those mothers have an additional challenge when it comes to being in the right state of mind with that baby. The right state of mind has been bombarded with all sorts of obstacles and anxieties, pressures, information, facts about your baby, which shouldn't be here for an ordinary mother–baby relation. So it's very difficult to have reverie with your baby, when you may have had a traumatic birth. How do you meditate with all that going on in your head and think of your baby the way you think of your baby in reverie, instead of thinking of the baby as a big, long list of diagnoses and behaviours?

MP: Wouldn't it be very interesting to set up a group for these troubled mothers and babies to foster a reflective, meditative stance in them, above and despite all the traumas going on, and to help them see their baby as an alive little person, needing their attention?

PB: I get very frustrated in my work with parents, when they only want behaviour techniques and it's a constant emphasis on behaviour management. It seems to me to put the cart before the horse: to manage the behaviour even before you understood it and understood its effect on you. They just want some techniques. Wouldn't it be more helpful to do some parent work that was about observation and helping parents to observe their child and observe themselves observing their child? How much rich information we might get from that to then help them accordingly!

MP: Some work for parents to learn about their own thoughts and feelings as they observe their baby or child as well as seeing him or her as they really are and freer from parental projections, this would be a real Buddhist stance, wouldn't it? But tell me more of your paper where you marry your psychotherapy work with your Buddhist ideas so smoothly.

PB: One thing I'm interested in and discuss in that paper is this question of suffering and, I suppose, because I've now worked with disabilities for so long that I'm often confronted with situations where I feel that I'm watching parents saying: "Why me? Why did this happen to us? It shouldn't have happened to us. I can't bear it that it happened to us. There's no way forward" and I suppose, as I said earlier, this is exactly what Buddhism addresses, you know, the reality of old age, sickness and death is what the Buddha realised. What's so difficult is that it's impossible to live knowing the reality of old age, sickness and death. We seem somehow to be programmed to think that life is eternal youth, eternal health and eternal life. So when we're confronted with all that and physical and mental disability, as the parents of these children are, where the brain will never be alright, you can't fix it, all that comes as a terrible shock. It shouldn't but it does and that's the absolute conundrum, you know. If we were to remember, which we can't, I can't anyway, that the human condition is, you know, old age, sickness and death, then it wouldn't come as a terrible shock, when things go wrong. You would be able to be more in the moment as we build these big castles based on something which is entirely wish fulfillment.

MP: You seem to be saying that part of your work as a child psychotherapist, who is also a Buddhist, is to try and help these parents who have severely disabled children to accept the reality which is not psychological and can't be changed: it has a physical component and is a hard fact of their reality.

PB: Absolutely. In a way, one is fixing something: if you fix the relationship with the disability, you have fixed something, but you haven't fixed the disability. If you fix the relationship with life, you've fixed something, but you haven't taken away old age, sickness, and death. That's what I feel psychotherapy can very usefully do, you know, you go into psychotherapy hoping that you will be able to somehow fix your childhood or something like that, but you can't re-write the past. You can change your relationship with your past, but if it is broken, then it is broken. That's the area where I feel there is a great overlap with Buddhism and being in the present moment, not looking backwards and not looking forward is a great achievement, which is extraordinarily difficult to get to, even for a brief moment.

MP: Indeed, but you also help to fix something in the child not just the parents' attitude to the disability, don't you? I mean, it's the process of psychotherapy, as you were saying early on, that produces some change.

THE BUDDHA AND THE BABY

PB: Yes, it changes their mind, a bit. When Bion talks about being without memory or desire, I think that's very helpful. He says "the capacity to forget, the ability to eschew desire and understanding, must be regarded as essential discipline for the psychoanalyst. Failure to practise this discipline will lead to a steady deterioration in the powers of observation whose maintenance is essential" (Bion, 1970, p. 51). When I was a trainee, I felt I was terribly important that I had to say the right thing at the right time and have a sort of rigidity, you know, about the setting; but the more I've gone on working, I think there's more of a trust in the process, in some unconscious communication, I don't know. Something in the patient which will respond, perhaps it has to do with this idea of having less ego as a therapist and more trust in the process and the patient and that this whole thing is much bigger than we understand. How children change in therapy as I was saying is quite mysterious.

MP: This is very Buddhist, to say that it's the process that counts, not the ego of the therapist. I find this in line with the Buddhist idea on no self. But to return to what you said, the quality of the attention given to a child in therapy, is a new experience; someone who observes them or contemplates on them, perhaps. What would be the difference in these two activities? Contemplation conjures up for me the idea of being together inside a temple.

PB: Contemplation and observation, I am not sure about the difference, but reverie combines observation and contemplation, I think. We do all the work inside ourselves, a psychotherapist used to say to me, so if you look at it, it doesn't look like anything very much, because it's all internal. I can really relate to that very much, especially if I get stuck with a patient, the question is not so much how am I going to get through to him but it's really: what do I have to do internally to release something in me knowing that having done that, it will release something in the patient?

MP: How do we deliver bad news, as you said earlier on? We have to have done the work inside us first, don't we?

PB: Exactly. I think this is a very spiritual model, isn't it, where you can't really change other people's mind but you can change your own mind. I feel in parent work, parents get too fixated with

THE CURATIVE FACTOR   105

changing their child, when what they need to do is something in themselves, changing and may be sometimes they need to love their child more, you know. None of this can work unless it's done in the spirit of something like love.

MP: We don't talk much about love in psychotherapy, do we?

PB: Freud does in "Mourning and Melancholia" (1917e) where the big problem with melancholia was the lack of love. Sometimes we get away from the basics, don't we? I see that parents feel very guilty about these very disabled children, because they know that they struggle to love them, that is in a very particular sense of the word "love". Chris Bollas talks about this as "perceptive identification" (Bollas, 2007). Actually, even Hannah Segal in further discussion about her paper said that that a good therapeutic setting must include unconscious love in the analyst for the patient. It's just not where she put her main emphasis (Segal, 1962).

MP: That's true also in my experience and the parents who do best are the ones who love their disabled children.

PB: Yes, and I think that links very much with the Dalai Lama, the importance of compassion, the Middle Way, having good relationships with the people around you make most things better. But in order to do such a simple thing, sometimes one has to do a lot of work internally.

MP: Yes, so many of us have had broken loves, broken relationships when we were children. This is a very different angle from what other people have said in their conversions here.

PB: Is this different from what other people have said?

MP: Yes, the perspective of love is very unique to our conversation. How to help parents to have more of a compassionate and loving stance towards their children who are not perfect or disabled and need help?

PB: I was listening to a Lacanian analyst, who talked about the problem of broken love. He said that most of the patients who come to him, come to him with problems of broken love. When they were children they grew up not feeling that they were loved. I thought

THE BUDDHA AND THE BABY

that was sort of quite simple but then looking at patients and at child patients, it's a big problem; they don't think they're lovable. They think something has goes wrong with their love relationships and one of the things that therapy fixes is that, I think.

MP: In my work with children under five and their families, I have come to the conclusion that, whatever the problem is with the little ones, if there is a loving parental background, the difficulties are most likely to be resolved quicker and lastingly. Many families with social problems coming from other countries, with different languages, losses, traumas, poverty and so on, when propelled by love towards each other and their children, they're already half way through satisfactory solutions even of emotional difficulties in their children. Diagnostically, the presence of loving parents is an essential factor, and I agree with you, Pamela, that love is one, perhaps the, curative factor.

PB: Yes, and I think that links very much with the Dalai Lama, the importance of compassion, the Middle Way, having a good relationships with the people around you. It makes most things better. But in order to do that simple thing, sometimes one has to do an awful lot of work internally.

MP: I was interested in your experience of egoless and spaciousness, can you say a bit more?

PB: I had a very good, young Western teacher for a while, it might have been at Rigpa, I cannot remember, and I am sure he must have attained experiences of emptiness by the way he spoke about it and in the meditations he led, I just felt it. I once came out of a meditation with a huge smile on my face; he looked at me and knew I got to something important. Unfortunately it didn't last and the next minute you're just worrying about banal things, whether your shoes match your dress etc.

MP: Yes, grasping to these experiences is so desirable but so unrewarding, and with this thought, I should not hold onto your time any longer, hoping that you have enjoyed sharing these thoughts with me as much as I have.

References

Bartram, P. (2013). Melancholia, mourning, love: transforming the melancholic response to disability through psychotherapy. *British Journal of Psychotherapy, 29*: 168–181.

Bion, W. R. (1970). *Attention and Interpretation*. London: Karnac.

Bollas, C. (2007). *The Freudian Moment*. London: Karnac.

Coltart, N. (1987). The practice of Buddhism and psycho-analysis. *The Middle Way, 62(2)*: 91–96.

Freud, S. (1912e). Recommendations to physicians practising psycho-analysis. SE 12, pp. 109–120. London: Hogarth.

Freud, S. (1917e). Mourning and melancholia. SE 14, pp. 243–260. London: Hogarth.

Huineng, in: Schumacher, S. (2009). *Zen in Plain English*. London: Watkins.

Segal, H. (1962). The curative factors in psycho-analysis. *The International Journal of Psycho-Analysis, 43*: 212–217 and 232–233.

Stern, D. (2004). *The Present Moment in Psychotherapy and Everyday Life*. New York, London: W. W. Norton.

CHAPTER NINE

The facilitating silence

Dialogue with Sara Leon

Be the change that you wish to see in the world.

—Mahatma Gandhi

MP: Well, this interview has to take place on the phone unfortunately but I hope we can meet later on and perhaps go to Amaravati Buddhist Monastery together at some point.

SL: Yes, that would be interesting for me.

MP: I'd like to begin by asking you when you started to be interested in Buddhism, unless you come from that family background and were brought up as such. Also how did the two choices of Buddhism and being a child psychotherapist come about for you?

SL: It must have been thirty years ago, a long time ago that I started with yoga. I lived in Germany at the time. I first became interested in yoga which in retrospect felt like psychoanalysis of the body. This lead to an interest in meditation, in Eastern philosophies and religions.

MP: Where you in Germany with your family?

110   THE BUDDHA AND THE BABY

SL: No, I went travelling with a friend and decided to stay for a while; it was a long time ago. It was there that I had joined a yoga class and had a very good yoga teacher. The more I practised the more my curiosity grew about the whole philosophy. Although my original intention was for physical health and calm, I slowly realised it was a way to learn and find out about myself. When I returned to England, I joined a local yoga class but for some reason did not really connect with the teacher, so I stopped. My interest in Buddhist meditation and philosophy took over so I turned to meditation instead. It was about twenty-five years ago when I joined a meditation group.

MP: Was that a Tibetan group?

SL: Initially I joined a Tibetan Buddhist group but then I went to a retreat in France. The retreat was run by Thich Nhat Hanh, who is a Vietnamese Zen Buddhist. There was something about simplicity in Zen that really resonated with me and I found it easier to apply to ordinary everyday life situations.

MP: How interesting, not many people in London go to Zen Meditation in my experience; it's more the Tibetan tradition that seems to attract people.

SL: Being grounded in the moment is what attracts me to Zen. When I am able, I enjoy week long silent retreats at Gaia House in Devon.

MP: Is that a Zen place? I didn't think so!

SL: No, but it is a Buddhist Centre. They offer a variety of retreats which are lead by different practitioners including Stephen and Martine Batchelor, who run a Zen retreat once a year. Stephen Batchelor wrote *Buddhism Without Beliefs* (Batchelor, 1998). I found this book interesting.

MP: I met Stephen Batchelor; he was my teacher at the Buddhist Society near Victoria Station several years ago.

SL: Well he impressed me. After going on the retreat in France I joined a local meditation group which followed Thich Nhat Hanh and Zen Buddhism. This group is also linked to the London Insight Meditation group in Golders Green. They offer a silent meditation day once a month on a Sunday, it is led by various teachers including Stephen and Martine Batchelor.

MP: Tell me, do you come from a Buddhist or a religious family?

SL: Not at all. When I was seven years old we moved house; our new home happened to be situated opposite a church. Every Sunday I found myself watching people going into and out of the church. I have no idea why I found this so fascinating but I knew I wanted to be part of it so I started attending Sunday school. Although my parents were not at all religious they allowed me to go. I stayed until I was fourteen or fifteen years and became a Sunday school assistant. I really enjoyed working with the children and still have fond memories. Without a doubt this is when I realised that I wanted to work with children and although I had no idea in what capacity, the seed was sown. The path to becoming a child psychotherapist was not so straight forward but I thought that one day I would work with children.

MP: That's unusual: it's from a spiritual path that you became interested in child psychotherapy. Do you know how that happened?

SL: It is hard to say. I remember liking the atmosphere in the church and how the vicar had such a good sense of humour and told the children interesting stories before we left the church for the Sunday school. The Sunday school teacher was a very kind woman and made learning such good fun. I still remember with much fondness all those good experiences. It is strange for me now to think that it was all those years ago and that the seed of becoming a child psychotherapist had been planted.

MP: What a lovely story about the origin of your desire and path to become a child psychotherapist and a spiritual child psychotherapist, if I may call you that!

SL: You may.

MP: Now back to the present day, how do you think Buddhism influences you as a child psychotherapist and vice-versa, if at all?

SL: I can see how it influences me as a person, so I assume this would affect the way I work. There is much to be learned from Buddhist philosophy but perhaps the most significant aspect for me has

112   THE BUDDHA AND THE BABY

been the silence. Week-long silent retreats have proved to be my most meaningful experiences. It is very hard to put into words how I have been impacted without reducing the experience. I remember feeling after one such retreat as if I had started to melt, in retrospect perhaps some of my ego or defences had melted, the defences which can keep me feeling separate and sometimes alienated from others. I felt connected and as if I had fallen in love with life itself. For me, it is as if I have learned the most from the silence, and silence continues to play an important part in my life and work.

MP: And here is me asking you to talk!

SL: When I trained as a child psychotherapist, in our first year, Priscilla Roth taught my group theory. She invited us to think about narcissism, suggesting that we would never understand anything about psychoanalytic thought if we did not understand narcissism. She questioned whether a person could ever carry out an act that was not narcissistic in some way. This thought has stayed with me over the years, and I think this is one of the ways in which psychoanalysis and Buddhism link.

MP: It's fascinating, isn't it?

SL: Yes. In Eastern philosophy, Buddhists talk about the importance of letting go of the ego. So for me at first, there seemed to be a contradiction between how we in the West aim to strengthen our ego capacity whilst in the East they aim to let go. It took many years and several silent retreats for me to understand this. The Zen retreats I attended were very well structured, and within the silence I felt very contained and able to deeply relax. There were no outside distractions, such as books, television, or social interactions, just me and my thoughts. I was therefore able to observe my thoughts day in, day out. After a few days, my mind became more settled, and as I observed my thoughts I could see how they were very repetitive and grasping and ultimately very narcissistic. I began to glimpse the Buddhist concept of emptiness, which I cannot do justice to in words, but it is a state of being, of non-grasping, not wanting to be clever or impress. It is a state of no thoughts.

THE FACILITATING SILENCE   113

MP: It's fascinating indeed: I find silent retreats such a healing experience, with such a sense of spaciousness despite their strict routine. I have to say they keep me sane and bring back home to me how we are almost subtly colonised by our work and finely consumed by the troubled lives of children and adults we take on to work with. Those ten-day silent retreats provide me with detoxification of that part of my life as well as with a very different dimension to existence. It's a different form of nourishment for us psychotherapists—or at least for myself—than analysis, supervisions, lectures, etc.

SL: I think so.

MP: Do you have any example or vignette of your work with children where meditation and Buddhism affect you?

SL: Yes I do. I think my work is affected in as much as, whilst meaning is important, I think I do not grasp onto it so much and for the most part I think I am probably more able to experience what it is like being with a particular child. I would like to think that more generally my presence is less intrusive but hopefully more enabling and containing.

MP: It's just "being", isn't it?

SL: Yes, just really being and perhaps having fewer expectations. I think that possibly what has really changed is the quality of the silence.

MP: And presumably the children feel that.

SL: Well, presumably. I think you're right, I can just Be. Obviously, children can be very anxious about being in the room with a therapist, but off the top of my head I don't remember feeling that any child was unnerved by silence. Perhaps they feel contained in the silence, or that I am alongside of them trying to understand.

MP: Do you have a specific example in mind?

SL: I once worked with a twelve-year-old boy for three years. He was three months premature and spent this time in an incubator. His mother suffered postnatal depression, and both parents suffered from mental health problems. His parents separated when he was ten years old, and at first he was looked after by his mother and her brother. Not being able to cope with him, his mother put him in a taxi and sent him to live with his father. He was not informed of her intention. His rage towards his mother prompted his teachers to refer him to the Child & Adolescent Mental Health Service where I work. For the first four months, he did not look at me or speak to me, so I approached the work rather like an infant observation. For example, he played mainly with two cars. Each week, the cars embarked on a fast and dangerous chase, often riding on the edge of the tabletop; they would inevitably crash and one would fall off the table. In some sessions, he attempted to stick objects together, such as pipe cleaners, but this usually ended in a sticky mess. His play seemed to communicate his anxiety about what happens when two people come together, that is, either there is a fear that one person will be annihilated or they will merge together in a very messy way. Perhaps in the face of this impossible type of human contact, he turned away from me into what felt like an autistic retreat. When he did start talking, it was sudden. He talked only about his computer and computer games. Although I was pleased to hear him talk, I often felt overwhelmed by his detailed and non-stop speech. It felt as if there was only room for one mind. In his omnipotent state of mind, he also refused to acknowledge any gaps which might suggest that I existed. He would never say hello or goodbye to me at the beginning and end of sessions. In his mind, everything had to be continuous as change and gaps represented danger. As I got hold of his anxieties, he slowly opened up to the idea that I might have something useful to offer. After about one year, his attitude towards his therapy changed; he began to look forward to it. He would burst into the therapy room and build a type of den, which he named his "special place". In this place, he was very playful, he played games like peek-a-boo. I wondered if he was in fact reconstructing a womb-like place in an attempt to re-experience the last three months in the womb which life had denied him. He enacted this scenario for weeks, in fact, right up until the summer break. He seemed to ignore all my comments about the pending break, and I was left with the feeling that he was unable to take in and think about the implications of the break. So it felt as if he was completely unprepared, perhaps like he had been unprepared for his premature birth. When he returned from the summer holiday, he did not speak to me for six months, apart from occasionally telling me how boring he found therapy and that he did not see the point in attending. In his six months of silence, I experienced a profound despair at being rejected. In fact, it was so excruciating that I often dreaded the sessions. In supervision, I sometimes wondered whether or not to continue the work. What helped was hearing from my colleague who worked with his father that he was making good progress in his external life. He had stopped soiling, lying, and stealing. In the following February, he suddenly started talking to me again. He announced that he wanted to "stop messing around and sort his life out". And he did. He began to excel academically at school and he made friends by joining various after-school clubs. His head of year informed me that he had become one of their best students, in his attitude as well as academically. For me, it seemed that a profound healing took place within the silence, through which the boy communicated enormous levels of rage and despair about whether or not life, his life, was worth living. It was a very powerful experience, and he taught me so much about the importance of silence.

MP: How beautiful and indeed how powerful silence is! Presumably your meditation stance must have helped you then with such relentless rejection.

SL: Well, yes. That's where meditation had really affirmed that for me: the value of a third position and be able to reflect on what was happening without feeling the need to impose myself.

MP: Now, here's a devil's advocate's question: what would be the difference between what we get in the training, supervisions, analysis and what meditation offers you in your work? Is there something extra that meditation offers you, in your view and experience?

SL: I had a very good analysis and a good therapeutic relationship and my analyst helped me to name my difficulties but I had to work hard on them and still do really, and it is meditation which continues to help. In particular, I find very helpful the precept on having an open mind to resolve conflicts in a community context. It's not always easy, is it?

116   THE BUDDHA AND THE BABY

MP: A lifetime effort or, rather, many lifetime efforts, that is! We all have our demons to work hard at; it is usually our most vulnerable spot that troubles us; that's where we need many hands from different sources and paths, I believe!

SL: I know that thinking of that precept, whose aim is to reduce conflicts, helps me to step back and think and be in the third position.

MP: To reflect rather than react.

SL: Yes, what goes on is bigger than me.

MP: Meditation in the Buddhist tradition helps to have a broader view, to go beyond our egos, our selves.

SL: Yes, and in that sense Buddhism gives me something extra to our therapeutic training.

MP: Perhaps that's the philosophical and spiritual aspect that goes beyond our small egos and selves. It's the realisation of the concept of *anatta*, no-self, isn't it? But to return to the boy you mentioned above, how did you have to change your therapeutic stance to contain his deep sense of not being wanted or loved?

SL: I really had to be in touch with my compassion towards him—despite him rejecting me repeatedly—and in realising the extent of his profound sense of abandonment I had to step back from myself and let him Be. It was not a matter of being right or wrong, rather there were weeks and months when I just had to Be and stay silent.

MP: I wonder about his attachment to you; now, how would you make sense of this, which is not fostered in Buddhism: no attachment they say, don't they?

SL: Well, the less I grasp, the less I have to be right, the less my ego is there, there is more of a revolution, I think, and I feel less attached to my ideas. That's how I understand this.

MP: From the point of view of the child: children get attached to you in your work, how do you think of non-attachment in Buddhist term, with regard to this fact?

THE FACILITATING SILENCE 117

SL: I'm not sure I can answer this: it's a big question. What I liked about Stephen Batchelor when I attend his retreats is that he stresses: "Don't attach to me or anything, you must find your own way and develop your own mind." This is what really appealed to me about Zen: "Don't think I've got all the answers."

MP: Well, that's your answer to my question, so far. Well, it's paradoxical this idea of attachment, isn't it? Look at Bion's idea of no memory or desire and his wish that analysts would not look up at him as a guru and yet, look what happened, a lot of people really look up at him as a, dare I say, semi-god, don't you think so? I suspect that's human nature.

SL: I think you're right, see what happened with Stephen Batchelor!

MP: Now, thinking of attachment and non attachment: this is linked with the idea of self and no self, isn't it? I wonder how one can apply the idea of no-self in the work with children.

SL: We help them to develop their ego and I think that you can only let go of it if you have developed it. When you have a healthy self then you can let go and that again is a paradox, isn't it?

MP: Indeed. Now, thinking of techniques that may come from your meditation, do you have a special one when you work with children?

SL: No, not directly; I don't apply mindfulness as many psychologists and other clinicians do in the NHS, I don't. But I have another vignette that I think might describe a different quality of silence. A colleague and I worked with a six-year-old African boy, his mother and younger step-sister for some months before I assessed him for psychotherapy. His father had died when he was ten months old and his step-father used to beat him and his mother up. One day he was beaten up quite badly and then shut out on the balcony for two to three hours. It was a cold day and he was wearing few clothes. Eventually his mother escaped to a refuge with both children. I agreed to see him for individual psychotherapy so my colleague and I took time in preparing him for the therapy and made sure we thought he was ready. On his first day of the therapy he was resistant and told his mother he did not want therapy. When I arrived in the waiting room he reluctantly

118   THE BUDDHA AND THE BABY

followed me to the therapy room. He sat uncomfortably on the edge of a chair wearing his jacket and his rucksack. After an initial introduction I asked him if he remembered why he was coming to see me. He said: "Feelings." I replied: "Yes, to think about your feelings." Pause. "I don't have any worries today." I said: "I think that is great that you don't have any worries today." Pause. I then showed him his psychotherapy box. He stood up and removed his rucksack and jacket. He opened his box and tipped some of the contents on the floor. He picked up a crocodile and studied it very carefully. Holding it in his hand he attacked the other objects, such as cars, animals, fences, figures in particular two men, who came in for most of the thrashings. Interestingly, there was a mother kangaroo, which had a baby in its pouch. Although the baby did get thrown about, he always placed it very carefully back in its mother's pouch. He was very engrossed in this activity. After about fifteen minutes I made a comment: "I notice that the crocodile is biting everyone and everything." "It's because he is hungry," he replied. For another fifteen minutes he continued with the play and remained very absorbed and focused. I then made another comment: "I understood that the crocodile was hungry but I wondered if it had any other feelings." "Yes, he is very angry because it is his home and all these things come in." "You mean they invade his home?" "Yes, and then they take over." I said I understood that must make the crocodile very angry. By then it was time to end. He put all the toys back in his box. We walked to the waiting room in silence.

MP: Here is your experience of the moments of silence, which were very important and together with your reflective comments you managed to engage him beautifully despite his initial resistance!

SL: Yes, that's what happened in this session. Although I have to say that sometimes I still say too much.

MP: On a more personal level: did you ever have any mystical experience, an experience of enlightenment or something particularly spiritual, unusual?

SL: Many years ago I had some premonition dreams. I would have a dream about something happening to people I knew and find out

THE FACILITATING SILENCE   119

that what I had dreamed had actually happened. The dreams lead me to go into a Jungian analysis.

MP: That must have been scary, the power of the unconscious!

SL: It was scary; yes, it was. It was the first thing I told my analyst as it was upsetting me. He normalised it and understood the dreams as being something that happens now and again. I have never had one since then. The more analysis I had and the more meditation I do the more connected with nature and with people I feel, and this can bring a sense of peace, at times. I think this is much more important to me now.

MP: I would imagine that such a sense of interconnectedness is also what gets through in your work with children.

SL: Yes, I suppose I do feel connected and perhaps more receptive and open.

MP: Well, with this we could perhaps end now this dialogue, a thoughtful interconnection between us two and the readers and interspersed with silences, which we could both tolerate as they were gravid with thinking and inspiring.

SL: As a friend once said to me: "in the words of the poet Theodore Roethke, may my silences become more accurate."

Reference

Batchelor, S. (1998). *Buddhism Without Beliefs: A Contemporary Guide to Awakening*. London: Bloomsbury.

CHAPTER TEN

Nothing fixed

Dialogue with Akashadevi

Body like a mountain
Heart like the ocean
Mind like the sky.

—Dogen (1200–1253 CE)

MP: This is an unusual venue to meet, Akasha Devi, a lay Buddhist community where you are living. It has always intrigued me since you've told me years ago of your choice of life. It's also particularly fascinating that you have been off work for a number of months to be on a long retreat and have come back having embraced a new "identity", if I am right. But I would like to start by asking you when you first started meditating, if that was before or while training as a child psychotherapist and if you come from a Buddhist tradition or other spiritual path.

AD: It was in the middle of my training, so I was quite stressed out and very driven, always overworking and feeling easily anxious and quite frantic about things. I just thought I needed to find something to calm me down and get me through this training.

122   THE BUDDHA AND THE BABY

MP: What about your analysis?

AD: Well, yes it helped me with many things but in a way it also
      increased those states because there was a lot of stuff coming to
      the surface which had to be worked through. I think I had been in
      analysis for three or four years when I learnt to meditate and then
      became a Buddhist. So it was quite interesting bringing that to
      analysis and talking about it in analysis and thinking about how
      the two, for me, were so complementary.

MP: You were not living in this community presumably at that
      time?

AD: No, I was living with a friend in a flat and then gradually got
      involved.

MP: When did you first come across Buddhism?

AD: As a teenager in Germany, I was vaguely interested in it as a
      religion without a God. I read H. Hesse's Siddhartha; I was in
      the peace movement and that kind of alternative circle. I came to
      this country when I was 18 to work in a Rudolf Steiner Camphill
      Residential Children Home in Aberdeen as my parents did not
      support me to go to university then because I was a girl and there
      was my brother to think about. I had also met an Englishman
      the year before in Ireland. So it was quite an impulsive decision
      to come to England. I was brought up as a Catholic but didn't
      believe in that. However, I was not an atheist, and I was very
      interested in Rudolf Steiner's antroposophic philosophy; that
      made sense to me at the time. In a nutshell, anthroposophy is a
      branch of mystic Christianity, which sees life as interconnecting
      flows of energy which can be transformed and directed in vari-
      ous ways—so quite a few parallels with Buddhism there, unbe-
      knownst to me at the time. I trained as a primary teacher then
      in Ormskirk, a little northern market town, nothing to do with
      Buddhism there, it all went underground a little bit. I was still
      reading about it, I knew there was something I was searching for
      in terms of a spiritual path. I was very interested and still am, in
      Shamanism and Native American culture—there's rather a paral-
      lel there with Buddhism, via the concept of interconnectedness,
      perhaps in a slightly more concrete way. But anyway, that's really

NOTHING FIXED   123

what interested me, so I went more in that direction at that time. Then I came to London and worked as a primary school teacher, got very disillusioned with the National Curriculum. I suppose my default thing, when I did not know what to do next in my life, was travelling, moving away; just like when aged eighteen I had come to England. I wanted to work abroad for a few years and just see what happened. I had this idea that I wanted to go to South America to explore Shamanism more deeply, but I didn't get a job because I couldn't speak Spanish well enough and they had many people who could speak Spanish very well. So I then applied for VSO (voluntary service overseas) and ended up accepting a job to go to Nepal as a primary teacher trainer and women's literacy facilitator. So I lived there in Nepal for two years. In Nepal, that's when I got very interested in Buddhism again. I lived in the hills and in Kathmandu, you see that picture there on the wall: it's the big stupa in Kathmandu. Just seeing the Tibetans practising was inspiring: there were lots of Tibetans refugees but also other native tribal groups, where people were practising something akin to Tibetan Buddhism. They had a spiritual path which was a mixture between a very old religion called Bonpo, which was more like Shamanism, and tantric Buddhism. I became very interested in all that and because I learned the language I could speak to people about it to some extent.

MP: You learnt Nepalese?

AD: We had an intensive language course. We went out a group of twelve of us, all doing the same job of teacher training in different districts, so the first two months we had this one-to-one or two-to-one language course with a native speaker. We were immersed in the language for seven, eight hours a day.

MP: They have a different alphabet also, don't they?

AD: Yes, It's the Sanskrit alphabet but we didn't learn to write very fluently; we did learn the alphabet because we were going to supervise literacy classes; we had to learn just enough to be able to write a little bit.

MP: What's the difference between the Sanskrit and the Pali, which are both used in Buddhist texts, aren't they?

124   THE BUDDHA AND THE BABY

AD: The script is the same; Pali is a different language but very related to Sanskrit. Nepali and Hindi both emerged from Sanskrit, which doesn't exist as a living language any more; it's a scholarly language like Latin. So I did that and I got very interested and just seeing Buddhism lived, I think, that's what struck me in Nepal. People didn't necessarily know very much about Buddhist philosophy or understood it very well intellectually, but they were very devotional and really believed in it and lived ethical lives because they could see very clearly that everything was connected; therefore it mattered what you did, and quite naturally those people simply tried to live by those principles. I thought that was fascinating.

MP: It was the real thing, a real, simple life not from the intellect, by the sound of it!

AD: Exactly. The atmosphere in places like Boudhanath—the big Buddhist stupa in Kathmandu—was incredible. I remember spending a lot of time there with a friend of mine in between language lessons watching people. You can climb up onto the round bit of the stupa and sit up there and just watch people walk round, the monks and the nuns walk round with their alms bowls, chanting Om Mani Padme Hum. And then there would be tourists, of course, walking around as well, and you would see that a lot of tourists wouldn't know that you walk round clockwise, so the monks would often just stand in front of tourists walking anti-clockwise, smile at them and turn them around. The tourists were really startled until they got it and said: "Ah, OK!"

MP: But physiologically it may be better to do it both ways in turn to balance the brain, isn't it?

AD: It's to do with the philosophy. In the Bonpo religion, they walk anti-clockwise, and in Buddhism clockwise. It's meant to be the direction to go up the spiral path, rather than going down, so it really matters. Again, it's such a concrete thing, the symbolism of that, but it was quite lovely how they did it: not at all pushy, just teaching. It's a completely different mentality. Yes, so I was in Nepal, then I came back and started training as a child psychotherapist with the Observation Course in 1995.

NOTHING FIXED   125

MP: So, you were not practising as a Buddhist, yet?

AD: No, I only learnt to meditate later on during my training.

MP: That was not a very long time ago, considering your radical choice of being part of a lay Buddhist Order and living in a community, isn't it?

AD: Eleven years ago? No, not very long on the scale of things, I suppose. I started living here eight years ago, after meditating for three years: I knew in my heart that I was a Buddhist and that I wanted to go with this particular Order, because I really liked the way they were doing things and I built up friendships. So I just tried it out for six months.

MP: Do you have to ordain?

AD: No, you don't have to, but I asked for ordination.

MP: Is that when you went away for four months not long ago?

AD: Well, you have to ask if you want to go all the way and join the Order. I asked in 2004 so then there's the whole process of particular retreats you go on, particular things you study and so on. There is a group of people around you, who know you well, have done retreats with you, taught you to meditate, who kind of keep an eye on your spiritual progress in terms of your meditation as well as living by the ethical precepts. So that process of getting ready took six years for me, and I was ordained last June. I was lucky to be able to be given a career break just before the cuts came in the NHS and it was hard on the clinic, but when I came back I was so much calmer and the people noticed it and the clinic benefited from that. The ordination was quite a big step, but it's kind of another starting point. Now that I'm part of the Order I can go on events like the International Order Convention in India in February 2013.

MP: What's the name of the Order?

AD: Triratna, that is, the Order of the Three Jewels. It was called the Western Buddhist Order until recently, because that was how it started—as a new Buddhist movement in the West. However, the name was changed at the request of the Indian Order

126   THE BUDDHA AND THE BABY

members—a third of the Order is now Indian—for the whole Order worldwide to have the same name, a name which would make sense to all Order Members worldwide. The teacher who founded the Order is called Sangharakshita—an Englishman who was posted in the Second World War in India and very early on he realised he was a Buddhist. His life story is very unusual.

MP: Perhaps it is linked with his past lives!

AD: When he read the Diamond Sutra aged sixteen, he did not understand it but he knew then that that was it: a kind of flash of light. He stayed in India after the war was over and there he was ordained as a Theravadin monk first, then spent twenty years in Kalimpong and was setting up various Buddhist groups and activities, linking in with lots of Tibetan Buddhists and Lamas, who were coming through this little Himalayan town. So he had some Tibetan and some Theravadin teachers, and a Chinese teacher too. He wrote a very good book called *The Survey of Buddhism* (Sangharakshita, 1957) when he was twenty-eight years old and living there. It's still regarded by Buddhist scholars of all traditions as one of the best books summarising the overall doctrine of Buddhism. He's quite brilliant intellectually, but also always had this vision that Buddhism needs to be practised, there's no point in just being intellectual about it. He ended up coming back to this country, because the English Sangha Trust and the Buddhist Society here in London—two Buddhist groups in the Sixties—had fallen out with each other and couldn't sort themselves out. Sangharakshita was well known in the Buddhist world by that time and was communicating with Buddhists around the world; so they asked him to come and act as a mediator. He came to try to do that and then he found that he couldn't do it; it was a completely stuck situation. He thought the problem was that both those groups were looking at their organisations more like a club, where people could just come for talks and learn a little bit about Buddhism but actually their lives didn't really change—it didn't touch the core of their lives. So he decided at that point that what was needed to establish Buddhism in this country was a Buddhist Order where people not only came along intellectually but really committed themselves to Buddhism and lived it. That's when he founded what was called the Western Buddhist Order.

He distilled out what he thought was the essence of Buddhism and tried to teach it in a way that made it applicable to Western, urban life—that was his angle. I think he did that brilliantly. I was very worried at first, of his being a kind of New Age missionary, but he isn't that at all and there is incredible depth in what he did.

MP: How does that fit in with the Indians, as they presumably don't need to learn about Buddhism?

AD: Well they do, because Buddhism, although it originated in India, had been completely forgotten about there and subsumed in a confusing and misleading way within the dominant religion of Hinduism for several centuries. Ironically, it was Western scholars who rediscovered around the turn of the twentieth century the history and significance of the Buddhist sites in India. When Sangharakshita was living in India in the 1950s, he met a politician called Dr Ambedkar, who was the Law Minister in Nehru's Government after India achieved Independence from British Colonial Rule. Dr Ambedkar led on writing the Indian Constitution at the time. Having been born into the ex-untouchable caste and really having had to fight for his education and for respect from his peers, he was more radical than Gandhi in that he actively criticised the caste system and wanted it abolished. Not many people, as you can imagine, went along with that.

MP: Especially the privileged castes, I would imagine!

AD: And what he did, he became a Buddhist from being born a Hindu, for political reasons, because he said that in Buddhism the caste system doesn't apply, while it's an integral part of Hinduism. He then encouraged the lower-caste people in India to become Buddhist, which would help them liberate themselves from the caste system. He called it "a peaceful Dhamma Revolution". Dr Ambedkar was incredibly successful: hundreds of thousands of people "from the scheduled castes", as they are now referred to, converted to Buddhism with him in a Mass Conversion Ceremony in October 1956. But those people didn't know very much about Buddhism, as they had converted for social and political reasons and were mostly without any formal education. Dr Ambedkar initially met Sangharakshita to ask for advice around the

128   THE BUDDHA AND THE BABY

conversion process, and they built up a lasting connection. Dr Ambedkar suffered from severe diabetes and died very tragically seven weeks after his own and the subsequent Mass Conversion Ceremony in Nagpur—his home town in the state of Maharashtra. Sangharakshita witnessed the plight of the converted Indian Buddhists, who now felt lost as their leader was dead and nobody else came forward to guide their next steps. So he tried himself to step in, giving many lectures on basic Buddhism during the remainder of his time in India. He also appealed to the other Eastern Buddhist countries to help by sending teachers, but there was very little response. So when he came back to England and founded the Order, he sent Western teachers back out to India to teach the Indian people. So it was an amazing cross fertilisation, of the Buddhist teachings being brought back into the country of their origin by Western Buddhists. By now, there is a vibrant Indian branch of the Triratna Order, continuing to put Dr Ambedkar's vision of a peaceful Dhamma Revolution into practice.

MP: So they have become quite proactive.

AD: Very much so, they're very politically active and very engaged with the potential of Buddhism for social transformation. It is an extraordinary Order, which is, as you might imagine, not free of its own scandals—including scandals around sexual acting out, particularly during the Movement's early years.

MP: It doesn't surprise me; it's part of institutions and human nature and you hear about scandals in all spiritual traditions and non-spiritual ones, as we know.

AD: Yes. I think that in trying to integrate aggressive and sexual energies through meditation, something very powerful happens and sometimes gets out of control. There's a quote from the Buddha where he says if there was a second energy as strong as sexual energy, then spiritual development wouldn't be possible. I can believe that.

MP: It's the life instinct, after all, that has allowed humanity to go on existing for millennia.

AD: That's right and something happens to it when you start to meditate, and to integrate it and to contain it can be very, very difficult.

NOTHING FIXED   129

MP: To continue with some of my questions: do you use your Buddhism in your psychotherapy work with children? Most people don't seem to do it directly.

AD: I don't use it explicitly myself, but some people I know do—especially teachers. There is a well-respected organisation associated with our Order called the Clear Vision Trust, which produces educational materials about Buddhism for school children of different ages, including experiential meditation exercises, like introducing a three-minute breathing space and so on.

MP: That's very interesting, yes; I'd like to learn more about it.

AD: The kind of inner space that is produced by doing the mindfulness of breathing meditation of just being in the present moment fully and being aware of the whole of your experience, that's also the state you have to be in when you are with a child in the therapy room, you know, not to be distracted, not to be preoccupied with anything else, to be fully present, aware of yourself and everything else that's going on in the child, so I think that's a complete parallel. So, although I wasn't explicitly using Buddhism in my work in terms of teaching it, I thought it helped my own mental state to become clearer. You know, I found it much easier once I started meditating to just naturally fall into that state when I was in the therapy room with a child. Some children pull you into a state when it's hard to concentrate and you start thinking about something else, somebody else; it happens to me much less now.

MP: But that's also part of the countertransference, when the patient pushes your mind away and then you come back and wonder what's going on for the patient at that moment. It's one of our tools, isn't it?

AD: It is, but what I found was that I could notice and become aware of my countertransference much more quickly, rather than going off for perhaps five minutes before I might notice; what gradually developed was a greater clarity and sensitivity to the child's and my own mental states.

MP: To move into this more theoretical arena: how do you reconcile the fact that we have to help our child patients to develop a stronger ego and the Buddhist idea of *anatta*, no-self?

130   THE BUDDHA AND THE BABY

AD: What Sangharakshita is teaching about that and what makes a lot of sense to me is that in order to progress to no-self, you have to first of all become a happy, healthy human being. So you need to have a strong ego and be stable and integrated as a human being, before you can go on to those higher levels of insight, where you realise no-self. So, I think there isn't really a contradiction, because first of all the foundation meditation practices are taught in most Buddhist centres—the Mindfulness of Breathing and the *Metta Bhavana* (Development of Loving Kindness). The Buddha did teach that in order to gain insight, you have to first of all develop a calm and concentrated mind and positive emotions: you have to be integrated as a human being, because if you're not integrated but are alienated or if you're very neurotic and have a lot of psychological difficulties, then you don't have a robust enough foundation on which to develop insight and use it in a good way. Instead it's actually likely to really disturb you; it can really drive you mad. Because insight is the gradual realisation that your ego, as a basis to make you feel safe and secure is an illusion, that actually it's not a real basis for feeling safe and secure. But first of all, you have to have a safe and secure ego and feel confident in yourself in order to then let that ego go, or whatever you want to call it. You realise the ego is not solid, is not something actually to be relied on; what you have to rely on is something much bigger than that and something that's more like the interconnectedness of everything; that everything is a process; that everything is energy.

MP: How do you use this idea in your work with children, then?

AD: To my mind, the aim of psychotherapeutic work with children is to help them to become integrated and to become happy human beings. I don't see my task as a therapist to help children or their parents with their spiritual development—they come for help because they are struggling with a problem on the psychological level, with not being integrated in some way.

MP: To help children and families to integrate better in their egos and lives: that would be your first step. Then they may chose, or not, their spiritual development. It is interesting that we, in the West, keep these two aspects of human life so separate. Deirdre Dowling will have something to say about this in her conversation in this book.

AD: Just to add something I've found very interesting since I've come back and have done this very concrete thing of having a new Buddhist name and using that name in all contexts. I discussed this issue with my clinical supervisor, as I was concerned about breaching technique through revealing something about my personal life and my beliefs. However, it felt wrong to simply state my new name without any explanation—too weird and potentially maddening, for the vulnerable children and families I was working with. She agreed. Not only had I changed my surname, which you might do when you get married, but I'd changed my name completely, which implied a major change of identity. Also, the families knew I had been away for four months, they did not know why I had been away, but I was coming back after that time and I was coming back with an Indian-sounding name. So between the two of us we decided that I would in effect breach psychoanalytic technique to explain to the children and families that I had become a Buddhist and that Akasha Devi was my new Buddhist name. My supervisor suggested that I treat any reactions to this as material like everything else, interpreting it. I didn't know how much people would ask me about it and it's been very different with different people; it's been fascinating, though. Some of the children and some of the parents started asking me about meditation. Some asked me explicitly what it means to become a Buddhist, and my reasons for taking this step. I tried to give very brief answers as well as interpreting the particular focus of their interest, and what this might potentially mean for them. But it has meant that there is sometimes an explicit conversation about Buddhism, due to my self-disclosure. There had been instances, even before I was ordained of seeing children, adolescents in particular, who had asked me whether I knew how to meditate and could teach them. So, they had probably unconsciously picked something up from me along those lines.

MP: Intuitively, I suppose.

AD: The difference is that before my disclosure I had never responded to these requests in any direct or concrete way but simply

132 THE BUDDHA AND THE BABY

interpreted them. This is definitely more difficult to do now that I have changed the parameters.

MP: The feeling that you had to tell them came from you, then, if I understand rightly?

AD: It came from me because I was concerned about what their phantasies would otherwise have been. What I thought, and what my supervisor agreed with, was that they would find it potentially quite maddening. Your name, and especially your first name, is so connected up with your identity, so it would have been like changing my identity after being away for a long time and coming back as a completely different person with this weird name. That would have been likely to have a very disturbing effect on them.

MP: But in the actual therapy they would have known that you were still more or less the same, sane person, presumably.

AD: But the children and families we, child psychotherapists see nowadays are very disturbed, at least in our clinic; they are on the psychotic rather than neurotic anxieties end of the spectrum. I didn't think that some of the children or families I saw would be able to have this kind of rational attitude and see that, yes, I was still the same person but they may have really believed that I was somebody else now. Something grounding was needed from my side, I felt, along the lines of: there is a rational explanation for this and the fact that I haven't suddenly transformed into an entirely different being.

MP: Perhaps also their identification with you having that name was affected: how will such a change of name influence their identification with you?

AD: Yes, and it's at such a concrete level. My supervisor was telling me that once she changed her hairstyle quite dramatically and, particularly one autistic child she worked with could not cope with that change for months; he felt as if she was no longer the same person.

MP: It's like a baby or a toddler not recognising mum's face when she puts a hat on: "mum is no longer mum" if she changes

NOTHING FIXED   133

appearance. Did you find that your patients spoke more about this new information they were given about you?

AD: Not much, interestingly. I was very worried that even just saying that it was a Buddhist name would be an intrusion into the therapeutic space, but it hasn't felt like that. Each of the children and each of the parents have taken it in their own way, and whatever it meant to them in relation to their particular difficulty, that was the aspect they picked up on quite quickly, and we didn't have to have long conversations. But I did have some more complicated responses, like one parent, with whom I mainly connect via long telephone conversations as she's quite unwell physically as well as psychologically. In the middle of a conversation about her son, out of the blue, suddenly she asked me to teach her to meditate or tell her where she could go and learn meditation, to help her become less persecuted and more able to relax her mind. I thought: "Should I? Could I? Why not?" I didn't know where my boundary was for a minute and said I just needed to think about that and would get back to her. Her sudden request but also my potential response felt quite intrusive and clearly like a boundary violation.

MP: She clearly wanted to take something from you: perhaps your meditative, relaxed way of being, and your state of mind. Perhaps she wanted to identify with you.

AD: Yes, but that might not be the right thing for her. Any information about us limits and closes up the patient's imagination. But it may also open up another dimension of imagination.

MP: Perhaps the answer of what to say and what not to say about oneself, under circumstances like you've described, really lies with the therapist's feelings; different therapists may have slightly different approaches and still work within therapeutic boundaries.

AD: Yes, that's true: different people may do different things. So, following this event in my life, a change in technique might follow, especially with some people who may ask me directly. We'll see; it will be interesting to observe how it will evolve. Perhaps we have to give up this idea that there's an ideal situation,

134 THE BUDDHA AND THE BABY

where everything can be completely open; there's always some kind of limitation, whether that's the gender of the analyst or the religious, or the sexual orientation or national and ethnic origin—something about the unique reality of a person that cannot be disguised.

MP: This comes back to my question about combining psychotherapy and meditation and the boundaries between the two.

AD: As part of my Buddhist teaching training, I am currently co-leading an MBCT course (mindfulness-based cognitive therapy), which they offer at the London Buddhist Centre, in a separate secular space downstairs. It's an eight-week course based on Jon Kabat Zinn's model. Basically, it uses a CBT methodology, in a very directive style. It's explicitly a therapeutic course and people come with psychological issues of depression, stress, addiction, and chronic pain, but at the end of the course they may also be encouraged to come back to the Buddhist centre for more explicitly spiritual courses and classes. I don't feel entirely comfortable with that. I wouldn't want to take advantage of someone's emotional vulnerability in order to coax them towards Buddhism, although, on the other hand, I do often feel the universal perspective offered by Buddhist philosophy could greatly help them.

MP: It is important for Buddhist teachers to be well aware of psychological issues and, as you said earlier on, for us psychotherapists to help with psychological issues, i.e. of ego identity and leave the spiritual issues to the Buddhists. This clarity is necessary to reduce possible damage and scandals.

AD: Yes, it could be damaging although there's more recognition in the Buddhist world, that some people may need psychological help. Buddhist centres do attract a lot of vulnerable people, who are really struggling either with severe psychological issues or with addictions, etc. and they really want to change their lives, but sometimes it's not enough just to learn to meditate and come to a Buddhist centre. Sometimes they also need therapy; they may have a huge reaction to meditation and this may not be enough to contain that. That's now well recognised in Buddhist centres.

MP: Another question I have is about attachment and non-attachment, which is so linked with self and no-self: what's your thinking about this?

AD: This is another very interesting issue. I was really struggling with this at first, misunderstanding it in a very concrete way. In the traditional Buddhist texts, the message is quite often categorical: attachment is a bad thing: we need to aim at non-attachment. However, when you explore the texts more deeply, you find a similar qualification as in the no-self doctrine; that actually, again, first of all, you need to be integrated and you need to be able to make good relationships, have good contacts with people, and feel connected and not alienated, before you can think about non-attachment. Non-attachment isn't saying you shouldn't have relationships with people, that you shouldn't love other people; it says don't fix on it; don't assume that this is going to be for life, that your intimate relationship is your refuge, basically. A relationship can never do that; another person can never do that. A relationship can be a very positive force in your life as long as you don't make it the centre of your life; you need to remain aware that at any moment something could happen, for whatever reason, to change the situation. The teaching advises you always to be aware of the impermanence of things. Within that you still have loving relationships; you can still have a family. It's much harder if you are in a relationship and choose to have children not to become attached in this fixed, ultimate way where your family becomes your life; but then you make that your practice: to be aware at all times that it may not last; that it's not for ever: illness, death, old age will occur as part of human reality. There was a practice with a certain order of monks, that each night they were turning their begging bowl upside down, because they might die in the night. This was their constant reminder of impermanence. So you meditate on non-attachment, but at the same time, your body is alive and you're looking after it and you're also having compassion towards it. It's quite a paradox to have compassion for human life but at the same time to realise that it is totally impermanent, not fixed.

MP: How do you link this with your work with children?

136   THE BUDDHA AND THE BABY

AD: Actually, I think in some work with children it can be really helpful. I have a patient at the moment, who had lots of disruptions in his life: from living with his mother to be taken into foster care quite inexplicably to him, then shipped off to Africa to be with part of his wider family: lots of inexplicable separations and disruptions, and he's now having a breakdown. When I was talking to this child about his experience and talked to his father, with whom he lives at the moment, it really did help me to have the Buddhist perspective on attachment. That child couldn't trust anybody after all that: he immediately feared that the assessing psychiatrist would take him away from his dad. This child has experienced impermanence in a very disruptive way all through his life and he is expecting catastrophes all the time. So, we proactively needed to tell him that his father was going to look after him for now and would continue to do so, "all being well". We then showed him that there had been many unexpected bad things happening to him, but also some unexpectedly good things. I try to help children to live with uncertainties but also with possible changes. Even to children you can say: "Yes, it's very frightening to think about the uncertainty of things, but it's not just fearful things that happen, also good things happen." You can also add that whatever happens, there's usually something and someone who will help.

MP: These children, who had not had a secure attachment, are bound to be so anxious all the time, aren't they?

AD: There is another child I saw, whose mother and grandfather both died, and he was totally preoccupied with death. I think he suffered from a kind of existential anxiety, in addition to some relatively mild attachment difficulties. This child, for some reason, had a particular sensitivity and what, I felt, he needed wasn't reassurance. He needed actually for me to tell him the truth: "Yes, it was true that they died, and we may all die at any point, but it's not the only thing that's true; it's also true that at any moment something good may happen. It's also true that things may stay okay sometimes!" That's what he needed to hear. Children don't need reassurance or they may feel patronised.

MP: Presumably you wouldn't say to a very young child, who's just lost his mother and is clinging onto his father that he is right in feeling anxious as his dad too, may die as we all have to die at some point, would you? I may, surely, verbalise his anxiety about the thought of dad's dying but would also give him the other thought that dad will hopefully stay alive for a long time and look after him.

AD: I suppose like with everything you have to be careful not to do it in a too reassuring way so that child feels you're not taking on board what he's saying but you're just trying to make him feel better, but actually you know, as well as they do, that you're going to die.

MP: I think we're saying something similar indeed.

AD: I do think psychoanalysis and Buddhism have something in common there, in being compassionate but also quite tough. Yes, you have to face the truth but at the same time be kind to yourself and be kind to everybody because the truth about life and reality is very difficult and very frightening as well as quite amazing. So, this naturally leads to a compassionate attitude towards all that lives. I think in a way for me they're very parallel like that, but with Buddhism you've got the perspective that this is human life. When you do therapy, it's very personal; it's this person's story and you're trying to make sense of their particular story and their particular fears. Buddhism can give you the bigger frame: "This is human life and whatever goes on in the individual story, it also goes on for all of us." That can be really reassuring to me: to think I'm not the only one. In this way, you don't fall into this self-commiseration attitude of: "Oh poor me, why did this happen to me while everybody else is perfectly happy?" This is clearly not the case: we all have to grapple with a version of this.

MP: To go back to the child who was existentially anxious about his dad also dying, perhaps the way to help him is to have a healthy attachment to his dad, who will hopefully go on living and looking after him, but also help the child to let go and face the fact that his dad may also die at some point.

AD: But also that even if that happens, there is another story i.e. that there are people, who will help, whatever happens. It doesn't have to be the end of the world; it doesn't have to be a catastrophe. It will feel like a catastrophe but there would be people that help the child even with those feelings.

138 THE BUDDHA AND THE BABY

MP: We're also helping children face a sort of dis-attachment when the end of sessions comes, or the end of term etc. Isn't that a way to help children accept impermanence all the time?

AD: Yes, we do that around holiday times of course. I did have a very interesting experience with one of my psychotherapy patients, who was very cross with me about my changed name. He said, when we had a three-week Christmas break, instead of two, because our dates were not quite matching: "But three weeks is too long, anyway what will you do and where are you going?" He was raging for most of the session: we spoke about it from all different angles and he couldn't quite get over it. At the end, as we were walking along the corridor to the waiting room he shouted: "And where are you going to go, and when you come back, are you going to change your name again?". This holiday had thrown him back to me having gone away for four months and I hadn't taken that on board. To him it was about the identity and that I could suddenly change again. At that point I said to him that I wasn't going to change my name and this was just an ordinary break.

MP: That was a reassuring reality that you let him know of. In this way, I see a link between Buddhism and psychoanalysis: to help children accept the reality of you going away, of mum having other children to look after; it helps children to accept separation or non-attachment and letting go. This is the other side of attachment, isn't it?

AD: It's not about not being attached in the psychodynamic sense, I don't think. It's a language issue here, a matter of definition. It's how you understand attachment or no-self. No-self doesn't mean that there's literally no self; it means no fixed self, not fixing on it. The same applies to non-attachment, which doesn't mean that there's no relationship and you're completely lonely all the time. It means don't fix on your relationship. Yes, that goes on in therapy: mum's love doesn't have to be exclusive, but that doesn't mean it's any less important and emotionally stirring.

MP: What are your thoughts about emptiness?

AD: To me emptiness means that there is nothing fixed in terms of an essence to anything; everything boils down to energy and we perceive the world as we do because of the limitation of our senses, but that's not the way it actually is—the way we perceive the world is a partial, distorted reflection of the way things really are. Eastern people don't have such a problem with emptiness as we do in the West because their understanding of the concept is positive: emptiness is an open space full of potential. Anything can emerge from it; it's actually freedom. We give this term a negative connotation in the West.

MP: Perhaps this idea could help us in working with hyperactive children, who have to fill any moment with action and movement for fear of their feelings such as feeling lost or frightened.

AD: The other thing that can help with such children could be an awareness of the body lying down. Again I'm thinking of another child I'm seeing at the moment: he is very hyperactive, very frantic and does quite a lot of moving around; sometimes he'll just collapse on the sofa and I will talk to him about having a rest. I could try to get him to become aware of his body at that point, and to get him to stay in that relaxed position for a minute. I have never actually done that with him, but I have often wondered whether this might be what he needs.

MP: Perhaps that would give him an experience of a pause, a moment of emptiness or of something else than frantic movements. Perhaps this could open up some new space for those hyperactive children? Perhaps we could be brave and introduce this new technique in our therapies at some point?

AD: I haven't so far. I was thinking of the receptive element and the active element in meditation: you both allow and observe whatever happens at that moment and at the same time you make an active effort to do a particular thing, for example, focussing on the breath. There is something a bit similar in psychoanalysis.

MP: The free floating attention of the analyst?

AD: Yes, that's the receptive element and Bion's concept of no memory or desire But I was also thinking of the active element: Bion's idea about the selected fact, i.e. something emerging out of that open space, which stands out, and you then have to make an active decision that this is the crux of the matter and you focus on that (Bion, 1967).

MP: This is interesting and it makes me think of what we have to do a lot in our work particularly with children. We may need to be concretely active, for example, in keeping the boundaries of the setting, when a child tries to run away from the therapy room or when we use more active techniques with children with autistic traits or other developmentally delayed children. We perform both a maternal and a paternal function, as you say, similarly to our stance in meditation.

AD: Yes, I often start in meditation just like I would do in a session: I sit and try to be aware as much as possible of my body, feelings and thoughts—my overall experience. Out of all that, something in particular will come into focus. I first of all see what happens and I decide, depending on what space I'm in, what type of meditation I need to practise at that moment. This kind of mindfulness exercise could be tried out with some aggressive, acting-out children. A teacher I know who works in a pupil referral unit has tried to do a very brief three-minute-long breathing exercise along these lines with the children, and she got some good results: the children got quite interested in that, and said it helped them feel calmer.

MP: On a more personal level, did you ever have some particularly extraordinary experience through meditation?

AD: Nothing dramatic, but I had glimpses of that when I first started meditating. I had experiences that showed me there is much more to my experience, to my perception, and to reality than I thought there was. For example, I did have experiences where I would be very concentrated during meditation and suddenly didn't know any more where my body stopped and started; I lost all sense of my body boundaries. It felt frightening but also very liberating. Your consciousness becomes bigger, and it's no longer limited to your physical body. The scary part is not recognising the territory and therefore not knowing what to do or where to go next from there.

MP: Perhaps this is a good point where to stop with this suspended thought. Many thanks Akasha Devi and I hope you enjoyed this conversation as much as I did.

References

Bion, W. R. (1967). Notes on memory and desire. *Psycho-Analytic Forum, 2*: 272–273; 279–280.

Dogen (1200–1253). Moon in a dewdrop—writings of the Zen Master Dogen. Ed. Kazuaki Tanahashi. New York: North Point Press, 1985.

Sangharakshita (1957). *A Survey of Buddhism*. Guildford, Surrey: Biddles. (Later editions published by Windhorse, Birmingham.)

CHAPTER ELEVEN

Walking with Buddha

Dialogue with friends

On the seashore of endless worlds children meet.

—Tagore

Three friends met for a walk on a coastal path in England and found themselves sharing their common quest of being involved with children and families with mental health issues and also of practising Buddhism. They're trying to find a way to combine their professional and meditative practices.

EMILY: Well, I've been introduced to Buddhism at the time of qualifying as a child psychotherapist and started regular meditation classes and retreats, which soon led me to notice the many common aspects between psychoanalytic psychotherapy and Buddhism.

CLARE: I have been interested in Buddhism since my trip to India in my teens, and although I try to apply it in my daily life and in my attitude to things, I have also got an interest in using mindfulness for mothers and babies and have just finished a group with them.

144   THE BUDDHA AND THE BABY

RICHARD: Oh yes, that's been a long-standing interest of mine also, but have not quite yet managed to gather such a group. Actually, I approached Buddhism in a very different circumstance of my life: I was facing death by a form of cancer and decided to enter a monastery to help prepare for dying. But when I left it ready to face the inevitable, alas, I had to face a new leaf of life: they had discovered a new drug that kept me alive till now.

EMILY: Well, that is indeed a more dramatic story, and as many people one hears about, it's the awareness of suffering and of the inevitable facts of life: getting old, sick, and dying, that attracts people to Buddhism. It sounds similar to what happened to young Buddha when he discovered those unpalatable facts of life, which he had been sheltered from by his family; but what about the mother–baby group, Clare?

CLARE: Yes, the embryonic idea of my group was rooted in the link between mindfulness and mentalization.

EMILY: Oh, that is interesting; please tell us more as I'm not sure I quite grasp the difference.

CLARE: Mindfulness as a practice is designed to help one to become acquainted with the functioning of the mind through stilling the mind by watching the breath and noticing how one's mind is constantly distracted by external events and also by internal events. From the mindfulness point of view, this is just grist for the mill; it doesn't matter the nature of the distraction, and the distraction is irrelevant, you know; it's becoming aware of the distraction itself that matters.

RICHARD: Yes, I experience that untamed monkey mind, as Buddhism describes the mind, which is constantly moving for distractions.

CLARE: That's it, and mindfulness is a technique that has its roots in Buddhism and it's being extracted to create a mental-health intervention, which is proving very helpful and has an increased evidence base; Bangor University and Oxford University in collaboration with Jon Kabat-Zinn in America are developing this evidence-based technique. Mentalising is this concept that's been particularly worked on by Fonagy and Bateman, and it aims at becoming mind-minded and at appreciating in an embedded emotional way, not just in an intellectual way, that we have minds which function individually and are separate. The more we can appreciate that other people have minds capable of thoughts, feelings, and affects, the more we can develop these soft skills, empathy, and emotional affect regulation. So, mentalising is a capacity we need to develop more and more to help the children and families we work with.

EMILY: It's interesting you talk about these qualities of the mind, and I'm thinking of my role as a seminar leader in the Psychoanalytical Observational Course at the Tavistock Clinic. The students in my seminar present their work situation and we often hear of disconcerting situations of abuse, neglect, traumas, and so on, that those children are subjected to. And yet, I always bear in mind Thich Nhat Hanh's idea that one can tolerate as much as one has been able to accept in oneself as part of human nature. So, I encourage students to be curious and interested in the stories behind being, for example, an abusing father, a cut-off mother, a violent grandfather, a neglectful grandmother, and even a sex abuser, without judging these people but with an open, spacious, and most necessary compassionate attitude.

RICHARD: Well, that's been my experience with a group of sexually abused girls, whom I saw in a group with a colleague some years ago. I was just at the beginning of my attempt to try being a child professional with a spiritual interest. I would go beyond the stories and the experiences of these girls to look at them just as young girls who were struggling to find their identity and to have relationships that they really wanted but were very frightened of, and were either a bit too advanced or a bit immature and mixed up about that, and that felt very real. We did role plays where the girls had to play out their relationships with boys and how they could be assertive and deal with boys. One had to be the girl and one was the boy and one was watching and giving advice, and it was very, very funny because of the way

146 THE BUDDHA AND THE BABY

they were role playing being the boy and they all laughed. They lost sight of being sexually abused when they were giving suggestions on how to deal with this boy: they all laughed as it was really funny; it all became much lighter and also hilarious at times. They came together as companions' coaches for each other. Some of the girls really learned a lot from these processes as it just felt like this was the beginning and the rehearsal for their actual life; and this was not theory-driven.

EMILY: I bet this will help them to grow up into better mothers, who may not need help later on with their babies, don't you think so?

RICHARD: Well, yes, I believe there is some research and evidence on treatment with sexually abused girls that can be resolutory for them. *A propos* of research, there is research that shows that in new mothers under stress, feeling particularly persecuted by their baby or overwhelmed by feelings of anxiety and depression, their capacity to mentalise and to remain aware of their mind and other people's minds becomes compromised.

EMILY: Well, and I've heard that these mother–baby mentalization groups have now got an evidence base for reducing the level of stress and depression in these mothers followed by healthy growth in their babies. In fact, it is Ros Powrie, who has a dialogue in this book (Chapter Two), who tells us exactly about these results. Yes, that's what I intend to study more systematically and to use mindfulness technique, to increase mentalization.

RICHARD: That's interesting: tell us more about your mindfulness group for mothers and babies, please.

CLARE: Yes, I've offered to run a ten-week group with mothers with babies: mothers who suffer from anxiety and depression; they are all known to mental health services and had already had individual therapy or parent–infant psychotherapy or therapy alongside the group. Some of these mothers are clearly very persecuted by these babies and

WALKING WITH BUDDHA   147

feel that the babies are out to get them and invade them. An important aim in using this technique is to allow them to see the baby as a separate being, as a little person with his or her own mind and not a rapist partner, for example. That's where the link is between mentalization and mindfulness, psychoanalysis and meditation. These mothers all sit on the floor on a blanket they have been asked to bring and put down their baby in front of them. The first ten to fifteen minutes are about a kind of mindfulness relaxation technique, including the body scan to encourage them to get in touch with different parts of their body, to really notice where they are holding the tension and then to actively direct the breath into those areas of tension. They are asked then to focus on the various parts of their body, to become aware of the stress starting from the head, the forehead, the face etc., down to the toes. The hands are used quite a lot as an object of focus: just to become aware of the sensation of the air touching their hands. They also have to focus on their breathing without forcing it and to notice how their breath becomes deeper and slower.

EMILY: That's interesting about the hands: I've heard other people using that in their work with girls with eating difficulties and how that object of focus can help to take the attention away from them being fat, ugly. It's Ricky Emmanuel, who's implementing that mindfulness technique and his dialogue is in this book (Chapter Fourteen).

RICHARD: Well, I also used that technique when I started to do mindfulness, although I didn't call it as such. The child or adolescent is invited to look at the room and to notice things, then to look at the palm of their hands and to do a breathing exercise. The attention shift from the environment to them as human beings and it is no longer bound to the symptom or the condition they have. What becomes focal is how they relate to their suffering, how they relate to their experience, rather than the actual content of their experiences: what, how, where, when, and how they tell their story. There is something about how people hold their humanity in the face of their traumas and tragedies and

148   THE BUDDHA AND THE BABY

about the qualities they've developed and cultivated via their relationship with suffering. This actually makes a big difference to how I see them and experience them, and I have seen changes in the way they report things and face things. This broader awareness and perspective helps them to feel more accepted; they feel that people say they have to change or do things that in their mind are connected with stuff they don't like about themselves. They feel broken, they feel different, they feel wrong and bad. There is a soft attitude and a kind of spaciousness about all of that that you don't get when you're just focusing on getting rid of certain things, the symptoms, and certain aspects of their experiences, which have become an enemy, something to get rid of. And that works and it is helpful and children become more functional.

EMILY: Richard, you certainly have a very broad experience and awareness of the whole gamut as you've worked with bereft children, children in war zones, in extreme poverty and traumatic situations in Mozambique, in Iraq, and other most troubled countries, and I can see how that has expanded your capacity to embrace their suffering and to explore—as you said—their relationship with suffering and what they do with such terrible experiences. You know, I'm thinking of something very different but linked here, that is, the Adult Attachment Interview (Main, Kaplan & Cassidy, 1985) that evaluates the types of attachments parents have by looking not so much at the experiences and traumas they had but at the linguistic and narrative coherence expressed in recounting such experiences. Similarly, you consider these children and parents' way of posing themselves in the face of traumas and tragedies: in that, I share your view that the healing process resides in such an attitude.

CLARE: To go back to the mindfulness group with depressed mothers and babies: when they have to attend to their babies—who surprisingly are quite self-contained and calm while their mothers focus on their self-awareness exercises—they are encouraged to do it, of course, but in a mindful way.

It's their way of relating to the baby's demand and distress that changes: the baby is no longer invaded by the mother's own projections and depression but freed through a mindful care.

EMILY: Oh, this is fascinating, so that mindfulness is not some sort of rarefied state that is only for when one is sitting in perfect conditions; actually, on the contrary, this is a state of being that one needs to develop practically at any moment in the day. And are the babies included in this mindfulness about the mothers' own selves?

CLARE: Yes, after the first part, I would say to them: "Now, let's spend a few minutes looking at your baby", and in the last few moments I invite them to think how they feel on that day and then to concentrate on their individual baby and to imagine what is like for their baby to be there. This is to try to increase their capacity to mentalise not just to be mindful about their own state but about their own baby, to observe their baby and to imagine how the baby may be feeling This may be more difficult for them to begin with, but less so at the end of the mindfulness exercises.

EMILY: This reminds me of a mother and baby who was rigid and on alert when he was with her; he could never sleep when alone in her care. She was severely depressed and had tried to kill herself more than once. In the first session, I only registered in my mind and body the horror shocks that she and her baby had been subjected to; I mostly performed a containing function with a soothing voice in the penumbra of the therapy room. By the end of that session, the baby was relaxed and asleep, while mother nearly fell asleep. I had practised mindfulness of mind and body silently and processed things inside me by transmitting them the atmosphere created by a calm and all-embracing mind. I was there with two suffering human beings—not just with their stories and their predicaments—and I had to help them out of that suffering.

CLARE: You've also been influenced by Buddhist ideas in your work with mothers and babies, I can see!

150 THE BUDDHA AND THE BABY

EMILY: Well, yes, the practice of meditation has widened and deepened my capacity to observe, to be in touch with the mother and baby's body–mind experiences, and has broaden my countertransference in its emotional and physical aspects. My therapeutic tools and insight also support the process of meditation as they help me to recognise, name, understand, and accept some disconcerting thoughts, images, feeling states, and awareness that emerge during meditation. The awareness of such states allows them to pass and a great sense of freedom and spaciousness appears. This process assists me when faced with very disconcerting and scandalous clinical situations; it helps not to stay caught up but to see it as transient and impermanent. In this respect, the practices of Buddhism and psychotherapy have come together in a mutually enhancing way in my clinical practice.

CLARE: Well, I am now thinking of the somewhat similar story of baby, Bruce, who was two months old when he was sent to an NHS clinic, by the mother's psychiatrist. In their first session with me, mother walked into my room half holding baby Bruce in her arms. He was agitated and mother plonked him at some distance from herself on the settee, where she herself slouched looking tired and fed up. Baby's eyes were wide open and his limbs were stretched out and rigid. He lay there alone on the immobile surface of the couch. He was in a hypervigilant state. My heart jolted. While telling me her story, she dragged Bruce along the couch towards herself as if he were a parcel and looked at him with hatred. Bruce stiffened up even more, looking alarmed, and so did I. Mother had not wanted a third child; she already had two teenage children from a previous violent relationship. Baby Bruce's father, too, was a violent man and a leader in a drug gang. He did not want her to have an abortion and she was terrorised by him. To get away from him, she overdosed soon after baby Bruce's birth. By the end of this first session, she had stretched herself comfortably along the couch, while baby Bruce looked a little less rigid. During this session, I listened with a sympathetic attitude (*muditta*), embracing them both with

WALKING WITH BUDDHA 151

my body (my voice, the vocal noises I uttered, my facial expression, body posture of leaning towards them) and with my mind (a compassionate, non-judgemental, loving attitude—*metta* and *karuna*). I felt their individual, separate struggles as I identified with both mother's story and baby's predicament with equanimity (*upekkha*). My body shook as baby Bruce's body startled and stiffened up; my heart raced breathlessly as mother recounted her story. In this first encounter, I offered this mother and baby what Bion called maternal reverie and containment. I did not say much but described the baby's body moves and feelings expressed bodily, and I also mirrored back mother's feelings. In this containing mode, a transformation had already occurred inside me: a physical and psychological shock lodged in my awareness without me reacting. I stayed with the shock and the unknown of this first encounter; intuition led me to talk softly, with deep voice and calmly while I listened to mother's dramas. A transformation occurred in mother and baby as they resonated with my inner state. As they felt cradled by me, they had a new experience of being homed in this new therapeutic encounter. Mother was very surprised at how both of them were relaxed, as it never happened when it was just the two of them, and she put it down to my soft, calming voice and to the atmosphere of the room. The work continued for years until Bruce settled in life completely well and so did his mother.

RICHARD: Oh, what you've described so clearly here, are the four Brahama-Vihara or dwelling in universal love, compassion, sympathetic joy, and equanimity, and I also find them useful in my work, which as you know is not quite psychoanalytic, but it has been refined by looking at my attitude and my relationship with the suffering of my patients. I find *anicca*, impermanence, a very useful tool: when I come to believe deeply in myself that all is impermanent: this body of mine as well as thoughts, feelings, and everything around us including the moon and the sun, then my grasping decreases. My grasping onto the idea of helping or affecting changes in children and families relents.

152   THE BUDDHA AND THE BABY

EMILY: But don't you think that this could become a sort of depressed giving up in the face if impotence and unbearable pain?

RICHARD: No, that's not what I meant by letting go; I suppose it's a fine balance between letting go into depression, being overwhelmed, taken over by the reality, on the one hand, and, on the other hand, by accepting things as they are, the reality of limitedness and impermanence, which, as you said earlier on, leads to a deep sense of freedom and spaciousness.

CLARE: OK, talking about impermanence of the self, I do struggle with this idea of no-self versus the need to help children develop their sense of themselves. In a recent conversation with a Buddhist monk living in a Buddhist monastery, I actually understood that there is no contradiction. He said that in Buddhism too, the self is taken great care of and the body too: one target is to achieve happiness in oneself. This is done not by denying the self but by dropping the idea of a self: "My misery, my depression, my joy, my excitement". It is dropping this state of mind into a more universal sense that this is part of human nature and not something specific to me, but this is the way things are at this moment. If one develops a capacity to observe the rising, the being, and the ceasing of such states then they pass away. The small individual self melts. Consciousness broadens beyond the small self and into and infinite spaciousness and freedom from non-attachment and non-clinging. Is that also your experience?

CLARE: Yes, I think that in psychotherapy we are dealing with what Buddhism would call the conventional self. The idea of *anatta* is an ontological position, you know, that if you meditate you're trying to find the object of negation and when you identify the object of negation then you realise emptiness of the self.

EMILY: What do you mean by: object of negation, I'm not familiar with that term?

CLARE: It's the self that we construct, so this idea of: I am I; I'm doing this, I'm, feeling that, and so on, you imagine these actions and have the strong arising sense of the: "I" that is doing that. So, you have to work hard to identify the nature of that "I" with which we so strongly identify, and, once you've really identified it, that becomes the object of negation and you understand that there is no permanent, inherent self. It is called the object of negation and—maybe that is a Tibetan Buddhism phrase—the object of negation is what we speak about a lot.

EMILY: So, does it deny that there is a permanent, inherently existing, independently existing self and does it affirm that there is a temporary self that changes all the time?

CLARE: No, it's not even a self: in Buddhism, there is a conventional self, a construct we have imputed on this idea, which I used to struggle with a lot: if you do therapy and all you do is talk about the self, something that does not exist … it is a complete confusion of definition. We are dealing with that construct in psychoanalysis; people have to be able to have a coherent sense of who they are. Buddhism also believes that but goes beyond that, as the Buddhist monk told me. I don't think it's useful to start thinking that the self does not exist. It exists in a different way to how most people think, according to the Buddhist point of view. It exists as an emerging phenomena based on causes and conditions. So the sense of self exists but, if you start searching, it's indefinable: there is no permanent, findable self, independent of the mental structure.

EMILY: I agree with that and think that Buddhist teaching breaks down this confusing idea of no-self by looking at what the self is made of. Rahula (1959) makes it very clear when he summarises this concept: I or the self is only a combination of ever-changing physical and mental forces or energies, which are divided into five groups or aggregates and encompass all that belongs to a person. The first aggregate is matter, which includes solidity, fluidity, heat

154   THE BUDDHA AND THE BABY

and motion. The second aggregate is sensations to do with the six senses, the sixth sense being the mind, that is, the organ that perceives sensations. The other aggregates are perceptions, mental formations (volitional actions: determination, will, ignorance, feelings, etc.) and consciousness of both physical and mental objects. Isn't this an amazing construct of the person, if you think that the Buddha formulated it 2.500 years ago, long before the scientific age with its knowledge of the human body and mind?

RICHARD: Earlier you talked about the observing of phenomena and the realisation of their impermanence.

CLARE: Actually, I'm quite taken by Thich Nhat Hanh's thinking on this (1987, p. 32). He reports the Buddha saying that "in order to understand, you have to be one with what you want to understand". Thich Nhat Hanh also writes that modern physicists "think that the word observer is no longer valid because an observer is distant from the object he observes. They have discovered that if you retain that kind of distinction, you cannot go very far in subatomic nuclear science. So they have proposed the word participant" (ibid., p. 38). Apparently observing is not enough to comprehend the nature of phenomena; one has to become that object, that feeling, that predicament, in order to be able to fully understand. Thich Nhat Hanh said that in order to understand anger, murderousness, joy, peace, and so on, you have to become anger, murderousness, joy, peace, and so on.

EMILY: I find this extremely interesting and linked with the concept of projective identification in psychoanalytic parlance. To be able to temporarily become what the patient projects on the therapist—and before the therapist moves out of this state—the therapist has to become at one with such projected state of mind, such experience, etc. In this state of oneness and union with that of the patient, the therapist apprehends the patient's ultimate reality, or "O" as Bion defined that state (Bion, 1959). To go back to Thich Nhat Hanh, what is impressive about his teaching is that he has been immersed in real and political life fully and since he was extradited from Vietnam due to his anti-war campaigning. He's lived

WALKING WITH BUDDHA   155

in exile ever since and, as a monk, has been involved in both teaching children and young people human values that embrace religion, politics, and philosophy, and has been a political activist.

RICHARD: What he says reminds me of the mirror neurons—although the language is different. Mirror neurons fire when we are watching someone else in pain; they become active in the watcher and allow empathising with someone else's pain. That's the basis of all empathy, but isn't it interesting how different strands of ideas come together in a sort of unity?

EMILY: Hm, yes indeed; now look at the lighthouse beaming on the horizon; we're getting closer to the end of our walk, and I want to share with you briefly something that I've started practising with some of my patients. It is the breathing exercise of focusing on the flow of breath going in and coming out through the nostrils and on the feeling of cool and warmth respectively. So far, a depressed mother has tried and it has helped her to contain her panicky states; it also seems to be working with a twelve-year-old girl on the autistic spectrum, who surprised me once, when she remembered the exercise and decided to practise it in the session at a point when I was stressing her out, so she said! I definitely want to learn more about mindfulness with children in the consulting room and to experiment more systematically; I shall keep you posted on this when we next meet for a walk and a discussion on these fundamental issues.

References

Bion, W. R. (1959). *Attention and Interpretation*. London: Tavistock.

Main, M., Kaplan, N., & Cassidy, J. (1985). Security in infancy, childhood and adulthood: a move to the level of representation. In: I. Bretherton and I. Waters (Eds.), *Growing Points of Attachment Theory and Research*, Monograph 50, Society for Research in Child Development, pp. 66–104.

Rahula, W. (1959). *The Five Aggregates: What the Buddha Taught*. London, Bedford: Gordon Fraser.

Tagore, R. (1910). *Gitanjali*. [Published in 2007 by Filiquarian LLC.]

Thich Nhat Hanh (1987). *Feelings and Perception: Being Peace*. London, Sydney: Rider.

CHAPTER TWELVE

The smug Buddha

Dialogue with Caroline Helm, whose Tibetan name is Gakyil Shenpen, which translates as Coil of Joy Benefiting Others

MP: My idea of this conversation, Caroline, is to explore together certain issues, which are dear to my heart and part of a struggle to integrate them. First of all, I'd like you to tell me how you first got interested in both Buddhism and psychoanalytic psychotherapy; whether you started as a Buddhist first, and then came to psychotherapy or vice versa; whether you come from a family tradition of meditation or other forms of spirituality.

CH: I have a Church of England background and was educated at an Anglo-Catholic school. I was quite a devout little girl: used to go to chapel, to confession, but I got disillusioned about, I suppose you might call it my Christian faith, in my late teens, when I was very unhappy.

MP: The healthy teenager's rebelliousness?

CH: Exactly. I remember praying like mad and, I remember, it wasn't doing anything at all. There wasn't anybody there and, if there

158   THE BUDDHA AND THE BABY

were somebody there, it didn't make me feel better at all, typical adolescent egocentricity. So, I stopped going to church and stopped practising Christianity. My interest in Buddhism came much later. For years I continued to be interested in things spiritual and I read the works of Thomas Merton, who became very interested in Eastern spirituality, particularly Zen Buddhism. Another influence undoubtedly was that my analyst had a very beautiful head of a Buddha in her consulting room. It used to make me angry because it was so serene when I was feeling very far from serene, but the fact that she had a Buddha became important to me.

MP: It's fascinating how the Buddhism stemmed from the analytic couch almost as if these two interests of yours were born together!

CH: Well, regarding my choice of profession—I had several years of analysis (actually in a different consulting room with no Buddha!) before making the decision to train as a child psychotherapist. When I decided I would like to try to train I had to start by getting a degree which I did, while at home with two small children, with the Open University and, having got the degree and got accepted on a training, I returned to my analyst for further analysis during my training. By then she had moved and acquired the Buddha! It was at the end of this second analysis that I knew I wanted to begin to meditate.

MP: It's interesting this process of identification for us all as human beings but also for us as patients. What we identify with, is not just what our analysts say or do but also something like a visual statue of a Buddha in the consulting room or a Japanese painting, as it happened to me. Sometimes we just absorb certain things by just being there, lying on an analytic couch!

CH: Yes, that lovely serene Buddha head when I was far from being serene. Yes, so I decided that I was definitely going to learn to meditate and at that point, a flyer came through my front door, for a short summer course in meditation at my local adult education institute, which was literally at the end of my road, a few minutes away. This is an example of auspicious co-incidence. I signed up for the course which led by a man who was a member of a London Tibetan Buddhist group. When those six weeks came to an end, I said: "now

THE SMUG BUDDHA   159

what to do?", and he said "well, you'll have to come to the Centre for some practice". And so I've been going there ever since.

MP: This is a lovely story!

CH: As I have said I read Thomas Merton, the Christian, who was a monk in the Cistercian contemplative tradition and who died while he was touring in Asia, he was found dead in his hotel room. During this trip he met the man who founded the Tibetan Buddhist Centre I go to in London.

MP: What's the name of its founder?

CH: It is Chogyam Trungpa Rinpoche. He was an amazing person who wrote many books, in English. He came out of Tibet at the same time as the Dalai Lama, as a very young man and the head of his monastery. He came to England and did a degree in Oxford and then went to USA but he always had a very deep respect for England. He gave up being a monk, married an English girl, which you can do in the Tibetan tradition, and led a westernised life for a time because he really needed to understand the western mind and behaviour and how our society worked, in order to know how best to bring the Buddhist teachings to us in the west.

MP: In what way in particular?

CH: He insisted on teaching in English so if you come to our Centre in Clapham, we do traditional Tibetan chants for different times of the day and different times of the year, and they're all translated into English. When he began teaching in the west it was a very hippy time but he was very clear that he didn't want his students in the west "tripping out" on the exoticism of Tibetan Buddhism. The first book he wrote was *Cutting Through Spiritual Materialism*.

MP: So he understood the grasping mind of the Western society!

CH: Indeed. I met him very briefly one year before he died. Following a serious accident he was left partially paralysed on one side; but he was a wonderful teacher, a very powerful man and actually lived for many years after the accident.

MP: How did your family see your move towards Buddhism?

160　THE BUDDHA AND THE BABY

CH:　They weren't alive sadly but I have a memory of my father, who was fascinated by the natural world and quite knowledgeable saying to me probably shortly before he died, "I think these Buddhists have something you know … ." He had been digging out a wasp nest in the garden and became entranced by the intricacy of the nest and found he didn't want to destroy it. We would have had really good conversations had he not died before I became a Buddhist.

MP:　What about your training?

CH:　Training as a child psychotherapist for me was really challenging. I started training with the Lowenfeld School which was closed down when I was in the middle of the training. And that was awful: it was not considered by the ACP to be a legitimate child psychotherapy training for many reasons. So we got a training, created for us five Lowenfeld students by the ACP, with input from all theoretical schools: a really eclectic training. This was so that we could finish our training requirements and qualify. It was a very difficult time for me as I had separated from my husband, was a single parent and one of my children had recently died from cystic fibrosis.

MP:　Was the experience of death that brought you to Buddhism?

CH:　Not consciously. Through my reading about Buddhism I began to find the teachings very convincing and very attractive and I remember thinking: "At last, somebody agrees with me". Now I can't believe the arrogance of that thought, basically that Buddhist teaching agrees with me! For me it was like coming home and finding where I belonged.

MP:　That could also be a sign of a past life: here it's you meeting with your other self again or something like that?

CH:　Absolutely.

MP:　How have you integrated Buddhism in your child psychotherapy work? Did you use techniques with children? Did you keep the two practices separate or not?

CH:　My first job was in what was then called a Child Guidance Unit in Brixton, and there was nothing specific about my interest in Buddhism that I would bring into my practice.

THE SMUG BUDDHA   161

MP: Did you think it affected your work, though?

CH: Yes, in the quality of attention.

MP: Nina Coltart wrote about that (Coltart, 1992).

CH: Yes, I completely agreed with her immediately when I read that paper. The form of meditation I practise and teach—I am an official Meditation Instructor in our tradition—is called Shamatha meditation, which translates from the Sanskrit as "peaceful abiding". It is very much to do with being in the present, absolutely on the spot, coming back again and again when the mind goes away, bringing it back to the present moment. It is a practice which slowly tames the turbulent mind and develops the ability to be present in a particularly attentive way. It is this I tried to bring to my work. There is another practice in our tradition—the Shambhala Buddhist tradition—which is called Tonglen. Pema Chödrön writes about this in many of her books (Chödrön, 1968). Tonglen is also called "Giving and Taking". It is a practice during which you take in negativity with your in-breath and you breathe out all the goodness you have within you while focusing on a person or situation that needs it.

MP: But that implies a very strong philosophical or existential statement, that is, that you have goodness inside you and breathe it out to the world, from which you breathe in negativity, doesn't it?

CH: I agree with what you say in your comment about the strong statement that we have goodness inside ourselves and the baseline of the Shambhala Teachings is the existence of Basic Goodness in all of us. I rarely but sometimes in a session with a child found myself doing Tonglen in an almost automatic, unconscious way. It was later in my career when I was working with children and their families on an acute Burns Unit that I used to use Tonglen consciously (but not formally).

MP: You are describing the process of containment and transformation of the projections from the patient within yourself and then a readiness to offer something back which has lost its malignant quality and has actually acquired a life quality. This is in line with Bion's thinking (Bion, 1961).

162   THE BUDDHA AND THE BABY

CH: Yes, and I'm seeing more clearly certainly in my later practice in hospital, that my main task was of containing parental pain and distress and my Buddhist practice was very useful for that: just to help me stay with their states. In a hospital setting where people are acting all the time, because they have to, I just sat there with patients without having to try to make anything better and, my meditation practice helped me a lot.

MP: Presumably that is also the function of our psychotherapeutic stance and of our supervision i.e. to bear unbearable states of pain, to bear the unbearable and only that can help, doesn't it?

CH: Yes, absolutely.

MP: Did you ever teach your child patients the technique of Tonglen or other techniques such as breathing?

CH: No, Tonglen is taught in the context of a retreat, where there is containment, support and regular meetings with a meditation instructor, because it is a very strong practice and can be quite upsetting. It is not something you would teach a child. We do now teach meditation to children in our tradition and there are many children in the community, who have been brought up meditating and focusing on their body breathing. But I didn't do this in my clinical work.

MP: It's not too common to find psychotherapists who use their Buddhist practices directly applied to children or their parents. It's usually more a mental attitude that is brought to the work. Although, having said that, the practice of mindfulness is also spreading in the work with children and adolescents, as we will see in some of the dialogues in this book. Now, thinking of the question about the ego, how did you reconcile the notion of helping your patient to develop their ego versus the Buddhist idea of letting go of the ego?

CH: Such a good question, and one that I've asked meditation teachers! I remember once putting my hand up and saying something along these lines: "My job as a child psychotherapist is actually in the business of strengthening the ego in children, but in Buddhism we do not see the ego as something to be encouraged, do we?", but the question wasn't really answered, and I don't think he understood where I was coming from in terms of child development. So, I had to work it out for myself. I think the situation is that, as a practising Buddhist, one task is the slow dissolving or dismantling of the ego in the Buddhist understanding of the word "ego". A healthy and functioning ego is a good thing from a psychoanalytic point of view, and a strong ego from a Buddhist point of view is not. The way Buddhists use the word "ego" is comparable, I think, with what a psychotherapist would call neurotic defences, a bunch of neurotic symptoms. So, in Buddhist practice, it's a slow dismantling, seeing through a false conception of the self, I think.

MP: Perhaps a narcissistic self, as someone described it?

CH: Yes, we think that all our neurotic bits are the self. You can do a contemplation of looking inside your body and searching for your self and where the self is. You really, really look for your ego in your body.

MP: Where did you find it?

CH: Not there, you find a bunch of organs; it's a gradual, deep understanding of the fact that, in one sense, I don't exist, and that is a state you can get to through meditation.

MP: The two concepts are then different for Buddhists and psychologists, aren't they?

CH: Exactly! Actually, I think that in order to embark on this Buddhist journey of slowly discovering that our thinking about, and experiencing of ourselves as a solid continuous self is perhaps misguided, you actually have to have quite a strong and solid ego in a psychological sense. Otherwise you could have a psychotic breakdown.

MP: Absolutely. It's interesting that you've used the phrase dismantling of the ego, which is that used by Meltzer to describe autism and psychosis (Meltzer, 1975). You used the term in the sense of peeling off the layers of our false self, of our preconceptions, projections, and so on, to get to the core nature of our true self, whatever that is, didn't you?.

164   THE BUDDHA AND THE BABY

CH: Yes, seeing through all the solid rubbish that makes up our idea of ourselves.

MP: Are you familiar with the experiment they did in Indian prisons with callous criminals with a history of abuse, neglect, and deeply mentally disturbed on the whole? An enlightened prison director, a woman, offered them a Vipassana meditation training that lasted ten days. Many convicts were able to become aware of what they had done, to feel regret, remorse and sadness for the pain and damage caused. It was a deep shift from a persecuted state of mind to a more thoughtful and reparatory state of mind, to use a psychoanalytic terminology. The results and effects achieved were beyond credibility. All this has been documented in the video called *Doing Time, Doing Vipassana*. They have expanded this experiment to prisons in other countries all over the world and, with amazing success, even in Western, materialistic countries. I suppose my associations to what you said is to this process of peeling off the disturbed and neurotic ego to reach a more essential and integrated ego.

CH: As I said before, there's a very important teaching in Shambhala Buddhism which is Basic Goodness; in more traditional Buddhist terminology the Buddha Nature in us all. So what is seen as the work of meditation has to do with dissolving the clouds obscuring the sun of our inherent goodness, which is there as an absolute basis not relative to anything else.

MP: Where would you locate that goodness, perhaps in the healthy ego?

CH: It's very difficult to say; because it's an experience beyond concepts, it's impossible to find words. It's completely basic. This is Christian too, isn't it? You have to believe in that, if you are to work with prisoners, with very disturbed people, with children etc., it's essential. For example, a few years ago there was a court case—the murder of a child by other children. I read an account in the press which described what happened when the defence counsel of one of the children was describing to the court details of his early family life. The child started to cry. This, for me, showed that within this desperately sick, callous child, there did still exist a soft centre that, we know well, could be accessed and touched and worked with, for example, in child psycho-therapy.

MP: Yes, that soft core is what we look for in our job. Now, to move on to a next question, still linked with the ego and letting go of it, how do you conceptualise the different versions of the notion of attachment and the need for children to be well attached with the notion of non-attachment in Buddhism?

CH: Gosh, that's a good one, and I haven't thought much about it! Yes, attachment is absolutely essential to become a person from a psychological point of view. The children, who are recognised as the reincarnations of incarnate lamas like the Dalai Lama when very young, are usually taken to the monastery with their mother at least for the first period, before they gradually wean them away. Their parents are taken to live very close to the monastery, so they don't break the relationship with them. So that attachment is recognised as being important. The image of the mother is very important in a specific practice where you're asked to conjure up loving feelings towards anybody in the world similar to those you have for your mother.

MP: Isn't that the Metta Meditation or Loving Kindness meditation?

CH: I think so. The Tibetans don't have the ambivalence we in the West often seem to have towards our mothers: just complete gratitude, honour, and devotion. They can't understand that we have difficulties with our parents! Yes, so you have to be attached before you let go, once again, like the ego.

MP: How did apply this to your work with children?

CH: I think the non-attachment teachings are for adults. There are degrees of attachment for adults. We are invited to give up a particular sort of neediness, clinginess, I think.

MP: But we can also apply this to children: the issue of sharing mum or the therapist, for example, and the feelings brought about by siblings in therapy, not just at home, perhaps? Could that be a link with non-attachment when we think of therapy with children? To help them tolerate the existence of another child or of

166   THE BUDDHA AND THE BABY

the father or whatever takes mum's total attention away from that child?

CH: Yes, I think so. They are not in conflict.

MP: How did you locate the concept of emptiness in your work with children?

CH: It's very difficult to think and talk about emptiness and there are degrees of it: absolute emptiness and relative emptiness. It's the beginning of seeing through the illusion of solidity and the effect this seems to have is a general lightening up. A lot of things which used to feel important don't any more. That's for me the beginning of emptiness. But it is a huge topic, impossible to do justice to here and now. The Heart Sutra describes the essence of it.

MP: Isn't that linked with letting go and also facing death, the death of our beloved people and ultimately our own death?

CH: Things which have been worrying all through one's life, gradually stop being so important and, in fact, can even become quite funny it's a sort of lightening. You reconcile with the way things are.

MP: The wisdom of life. On a more personal level: did you ever have some particular, transforming experience linked with your Buddhist practice?

CH: Well, not really, just an ordinary experience when I have moments of being absolutely present, there, mind and body synchronised completely. This I experience with practising more and more. I went through a period of thinking that everybody else gets amazing experiences and I don't; what's the matter with me, there must be something terribly wrong with me. Well, I don't feel that any more.

MP: On this note of acceptance and letting go we can end with many thanks, Caroline, for sharing your experience with me and the readers.

References

Bion, W. R. (1962). *Learning from Experience*. London: Tavistock.
Chödrön, P. (1968). *When Things Fall Apart*. London: Elements.
Chogyam Trungpa Rinpoche (1973). *Cutting Through Spiritual Materialism*. Boston: Shambhala Publications.
Coltart, N. (1992). *Slouching Towards Bethlehem*. New York: Guilford.
Meltzer, D., Bremner, J., Hoxter, S., Weddell, D., & Wittenberg, I. (1975). *Explorations in Autism*. Perth: Clunie Press.

CHAPTER THIRTEEN

What works for whom?

Dialogue with Myra Berg

Never turn away … Just turn towards as all
you really have is your own experience.

MP: I am very grateful that you have agreed to meet again since the previous recording got some glitch and wasn't useable. Perhaps we could start again by how you got into Buddhism, whether you come from a Buddhist or a religious family background.

MB: I don't come from a religious background and certainly not Buddhist. I think I became aware of it when I was probably a teenager; it was actually the Buddha himself, the icon of the Buddha, his feeling of calm, wisdom and a lot of associations I had to that, so that was something I was aware of but didn't take it any further. Then when I was older I went to a couple of Buddhist countries and went into Buddhist temples.

MP: Which countries were they?

MB: Ladhak or Little Tibet and Vietnam. I also did martial arts and that's got sort of Zen connotations and a meditation part and an Eastern way of thinking; so bit by bit by bit, when I finished

169

170   THE BUDDHA AND THE BABY

analysis after doing my psychotherapy training I wanted to do something that took its place and to give me some space and provide me with some grounding; so it happened I came across a Buddhist meditation group, which was very close to where I live and on a night that I could manage. So I started to go there and I've got a couple of friends, that are involved with Buddhism, so I've been to their Buddhist centres with them and I quite liked the atmosphere and the ideas, so that's it.

MP: A very nice introduction then, gradual as you said, and grown from inside slowly. When we last spoke, you mentioned the Lion's Roar, the nine Gates, and your approach; can you say a bit more about it?

MB: Yes, it's a small group of Buddhists called Longchen, it's a form of Tibetan Buddhism, which started when a lama from Tibet called Trungpa Rinpoche came over to Oxford University, escaping from Tibet and set up a little meditation group and had many followers. He's dead now, but one of his students was designated by Trungpa to be the leader for Great Britain and this guy lives in Oxford and set up many classes; so the people who teach us are his students and it's quite hierarchical. He's got a course of studies and the first course is called "The Lion's Roar", which is about the heart of the Buddha nature, like the lion that roars out and finds expression. It's about beginning to awaken your heart like a lion's courage to vent, so it's about openness, and the view of Longchen is about openness, compassion, and wisdom. That's a three-year course, which I've just completed, and if you do that, you can go onto the next stage, which is called "Endless compassionate vision, the awakened heart". To do that, you have to take refuge in the Three Jewels and I haven't done that because I don't feel ready to take refuge; I don't feel I can do any more at the moment, so I'm doing the third year again; I feel there is a lot there.

MP: It takes time to digest and assimilate these teachings, similarly to what happened in our training and analysis, they go along with an internal growth or a spiritual journey, they're not theoretical courses and one cannot cram stuff in by reading books and so on, it's a process that takes time.

MB: That's it, so it doesn't feel right for me to go on at this moment.

MP: You have quite an innovative way of working with your psychotherapy patients, and I wonder whether you bring your meditative experience into your sessions with children, somehow.

MB: Well, I think some of it is very similar to analysis in the sense of withstanding things that are difficult and slowing down and not having to do, so in that sense it wouldn't be any different from what any psychotherapist will do, but I think I add on things like: there is no time and space, and this I think wouldn't be normal for any psychoanalytic psychotherapist. Where time and space are very important boundaries. So, within the therapeutic boundaries, which would be the ordinary ones, I would work differently, especially because I see many children with traumas and trauma doesn't have the concept of time and space. In the "Lion's Roar", there are nine Gates: each gate leads to the same place but there are different ways of accessing it. Conceptual thinking collapses in the gates, so time will be one concept that would collapse: there is no such thing as time, no such thing as past, present, or future.

MP: You're talking about the nature of the unconscious, where there is no time, aren't you?

MB: Yes, I've become much more in touch with that and I've got lots of ways of thinking about it that I didn't get from my more traditional therapeutic training and analysis. So with my patients, there is a way of thinking about no time and being guided by not-knowing and a sense that things are not being fixed or determined or structured.

MP: Can you think of a vignette, where this becomes manifested in the actual session with a child? How would this idea of no time and no space apply in your sessions with children, for example?

MB: I tend to work intuitively and with what comes out, I don't plan anything. I would say something or give an idea that doesn't come out of the transference or countertransference, not out of an emotion or the bodily reaction but out of a thought process. Another thing about the Gates is that thoughts don't exist in time, they come and they go; so I would be looking at situations that children might bring, a conflict for example, and would

172   THE BUDDHA AND THE BABY

think that all things pass and go. Whereas I might have known it intellectually before, I can actually experience it, and I might get them to do something, like to stop for a few minutes, as if they were meditating really, and think of what they were talking about and their body sense of it, so they're quite full up with it.

MP: So you get them to feel and think about their body.

MB: Yes, well, I've always done that and been interested in bodily feelings as I've always thought there is not a body–mind separation. I would have a child just sit and notice her feelings and become observant of what goes on in her body and thoughts without necessarily saying or acting. Then you get to see patterns. This is very similar to what we call psychoanalytic observation.

MP: That's very interesting.

MB: Some children can't do it and it's very interesting when they can't and they cut off but when they can do it even for two or three minutes they can see that particular sensation has changed, it's not the same. Everything is fluid and when they have very strong feelings they cannot manage, it feels that everything is fixed, immovable. This helps them to be more realistic and also separate from them as well as relaxed. Feelings, sensations come and go and they come back and they go.

MP: Would you do this with what age in particular?

MB: Any age starting from eight or nine years old, not just adolescents. But if there is a particularly thoughtful six-year-old you can do it because it's experiential so anybody who understands language, will be able to do it. It would fit in with whatever play or talk the child is doing in the session. I have come to look at repetitive play differently because as there's no past, present or future and nothing is ever the same even if someone does the same thing, say three times, it's different and it's moving in a flux. I might think: "Well this play looks the same but is it really the same?" and "what differences might there be?"

MP: This is also very psychoanalytic thinking because in spite of the apparent sameness and repetitiveness of the most boring play or action, there is always something at least minimally different

WHAT WORKS FOR WHOM? 173

and new either in the child's state, in their projections or in the therapist's mind.

MB: Well, if it's repetitive and akin to –K (Bion, 1962) anti-thought, the therapist's countertransference would be of wanting to go to sleep with boredom, then one might move the child from that into something else, which I still do sometimes.

MP: Especially with children with autism or on the spectrum; but what would you say to the child when that occurs?

MB: I would say: "That feels rather boring, you doing that over and over again; I just wonder whether that's helpful to you if I let you do that over and over again, is that helpful?"

MP: And the child's response?

MB: Sometimes they'd move along and change and sometimes they'd completely ignore me and would do it anyway. Well I might make a comment about what it feels like to be ignored. It's mostly the children on the spectrum who wouldn't change easily. Those who change eventually will begin to notice it themselves; some would disagree with me and say why they do, then we would have something to think about and help the child to be aware of my thoughts and of his or her thoughts; then things get unlocked. I have also trained in EMDR and use that when I get stuck with some children: I like to be a bit eclectic so I don't get bored with myself with the same interpretations that make me crazy, so it's good to have a few techniques that I can use as needed.

MP: What works for whom is a fundamental and much needed approach with the child population that is changing so much nowadays! Rare are the patients who respond to traditional analytic interpretations. Now, thinking of the idea of ego development and the Buddhist non ego, would you be able to expand of these ideas?

MB: Sometimes I struggle to put psychoanalysis and Buddhism together. Something like the ego: in Buddhism you try to lose your ego while in psychoanalysis you don't. I struggle with that but I'm now using different words. The word ego in Buddhism, I think equals the word narcissism in psychoanalysis. And I

174 THE BUDDHA AND THE BABY

call the psychoanalytic ego in Buddhist terms, something like honesty and openness. But that is my personal way of thinking of the ego. I try to deal with these two conflicting ideas and find a sort of bridge for the two meanings. If you expand your awareness through meditation and you lose your sense of finite boundaries, which includes the ego and narcissism, you would be able to really feel the inter-connectedness with the universe: that would be the awakened heart: the heart that has no boundaries.

MP: Oh I see, did you ever have such a deep and expanding experience?

MB: No, I never had, I can understand it intellectually and it makes a lot of sense to me and I think it's true, but I'm aware that when things start to expand I'm aware of my anxieties and am too frightened, yes, of losing my boundaries: I think I might fall apart. I know that's how you're supposed to feel but I fear I'm going to crash and not to fly … don't have enough strength or courage yet.

MP: This is part of the practice, isn't it? The practice that you're not going to die, crash, go mad, and lose yourself, presumably. When I had a fleeting experience of not-me, it was actually an experience of awareness of spaciousness and of something bigger than me; far from being a catastrophic feeling, it was a very pleasant one.

MB: I think that comes naturally it's not something I have control over. It links with Esher Bick's idea of second skin formation (Bick, 1969) and with psychotherapy. I pick up the fear of madness, catastrophe, and fragmentations in some adolescent patients and in some parents. My awareness helps me work with that, to understand it and not be frustrated, irritated or feel rejection. Meditation helps me to keep working in a safe way because you can only go as far as you can and it's about trusting yourself and your own mind.

MP: What about the attachment that we foster in child development and the Buddhist idea of non-attachment?

MB: Where we start from in the human realm—if you think of the six realms in Buddhism—we are not Buddhas and the idea of enlightenment is that you achieve non-attachment, you know, in the sense of inter-connectedness that we are all part of an interconnected state with no-separation; but that's in the future, we're not there yet. We're not Bodhisattvas, we're not enlightened so we are attached and that's why we are in the human realm. We all have aspects of the Buddha inside us but that's been clouded over like a dust, by distortions, delusions and so on. So what we're doing by meditating is uncluttering that, like spring cleaning and this releases the Buddha nature which is non-attached by nature. So it's not something that we try to do; your attachment will naturally decrease, while the ego needs to attach and grows strong. I think there is a difference between attachment and connection and I think that, where in psychoanalysis they use one word that means a lot of things; in Buddhism they are a bit more precise. Attachment is grasping and grasping promotes the ego and promotes selfishness and self-interest, whiles connection is the other aspect: one needs to be connected to one's teacher in order to learn and that would be more like the analyst-patient relationship. I call that a connection rather than an attachment because I think it's important to differentiate the quality of the attachment.

MP: But one has an emotional attachment to one's parents or one's analyst, don't we? It's different from the attachment as the grasping state which Buddhism refers to, isn't it?

MB: It's also like the paranoid-schizoid and the depressive positions (Klein, 1942), where the paranoid-schizoid does things for its own sake in order to fight or flight; survival is the frequent reason for beginning to study Buddhism; the depressive position has an idea of a two-person relationship, a whole object, it has a capacity for concern about the other and so that would be much more like the Buddhist notion of connectedness and the relationship to the teacher. So we would like our patients to be more in a depressive position state as the Buddhist guru would say: it would be good if you are more in this connected state rather than an attached state but we recognise that you are in the human realm as a human being and are going to fluctuate. I think that's the same in both. I haven't thought it quite like that before, so that's good as this question made me have to think.

176   THE BUDDHA AND THE BABY

MP: It's a very interesting direction our dialogue is taking and I am also learning a lot.

MB: My kind of thinking is that my idea about these two have got to be able to work together, otherwise there's not such thing as holistic and I have to find out more about how they do it.

MP: How do you think of attachment and connectedness in your work with children?

MB: I don't want them to be attached to me but I want them to be connected to me so obviously using the normal techniques of transference interpretations, if I feel they can manage that, and commenting on things, even if they call it "rubbish".—that I think are likely to be true and which promote the connection. I don't want to promote entanglement and grasping.

MP: What about if a child is entangled in his object relation and reproduces that in the transference, how do you manage that?

MB: I make a comment about that and use Anne Alvarez' technique and the stuff she describes in her writings: "It's hard to believe; withstanding survival" By this I mean taking up a stance that is the opposite of the overt. "It is hard to believe that we will survive this long break" in order to draw attention to the reality of the break (separation) and also acknowledge the patient's difficulty with separation. I find that quite helpful. I will talk for example, about that patient's stickiness at the end of sessions and not wanting to leave: "I know you don't like it but it's important that we end because without ending you cannot have beginnings and without beginnings we are not getting into the real world and no development can take place".

MP: The notion of time comes then into the work.

MB: No, it's not the notion of time but of beginning and ending; it's got an aspect of time but the real aspect is the idea that we cannot have everything all the time. But we can have trust, trust that I will see her next week. It's much more than the concept of time. The reality of the situation hasn't got to do with time but with loss, the separation and how to help the child manage the separation and it doesn't have to do with space either. We can sit next to each other and be in completely different spaces or we can be very connected even if we are very distant.

MP: Well, on this note of time and endings, we need to draw this most enlightening dialogue to a conclusion, with many thanks Myra and many good wishes along the path.

References

Bick, E. (1968). The experience of the skin in early object relations. *International Journal of Psychoanalysis, 49*: 484–486.

Bion, W. R. (1962). The theory of thinking. In: *Second Thoughts*. London: Maresfield Reprints.

Klein, M. (1942). *Love, Guilt and Reparation*. New York: Delta Books, 1975.

CHAPTER FOURTEEN

Mindfulness and meditation in the consulting room

Dialogue with Ricky Emanuel

There are only two days when things are impossible—
yesterday and tomorrow.

—Dalai Lama

MP: Ricky, thank you for meeting me to talk about your ideas on psychotherapy and meditation as I know you have been meditating for a long time and have been interested and written on psychotherapy and Buddhist ideas.

RE: I don't practise Buddhism, but I practise meditation and am interested in the Buddhist thinking and constructs of mind, not in the religion.

MP: How did you get to meditation in your life?

RE: Very early at university, I did transcendental meditation, but I didn't keep up with it.

MP: Did you have a mantra then?

RE: Yes, I did that for a while then left it. It was part of all that was going on in the sixties and seventies. How I came back to it

179

recently, I really cannot remember, but as you know I have always been interested in it, in particular in the intersection between psychotherapy and meditation. A book I really like is the Epstein book *Thoughts without a Thinker* (Epstein, 1996), I think is a brilliant book.

MP: He is inspired a lot by Bion's idea, isn't he? But please tell me more.

RE: Thoughts exist prior to the thinker; there is no such thing as a thinker, that's the no-self idea in Buddhism; thoughts exist and thoughts are really about emotional experience in general. Bion's idea is that thoughts are about emotional experience and that the thinking process is brought into operation to deal with what he calls the pressure of thought, which is about processing emotions. So, emotion is at the heart of things in Bion's idea and from the neuroscience point of view it's true: emotions are the core aspect of being and are body based. Thoughts are things in themselves and are transient and change and thought without a thinker means the whole idea that we get absolutely hooked on the sense of identity based on the thinking process of what we think we are. And yet, who we are changes every single minute and that is a very Buddhist idea: transience, impermanence.

MP: Indeed it is and also no-self as you've mentioned.

RE: No-ego and the ego passes. In Epstein's book, the link between ego and narcissism is that we are all very attached to whom we think we are and we hold onto this idea of whom we think we are and to particular identities: I'm a psychotherapist, I'm a Buddhist, I'm a Jew, and all those things. So, I think it's very compatible with psychotherapy, although I've never ever read any proper Buddhist text, the Dharma; I've never studied Buddhism as such. I've been to lectures, to monasteries, been listening to people, but I think it's become transformed into an interest in mindfulness and obviously mindfulness is one aspect of meditation, one aspect of Buddhism. So I don't think it's Buddhism; but mindfulness is a massively growing industry. I met somebody at a New Year's party, it was a young girl who was doing a sort of Buddhism to do with chanting, I can't remember, I went with her to one of her meetings, I didn't like it: chanting in front of an idol, it was too bizarre for me all that, as it brought up my

MINDFULNESS AND MEDITATION IN THE CONSULTING ROOM   181

long heritage of Judaism and it was absolutely not OK. So, when I went to Amaravati monastery, no way that I would bow down to the Buddha statue. I know that they've explained that you're not bowing down to a god, but it's really a devotional thing of thanks and gratitude, and I understand that it's ingrained for generations, but the idea of bowing down to a statue is really out of the question for me.

MP: I understand that, it can be daunting with all the rituals and prayers, a reminder of Catholicism for me too! But I take to the simplicity and essential aspects of this spirituality.

RE: I decided one day that I had to start meditation again, it requires discipline and so I started and tried different kinds because I think it's very easy to get stuck in meditation: it becomes a ritual in itself.

MP: Presumably you focus on the breath when you meditate and that's not an easy task as the mind goes, doesn't it?

RE: Yes, the mind goes off and that's a concept I use a lot in psychotherapy: that of the mind going and bringing it back.

MP: With children also?

RE: With children and anyone because I think that's one of the essential things in getting stuck into mental processing and to come back to the present: the wish to live more in the present, I think is also very Buddhist.

MP: Absolutely, only the present exists, they say. The past is gone; the future has not come yet.

RE: The anxieties are usually about the future and the grievances about the past, so trying to help people to notice, as one does in meditation, is part of what I do in psychotherapy. I use the sort of structure of meditation where you notice that you've gone. Some people don't notice that they've gone, that they're now in the past with the grievance or that they are in the future.

MP: You have to work on the past in therapy; you have to work on past grievances to then be able to come back to the present, don't you?

182   THE BUDDHA AND THE BABY

RE: You have to pay attention to that but I like Bion's idea of the past re-presenting in the present; he splits these words in an amazing way: represent and re-present; the past re-presents. You need to attend to the past but it's the past as it's affecting your ability to live in the present, not the past for the sake of the past; that's why I like his word re-presenting. The past is represented, in other words it's the past re-presented in the present. When you're stuck in the past, then you need to look at the grievances, as you can't be in the present.

MP: Well, yes, in therapy we work with the *hic et nunc*, that is, the here and now of the session and how the past is brought into the present in the session, don't we? But perhaps this applies less to children than to adults.

RE: Not adolescents: I work a lot with eating disorders now in adolescents and they have lots of thoughts on the future, how they're going to turn out to be; will they be fat or will they be thin, and there's a lot of pressure from schools in terms of: "If I don't get my twelve A stars, I won't be able to get into a good sixth form, and I won't get into this university and I won't get a job", so it's very future-orientated. I think the pressure now on young people is immense and the job insecurity, and we lived through an era when we had jobs. Young people now aren't in that position; fixed-term and short contracts and not permanent jobs. When a programme or a project comes to an end, then one has to get another job.

MP: This somehow forces young people to live more in the present, in a paradoxical way.

RE: Possibly, but it's also terribly insecure, for example, it's hard to get a mortgage with this system.

MP: It trains one to impermanence; I would like now to think of another question: you use mindfulness in your work, don't you?

RE: Increasingly: it's harder with children, and I tend to do some breathing with children, when they've got a lot of panic and help them to focus on where they are. What I find really interesting is that we, people who do meditation, like the feelings that meditation engenders; it makes people calm. If you've been quite traumatised, to be in a situation where you feel you are calm, it

MINDFULNESS AND MEDITATION IN THE CONSULTING ROOM 183

means you're not alert: that's what you experience. If you keep moving and keep talking and keep thinking and keep talking: the image is of riding a bicycle: when you stop pedalling you fall. You keep moving etc. and when you stop thinking and you stop talking and doing all that, you think you lose your sort of second skin, and it feels very dangerous. It's what I wrote in my paper on the Void (Emanuel, 2001), that was very important for me to write that paper, which was about trying to address nothingness, the creative aspect of nothingness, which is what Buddhism calls emptiness: that things arise from emptiness as a source of creativity. Our patients cannot bear that feeling, so I think calm becomes associated with emptiness and danger. I use mindfulness increasingly—we do it anyway, Maria, as it's part of our psychotherapy training, anyway, that's why I find it so easy to incorporate, just to be able to pay attention to what's going on.

MP: Are you actively using it with children? How would you use mindfulness with a child?

RE: With an adolescent it's very similar to an adult; for example I use it with an adolescent with eating disorder: they tend to be stuck in a very negative gang-like mentality with a narcissistic organisation: they think they don't deserve to have food; they're fat etc., a lot of very negative ideations in their mind. I suppose an attentional shift is what the format of meditation provides i.e. a standard template. In meditation, you have an attentional shift, when you notice that your mind is everywhere, you chose to shift you attention back to something chosen.

MP: Is that what you call mindfulness?

RE: It's one of the aspects of mindfulness: it's to shift the attention; but you've got to first notice. Last week, I had a fifteen-year-old girl, and I asked her if she'd noticed her mind was gone; it was her first session and she was describing how her mind was in that very negative place: she shouldn't exist; she doesn't deserve to learn; she was full of grievances and full of hate. I asked if she could notice when her mind was in that place and she said she couldn't; she's just in that place. So I think the first thing it to get them to notice that their mind is in that space, which is the observing self, as they call it in psychoanalysis, which is the same as meditation

184 THE BUDDHA AND THE BABY

when you notice that your mind has drifted. That's the key thing, I think. It's not that your mind has drifted or that you stayed only for so many seconds on the breath. It's to develop the capacity to notice.

MP: And not to be identified with your thoughts, negativity and so on, as the Buddhists says; not to be your thought but to watch it.

RE: But they're so identified with that because their sense of identity is linked to that thought: "I am an anorectic; I am different from other people; I am a sexually abused child." It's very difficult to ease off that identification.

MP: If you have a child or adolescent to observe that state of mind and then the child is no longer identified with that state of mind, what is there then for him or her? Oh dear: emptiness!

RE: That's the problem: exactly a lack of an identity and the "what is there?" Phil Mollon is not a Buddhist at all but he does psychoanalytic energy therapy, the Tapping technique. He asks some questions that I think are incredibly helpful, which I use a lot, for example: "Would you still be yourself if you didn't have your problems? Would it be safe to be rid of your problems? Do you deserve to be free of your problems?" They are all about identity. I asked these questions to that girl last week and her answer was: "No, no, no", she wouldn't be herself, it wouldn't be safe, and she doesn't deserve it. So, you know that she's in the grip of very powerful maintaining forces, that will require her to be wedded to her identity as an anorectic and that she doesn't know, if she's not that, who she is. This is exactly the problem, and that is where the void comes into it.

MP: And as you said also in your paper, the void is not nothingness, it's not emptiness, as the Buddhist say; it's spaciousness where lots of things can happen, isn't it?

RE: Exactly, but you've got to be able to tolerate it; it's a negative capability. So I think Bion is so wedded to this kind of thinking. I think he was to me the saviour of psychoanalysis; if it had stayed with the Kleinian view it would have been very limited for me. It's the way he brought this thinking into psychoanalysis, he opened up vistas that people had not opened up but that other traditions

MINDFULNESS AND MEDITATION IN THE CONSULTING ROOM   185

had and the Buddhists had. It's the way he'd brought it into psychoanalysis; I think. I feel I could spend the rest of my analytic life understanding Bion. He was influenced by this thinking in his upbringing in India with an Indian nanny. They've made a film about him: Martha Harris and Don Meltzer, I've never seen it and am not sure what ever happened to that film on his early years in India. Buddhism is a way of being able to name essential truths, and it is more comfortable for me to process it through a psychoanalytic framework than, you know, be part of a Buddhist monastery or a Buddhist tradition. But I have a great deal of affinity with that, more than anything else, more than Judaism. I don't relate to that at all.

MP: Perhaps the mystical traditions in Christianity, Sufism, and Judaism have something in common with Buddhism, apart from talking about God, which Buddhism doesn't do.

RE: I think all mystical traditions are overlapping. I got interested in the Kabbalah tradition, the Jewish mystical tradition; the Hindu tradition and the Kabbalah are probably the oldest mystical traditions, except they do have an idea of the Creator, and in that sense I'm much more akin to the Buddhists in not needing that Creator. I don't know as far as the Buddhists are concerned if they have a Creator in their thinking, perhaps you know?

MP: I don't know actually: they believe in reincarnation in different forms and realms but I don't know about the original beginning. I must ask my Buddhist friends sometime.

RE: Yes, you should ask. I avoid those questions, you know, my background's in sciences and I'm more of a scientist and becoming more and more atheistic in not needing the idea of a god. I find the ideas of god very difficult.

MP: What do you think happens when you die? You die and that's it?

RE: Well, I don't know, but I mean, I think, you're recycled in some form, but the reincarnation concept is not a very real one to me, I think it is for you, perhaps.

MP: Not really; I'm more of an agnostic, even though the idea of reincarnation fascinates me: I play with the idea that in a previous life

186 THE BUDDHA AND THE BABY

I was such and such, but really, deep down, I do not know. But if we are recycled in some form, it's the energy that gets recycled isn't it?

RE: Well, it has to, because matter cannot be created or destroyed; so you return whatever, if you are cremated or you decompose etc., the atoms return into the universe and there is only a fixed amount of matter, and matter cannot be created or destroyed, only transformed; so in that sense, there's a recycling.

MP: Yes, but the question is: who created matter at the beginning or how did it create itself and from what? In other words: who created the creator?

RE: Of course, it's a huge question, but there's always the question of first causes; we need to be able to think and to create a god; it seems to me to be an infantile need to feel that there's someone, who's in charge of things. I hate it when you sort of look at these people praying to go into battle and their god will protect them or slaughter their enemies and the other one will be their god, who slaughters the other side: it's offensive. So, I don't like it and Buddhism frees you from all of that.

MP: And it frees you from guilt, the guilt of the original sin in Christianity. There is no sense of guilt being fostered in Buddhism.

RE: Just responsibility. There is tremendous guilt needing to be attended to in our patients and it is linked with aggressive phantasies or perverse phantasies. Coming back to the use of this, I would use mindfulness with patients in lots of ways: as a concept, you know, in this overall way of bringing yourself back to the present, living in the present. But regarding actual techniques, I do sometimes do breathing when they're panicky.

MP: Would you ask a seven-year-old to do breathing?

RE: For example, I had a little boy, who was doing very badly at school, and he came to see me that day: he'd forgotten his school blazer and he was getting into a real state about what was going to happen to him, when he got to school. So I had to use a breathing technique, which is called collarbone

MINDFULNESS AND MEDITATION IN THE CONSULTING ROOM   187

technique, of stimulating the acupressure points that connect to the sympathetic and parasympathetic nerves. Within all this, I integrate the neuroscience view, so if you push these points here on you collarbone, it stimulates the autonomic nervous system, the parasympathetic nervous system, which is the rest and digest system as opposed to the fear system of flight or fight, that is, the sympathetic system. So I would say to that child: "you're very worried about going back to school, so I will show you something which is like a first aid, which is a way of calming you down, so that you're in a different place when you come to the school." So I just teach them and ask: "Do you want to try this now?" And they usually do and some children get an immediate sense of calmness from it; it's a very powerful breathing technique and they like it.

MP: So, the breathing together with pressing?

RE: Yes, you half breathe in and half breathe out, breath in fully etc. and your hands are crossed, it's a bit of EMDR technique. It calms you down very quickly. So in terms of the panic, I say: "As you're going into the school you can do this so to calm down and it makes your entry into school not in this kind of anxious state." It's very basic.

MP: Do they come back saying it helped them?

RE: Yes, they do and most are fine but some of them hate it for the reason I was saying: they don't want to be calm. With adolescents we ask them to do a basic body scan in order to bringing them back into the present. We would ask them to sit up and to focus and to pay attention, for example, to their shape where the chair touches their body. Now, depending on the patient: with anorectics you can't ask them to think about their legs as they're too phobic; their ideations about their legs cannot be focussed on. The thing they can focus on is their feet. So we found that asking: "What shape your feet are making on the floor now?" grounds them and you can then see if they become aware of their breath. Sometimes they can and sometimes they can't. It's about attentional shift: only one aspect of mindfulness is attentional shift so you can say: "When you notice that you're in this space of negativity, you try to give a name to the place you're in your mind". So, for example, a girl who used to ruminate would say that she was in the deserved

188   THE BUDDHA AND THE BABY

place; "I don't deserve to eat; I don't deserve to enjoy food" and so on. In using some of the mindfulness aspect, an attentional shift takes place, as you would do in meditation when you notice that your mind has gone and you'd bring it back to your mantra, breath, or whatever it is, that is in itself a helpful thing to come back to. The other aspect of mindfulness practice has been to be able to learn to label some of the places where your mind has gone to and your preoccupations such as: the exam place, the fat place, the sex place, the greed place and so on. When you've got into that ruminative way of thinking, you name the places of the rumination; you ask the patient to have a view of what the thought is. That's a different aspect of mindfulness: to be able to observe what is that place the mind keeps going to—as well as the attentional shift mentioned earlier. This is developmental psychotherapy.

MP: It is a type of Buddhist meditation: to notice that the mind has gone away from the object of meditation and to name the activity the mind is performing such as: thinking, planning, remembering, fearing, and so on, this is before one brings the mind back to the chosen object of meditation. But now, thinking of attachment in psychology and psychotherapy and the non-attachment encouraged by Buddhism, the two seem to be quite opposite, don't they? What are your thoughts about this, Ricky?

RE: I think it's more its negative, you know, the idea of identification with ideas such as: "I'm fat, I'm crap, and I'm useless". I had a girl, we were talking about her personality, which seemed to disintegrate when she went to secondary school because she was very happy in her primary school; when she got to secondary school, there was a sort of cool group, and she needed to try and fit in to what was required of her. So, she tried to metamorphise herself, which is the negative side of non-attachment in terms of rid herself of what she felt she was her core being and she had to get rid of that and become a kind of chameleon self; so she had to adjust herself to what was required of her. So this is a very perverse use of non-attachment, I think, in the sense of: "I will become whatever everybody wants me to be".

MP: That's an interesting vertex of non-attachment and is actually creating a false self, isn't it?

MINDFULNESS AND MEDITATION IN THE CONSULTING ROOM   189

RE: Yes, but then, is there a true self? Nick Carroll talks of illusion and they're all self-constructions. Bion talks about invariants in a mathematical transformation and the invariant doesn't change in the transformation; it's something about what remains the same about a person and what is the core aspect of them. From the Buddhist view, they are probably all illusions. The chameleon girl I just mentioned, who changes according to what is expected of her, now complains that she has nothing, absolutely nothing. This is more the terrifying void experience of persecutory emptiness than an experience of potentially creative emptiness.

MP: Yes, emptiness of thoughts churning on and on in the mind; so emptiness in the Buddhist sense of spaciousness and not of black-hole of nothingness and despair, you mean.

RE: Yes, that's exactly what I tried to say in my "Void" paper (Emanuel, ibid.), which is very different from that negative state and it's the emptiness of the self, yes, *anatta*. So the non-attachment idea is quite complex, because you could say that my girl was not attached to her sense of self when she went to secondary school; it was catastrophic for her because it meant completely abandoning everything about herself, her authenticity.

MP: Her little-girl self of primary school, presumably.

RE: Her authenticity was lost when she had to try to adjust herself according to whom she was with. Adolescents try out different ways: being rebellious and so on, but if you lose your core, that can really be catastrophic, as it was for my girl.

MP: In which form are you practising mindfulness with your patients?

RE: We—in a little group at the Tavistock—are thinking quite a lot about the contra-indications to mindfulness, which has become so popularised and also in a way, a bit trivialised. We assume, like people did in the early days with psychotherapy, that is can be helpful to everybody, but it's not. There are a lot of times when people find it just not helpful. What are the preconditions needed

190   THE BUDDHA AND THE BABY

for mindfulness? Recently I did the course at the Anna Freud on mentalisation and I was really impressed—unexpectedly so—by what they've done: they talked about mindfulness. From my point of view, you need a capacity for mentalisation which is a capacity to make sense of emotional experience; you need to be able to have a container and to receive whatever you are receiving. You need not to be in what they call a non-mentalising state, a non-thinking state, and we have many patients who are in a non-thinking state, and they cannot use mindfulness as you need to be able to observe what you have on your mind: thoughts, sensations, breath, your present consciousness; you need an observing ego or consciousness and to be able to stay with something. Now, many of our patients cannot stay with a thought, can't stay with a feeling; they're on action mode and they're completely dominated by a superego structure or judgement. You have to be able to have an experience and to notice that. Mindfulness requires a noticing capacity.

MP: As you're talking, I'm thinking of my patients and which one could benefit or not from mindfulness and I am wondering whether mindfulness is just impossible to practise with very disturbed people, and unless they are able to observe and think of their experience or whether it's actually negative and counter-productive in itself.

RE: One patient of mine, who had an eating disorder, when I proposed to try some very simple breathing and body awareness, experienced just a little sense of calm, which gave her a tremendous panic because it means you're off guard and no longer in control; she couldn't stand calm and got very angry and said: "I don't like that and I'm not doing it" and felt very persecuted. It was the wrong thing for her. She's got to be on her toes and it's like a second skin; it goes back to Ester Bick (1968). What happens if the second skin defences, which may be hyperactivity is one of them and being in constant movement, what happens when that stops? You've got a real threat of disintegration, a real threat of fragmentation and that is extremely persecutory; it's something in that kind of order. That girl is a dancer so she holds herself together by movement quite a lot and her mind is constantly busy, so she doesn't want to stop, she can't stop; so mindfulness is counter-indicated for her.

MP: It is like taking away her defences and she has nothing else left, isn't it?

RE: Exactly, so I think one has got to build first, if that's possible, a capacity to think about her experience and be with her emotions.

MP: To build an ego?

RE: I think it is: an observing ego, a core, something like that. So many of my patients don't have that. What I've learnt in the mentalising course was that it's no good trying do anything with someone who's not mentalising other than try to get them mentalising again and there are techniques for doing that because you can't give them an interpretation, you can't give them understanding, you can't do anything because they haven't got a way of processing anything you're giving them; so you have to do something more basic to re-boot the computer, if you like, re-boot to get going; that's very helpful.

MP: Or creating a capacity if they never had it; to do developmental psychotherapy as they call it at the Anna Freud, to build up what has never been there, i.e. a capacity to think, a sort of ego.

RE: That's right. It comes from the Anna Freud Centre and Anne Alvarez has very much developed it and I think we do that a lot; we need to do the developmental work first as the capacity for mindfulness implies some of that cognitive stuff. CBT is the same; it requires a capacity to think beforehand. In that training, they include mindfulness as part of they mentalising package they offer. Mindfulness is not thinking about an emotional experience but is awareness of the emotions, not thinking about, nor trying to process them. Mentalisation is a treatment that includes psychoanalysis, transference interpretation, countertransference, and mindfulness: that's where change will take place, they believe, but they say that you cannot go there until these other structures that is, a capacity for thinking, is put in place. Once this is in place, then you can go to the transference as a place of change. They recognise something, which I think we often fail to, which is that we go much too early and assume that people can actually process transference interpretations, when they cannot. Anna Alvarez has really got there in the best way.

MP: Those patients need to have a mind and when we work with kids on the autistic spectrum, we know they don't have a formed mind that thinks conventionally.

RE: That's right: a different mind that doesn't mentalise concepts. Mark Epstein says that one can use this whole process of mindfulness in such a defensive way that you don't get to the core psychopathology, that's why Epstein wanted to incorporate Buddhism methodology with the psychoanalytic one. I think that sometimes people use these paths as defence structures and there is great psychopathology underneath, that's why I think you need a dual approach. For example, becoming completely attached to the Buddhist way can be as a defensive way of living; Mattie Harris used to say the same thing about psychoanalysis, that she'd wanted training analysts to be people who don't think analysis is an alternative to life. It's the same sort of thing: you've got to be able to live your life and not be in some defensive-like psychic retreat.

MP: Yes, to use it as a narrow church to hold on for pseudo-protection not for true growth.

RE: So, I think it's important to think of the complexity of it and that mindfulness is not right for everybody. We have a programme in our eating disorder clinic—it's an evidence-based programme called "Food and Me", which is a mindful eating programme, but we've found that it's only useful for patients who have already started the recovery phase. When someone is in an absolutely obsessive, negative, destructive, super-ego-dominated phase, they can't use it; only when there is a little bit of space in the mind to have an alternative perspective, that's when mentalisation can work, because we want mentalisation to be able to have different perspectives: this is my mind and this is yours not just mine. What the Buddhist would say about that, that is, that you need a mental structure to be able to do mindfulness, I don't really know; I would imagine that they could say that those structures are just as illusionary and need to be dismantled as seen as illusion and in order for an absolute at-oneness to occur.

MINDFULNESS AND MEDITATION IN THE CONSULTING ROOM   193

MP: I believe, from what I've learned about Buddhism, that they think one has to be able to think and not be simple-minded or weak-minded to be able to meditate, and this doesn't mean that one is not worthy of compassion or love but cannot get to this awareness of oneself.

RE: In my "Void" paper, I mention Bion's "cloud of unknowing" taken by him from the Christian mystic Master Eckhart, and I say that we need to have a containing system to be able to tolerate that level of unknowing, to contain the "cloud of unknowing", the negative capability. Those structures, which we say are so necessary for this stage of mindfulness, I would imagine the Buddhist would say they need to dismantle.

MP: I would imagine so: the ego we help our patients to strengthen may have to be let go of in the spiritual path and after it has been firmly established. That's where the spiritual path takes off with a very deep understanding of the human mind and into the realm of unknown and mystics, I would say.

RE: It's very esoteric and very few people can travel there. I suppose is what Bion would call "at-one-ment", which he uses as the same word as atonement, which is very clever. It's the same word. There is a new book by Michael Eigen called *Kabbalah and Psychoanalysis*, he said he met Bion when he was in San Francisco before he died, and Bion said to Michael Eigen: "Do you know about the Kabbalah (which is the Jewish mystical tradition)?" Michael Eigen said: "Know about, no, I can't know about, I know of it". To know about something is very different from knowing of something. Bion said: "Yes, the same is true for me, but it's the basis of all my psychoanalytic formulations." He feels that the Kabbalah is the most evolved mystical structure. He knew about the Eastern traditions: he quotes them quite a lot, you know: "no memory and desire" is a very Buddhist idea. The Kabbalistic tradition is the oldest spiritual tradition and comes from the same sort of period as the Hindu tradition, and Bion said it was the basis of his psychoanalytic thinking. His idea of "O", the unknowable, the "Godhead", idea is very Kabbalistic. There is this idea in the Kabbalah of either complete nothingness, an infinite kind of space like the universe and the actual point, which is either miniscule

194 THE BUDDHA AND THE BABY

or huge. Bion had been very influenced by the Kabbalah in his writing. Have you ever met him, Maria? Just to be in his presence, was an amazing experience: I went to a three-day event with him at the Tavistock, when I was just beginning my training as a child psychotherapist: it was an extraordinary and very frustrating experience. I remember him saying: "People asked me how you recognise the truth", and he started free-associating on that question and talked for a bit. Meltzer wrote a brilliant paper called "The diameter of the circle" in the book *Sincerity* (Hahn, 1994), which is trying to look at how Bion thought: it is a fantastic paper and he would say that he would start with a subject and would say: how do you recognise the truth of it, and he looked at it from here and would illuminate it from there—this is Bion's multiple vertices or perspective—and then he would go on to, say, Alexandra Palace and he would look at it from Alexandra Palace and then he would look at it from there and so on, and if you got a sense of what he was doing, you could see he was illuminating it from various perspectives and it would come alive like this in your mind because he's given you so many different ways of looking at it that the dimensionality of the problem would kind of become clear. Bion would say that the answer kills the question, and he would want to keep the question open all the time; openness, openness, openness all the time. He would not want to close that question; any attempt to close the question, he'd open it again. Actually, it's what mentalisation does. You may be able to discern the invariant in the object, and he was interested in the invariants in the object, in what doesn't change.

MP: Is that the truth then, that is, what doesn't change even when you look at the object from different vertices?

RE: It's partly. Most of the time, I was completely lost then, in being with him because the sense of frustration: how is what he's been talking about now has got anything to do with that question? Most people would come out feeling incredibly frustrated and thinking: "Has the emperor got any clothes? Is he talking complete nonsense? Is he trying to be a mystic? Is he trying to make things as complicated as possible?" It was very frustrating, like his writing. That was a very common experience: people coming out of his lectures cross: "What is this?" When you got it, maybe one or two times in a day, I felt it, I got it, then, this is like another

MINDFULNESS AND MEDITATION IN THE CONSULTING ROOM 195

dimension: you had a sense of someone who was a genius; I've been very few times in the presence of a genius, and I felt he was a genius, whatever that means. But most of the time, it was incredibly frustrating, but it was worth letting it come over you and not think so much; so that's where I think he was a mystic, he was absolutely a mystic. I don't think he would think he was. Francesca Bion published books on his Tavistock lectures; he was an amazing presence.

MP: This is so illuminating, Ricky, but now to end this deeply interesting dialogue, can I ask if you ever had any special or mystical experience yourself?

RE: Well, yes, I had an unbelievable experience of cosmic beauty and at one-ness, once when I was in Crete during a spring holiday and during a particular period in my early age. The beauty of the spring field with amazing flowers gave me an amazing experience of interconnectedness with all. That's all I can say: a state that one may be experiencing through intense meditation, I would say now.

MP: Well, although you do not call yourself a Buddhist, I think you embody in your thinking and in your clinical work the realisation of the Buddhist acception on the ideas of attachment, no-self, emptiness, and mindfulness in a way that is both mind-full and mind-less—in the sense of emptiness—and as you have so clearly demonstrated in your paper on the Void (Emanuel, 2001). With this note of mysticism, we could now draw to an end, with many, many thanks and good wishes for the journey as a meditator and as a very original psychotherapist.

References

Bick, E. (1968). The experience of the skin in early object relations. *International Journal of Psychoanalysis, 49*: 484–486.

Emanuel, R. (2001). A-void—an exploration of defences against sensing nothingness. *International Journal of Psychoanalysis, 82*: 1069–1084.

Epstein, M. (1996). *Thoughts without a Thinker: Psychotherapy from a Buddhist Perspective*. London: Duckworth.

Hahn, A. (1994). *Sincerity and Other Works: The Collected Papers of Donald Meltzer*. London: Karnac.

CHAPTER FIFTEEN

Vagal superstars

Dialogue with Graham Music

> You can hold yourself back from the sufferings of the world,
> that is something you are free to do and it accords with your
> nature,
> but perhaps this very holding back
> is the one suffering you could avoid.
>
> —Kafka (1917–1918)

MP: Well, Graham, I'm not sure about your interest in meditation, whether it comes from a Buddhist practice or a more generic form of mindfulness?

GM: I'm not a Buddhist but I first got interested in Eastern thinking when I was at school, a very typical adolescent thing to do at the time. When I got to university, my intellectual passions were more about politics. However I had a fantastic sociology teacher, Bob Witkin, who was very interested in aesthetic experience and also in what we would now think of in terms of right as opposed to left hemisphere dominated ways of understanding the world. He in fact introduced me to very early books on right and left

198   THE BUDDHA AND THE BABY

hemisphere and this was back in 1977. When I presented my thesis on a Marxist analysis of the educational system, as one did in those days, we used to have discussions in his house, and he helped make links between the early Marx, people like Theodore Adorno as well as Suzuki's work. This got me hooked, mostly intellectually, but I also met several people when I was at university who were practising. I just dipped in and out of meditation from then on for many years, but it was always there, alongside other forms of spiritual thinking, which did not entail swallowing whole belief systems.

MP: You come from a Jewish background, don't you?

GM: Indeed, at least in terms of ethnic origin. My family practised minimally, but were unusual. For example I was a Jewish boy whose dad was a pig farmer, not terribly kosher.

MP: You don't mean metaphorically, do you?

GM: No, literally. So that was the origin of my interest in meditation and I think I have a long, and slightly chequered relationship with meditation and Eastern thought. There were periods in my twenties, when I would go off on retreats, but then I would lapse into late adolescent and slightly manic life choices.

MP: Buddhist retreats?

GM: Yes, but in-between I would often not do very much for a long time, just occasionally I would sit. So it has been around for a long time but it is only for the last few years that I've had a very regular daily practice, I think.

MP: What has brought up this?

GM: I've always been interested in the interface between psychoanalysis and Buddhism, sometimes a rather intellectual and cerebral one. However I think there are profound links between the two practices, when they are done with depth and integrity. Interestingly when I came to train here at the Tavistock, I knew that I wasn't going to fit in easily with just a post-Kleinian way of thinking and I went to Nina Coltart to help me find an analyst and of course we ended up talking about the relationship between free association and meditation. I've always tried to keep the therapeutic thinking and this, slightly separate over the years, but I've always been interested in people who manage a degree of integration. I think Bion did, I'm sure other people have talked about this, but I also got interested in other thinkers and traditions. Michael Eigen, for example, in the States, really made big links between his psycho-analytic practice and his spiritual beliefs.

MP: They call him a mystical analyst, I read somewhere.

GM: Oh, I see.

MP: And when did you decide to become a psychotherapist?

GM: I suppose I was always interested but thought about it seriously in my early twenties, after having done the common adolescent thing of travelling, and then going on to work, in my case for a local authority: I ended up looking after a block of flats in which they placed people, whom they wouldn't place today together. They were people they would not give a permanent home to; it was quite a prejudiced time. The block of flats was made up of prostitutes, drug dealers, young people out of prisons, young single mums, people with severe learning disabilities; most of them had massive rent arrears etc, a kind of dustbin for those who were deemed somewhat unsavoury. My job was partly to take the rent, look after the flats but I also had a pastoral role and people would come and to talk to me and I would be their first port of call. That was interesting, but I was 23, I was a baby and these people had really complicated issues. The thing that moved me away from that world—I'd been thinking of doing a psychoanalytic-orientated social work course at the time, there was one man who had spent twenty-plus years in Friern Barnet, who was a paranoid schizophrenic basically, who used to come into the room and worry about all different machines that were recording him, and spies and those sort of things. Then one day he didn't turn up: he used to turn up like clockwork with his rent and I knew that something had happened. Interestingly, even then, at twenty-three, I'd realised that he needed more help, and I had several times phoned up the social worker and said: "Look, this person has got no one supporting him; he hasn't got a single person in his life; this isn't good enough." But anyway, I found him dead in his flat.

200   THE BUDDHA AND THE BABY

MP: Oh, what a shock!

GM: That really was such a trauma for me that within a year I changed direction. There was no support, no one knew what to do, no one to help make sense of this. I remember going to the funeral, I was the only person there.

MP: What a sad story.

GM: So I left and I became an antique dealer but even then I would read Freud with my tea and chip butty at 7.30 in the morning in little Northern market towns, having already bought my goods; also Eastern things interested me: I remember reading Rumi and I started doing small courses but also having a good time.

MP: It's interesting: the antique dealer, you were already interested in the past, in the history or furniture, and then you moved onto the history of people, children and so on.

GM: Like Freud's interest in archaeology. During that period I did things like an art therapy course; an introduction to psychology alongside other kinds of seeking and even then I always found them very linked. Then a crisis in my personal life in my late twenties brought me back in therapy myself: I also did more courses, I went to the Institute of Psychotherapy and Social Studies, which is more integrative and politically orientated; then I went to the Minster Centre which is a much more integrative and humanistic body-based therapy: it had a lot of transpersonal, spiritual stuff as well as body therapy and psychoanalytical thinking. I found the body stuff much more useful than the spiritual ideas in terms of therapeutic practice and then I came here, afterwards, to do the observational course and then the psychotherapy training. So that's my path, really.

MP: Psychotherapy intermingled with the spiritual path from very early on. Tell me, how does your spiritual inclination affect your work with children and adolescents now?

GM: It's taken this long since qualifying, I think, for me to really think that there are serious possibilities of integration, even though I've always felt that something about the free-associational process was very similar to watching your thoughts in meditation, especially in being aware of one's body states. I've always found this very helpful in terms of countertransference.

MP: Can you say a bit more about this point?

GM: When I was practising meditation, I found myself much more aware of my responses to other people, so I could more easily know if the states being stirred up in me were such as if I was feeling more flattened and dulled down, or if I was feeling sympathetically aroused.

MP: Indeed, in meditation practice one becomes very aware of the body–mind. I share with you this idea of the body countertransference and the increased sensitivity and awareness fostered by meditation.

GM: It's just astoundingly powerful learning, I think. Then more recently one of the things that got me interested again and gave me a bit more hope that these things could be integrated a bit more, was the mindfulness movement. As you know, I'm really interested in neurosciences and attachment and developmental thinking and many of the people who have been looking at that area, were finding really exciting and interesting things about the brain as we know, and attachment patterns. A few of them, who researched the brain, suddenly got really interested in the mindfulness research and the meditation research and its extraordinary effects on the brain, even sometimes after quite short periods of time. So, suddenly I thought, there are important connections here and this is very exciting and the amount of research that is going on is quite extraordinary.

MP: Mostly in America, isn't it?

GM: Yes, nearly al in America, some here like the mindfulness-based cognitive therapy (MBCT) which has an impressive evidence base for preventing depression relapse. There are many courses based on the Jon Kabat-Zinn MBSR model, which has been the predominant one. Having already, anyway, been interested in mindfulness and the brain, I was finding all these extraordinary connections, which linked with the work I was doing with the children, who were not necessarily being reached by interpretative ways of working: I work a lot with trauma, with children who have been in the care system and whose autonomic nervous systems are often very hyper aroused, indeed often too over aroused to take in anything one says. They really need a place of safety inside themselves before they can begin to think about anything else. These are children who also have a very profound effect on the people around them, their carers, teachers, and all those people, who often get into a terrible state. I was very interested in some of the research, for example, by Davidson about how kids who are more confident and outgoing have higher left pre-frontal activation than kids who have more depressed, neurotic presentations, who have higher pre-front right activation.

MP: This is in adults, isn't it?

GM: And in children as well: they found it in nursery kids in resting states; but this shift is also what happens if you do a course in mindfulness, you have this leftward shift in terms of certain areas of the pre-frontal cortex. So even if mindfulness takes place mainly in the right hemisphere, there are certain areas, which have to do with feeling better about yourself, which are affected by meditation. All these amazing links are going on!

MP: So much more could be done with children.

GM: No question about that but lots of people are already doing quite interesting things with children. All the rigorous research about mindfulness and its effectiveness as a therapeutic modality is currently about adults, but there are increasing numbers of experimental ways of working that are also beginning to be researched with kids. There are some people in the States, like Susan Kaiser Greenland, who have been developing mindfulness with kids; she is one of many who have described techniques and exercises. These have been carefully adapted for children: you don't sit and meditate for half an hour with children, but you may ring the meditation bell and get them to sit quietly, listen and put their hand up when bell stops. This is to help them develop the capacity to concentrate, which is very linked with the executive functioning, and many of the kids we most worry about have big struggle with their executive functioning: this is an area that we haven't thought enough about in psychoanalytic child psychotherapy.

MP: How do you apply this in your clinical work? Do you do breathing exercises with the children or something?

GM: Ok, let me come to that in a minute. Going to see some of these people like the psychiatrist Daniel Siegel, who is very interested in the brain, who is very interested in attachment and then got very interested in mindfulness, a few of us psychoanalytic psychotherapists—a few child and a few adult therapists— formed a monthly group that meets to think about the interface between psychoanalytic psychotherapy and mindfulness. This has been going for about two years now. We do a little bit of sitting together and then we take it in turn to think about how we use mindfulness in our work directly or indirectly. We've given each other a bit of courage. Some in the group do more active, body-aware interventions; others just use it inside themselves.

MP: This is fascinating!

GM: Then setting up a new course here, called Psychological Therapy with Children, Young People and Families, a course with an aim to train people for some of those CAMHS jobs, which are around nowadays. That course had to be shorter than the child psychotherapy, much more eclectic but with a psychoanalytic core, so they get child psychotherapy supervision, teaching and theory.

MP: It probably wants to counteract the IAPT (Increasing Access to Psychological Therapies) training and its generic approach.

GM: Exactly and it wants to give people other strings to their bow, when they leave, and have something which you may call evidence-based or on the verge of evidence-based. So we decided to bring mindfulness into this in the second year. So they get one year fortnightly of the equivalent of the eight-week mindfulness-based stress reduction or cognitive therapy. So they get experience themselves, they get given home practice, and then some basic tools for applying this thinking. In addition, they all have to be in their own therapy; they're trained mainly in psychoanalytic thinking, but also they get some systemic input, and a bit of CBT. Mindfulness is there experientially primarily. They have an experience of an eight-week course, gain some practical skills, and then some may want to do a whole longer training.

204   THE BUDDHA AND THE BABY

MP: Do you have somebody who's done the mindfulness training to teach them, or did you do the eight-week mindfulness course yourself?

GM: No, we have brought someone in to do this, Bill Young, a child psychiatrist, who in fact trained here long ago. I am not qualified or experienced enough to teach very much yet. I have done the eight-week course with someone from Cambridge; this was organised by Ricky Emanuel for clinicians at the Royal Free Hospital. The teacher was Michael Chaskalson, who also worked alongside John Teasdale and Mark Williams. So I've done that, and then I've been practising very regularly, but my practice would need to deepen to teach more, and I have just started doing teacher training.

MP: Are you now talking of practising meditation or mindfulness, and what difference do you make between the two?

GM: Mindfulness is more like the beginning of a long meditation journey, I think; it's much more based on the elements of learning how to pay attention, to focus, to shift attention. The exercises are quite basic, and start with the body scan; people have two weeks or so to do their own practice, then they move into following the breath, listening to sounds, watching thoughts, and those sort of exercises; they also have lots of tips and tricks like three-minute breathing spaces, which you can do any time during the day; I sometimes do it in between patients. For example, you sit for one minute and become aware of what thoughts and feelings you have; then you concentrate on your breath for a minute, then on your body breathing for a minute, just little breaks in the day. Mindfulness is not the same as the depth people reach with long-standing meditation practices, but in order to deliver mindfulness training and in order to do mindfulness training, you have to do your own practice.

MP: Would you say that perhaps mindfulness teaches more techniques?

GM: Yes and no: there are also techniques in meditation as there are techniques in child psychotherapy; when it flows, it's not about techniques and I think that if you learn to sit and be interested in, and alert to whatever your breath happens to be doing; that isn't really technique, it's a way of life, a way of being, I think. So the people who are very keen on mindfulness and who developed it in this country, originally in Bangor, and then Cambridge and Oxford, they're very keen that people have a very serious and regular practice themselves. So it's got to be integrated into the personality. Maybe with children it will be necessary to develop techniques for helping them. I think there might be two ways of intervening with children: both working directly with children, individually and in groups, and also working with parents or carers, helping them develop a mindful awareness, which in turn should allow the children to be more self-regulated.

MP: You mean more self-regulated as adults and more contained in their dealing with children?

GM: Yes, it will then transmit to the children. I've also started a weekly workshop here for child psychotherapists and other trainees about the clinical implication of attachment, neurosciences etc., and this morning, for example, we've just had a presentation by somebody who works much more bodily with traumatised children. She was taking the group through some basic somatic awareness exercises: how do you feel in your body when you're under stress, this has good links with mindfulness practices, I think.

MP: It's fascinating this opening up to the body and the meditation is breaking the ice, somehow.

GM: We're just beginning and it's not many of us doing it yet.

MP: Years ago, Ricky Emanuel invited an Indian psychiatrist to talk about the experiment they've done in Indian prison where they taught eleven days of Vipassana meditation to the most callous people serving long prison sentences. The tape they've now made is called *Doing Time, Doing Vipassana*. The results were unbelievable: some of those prisoners shifted from feeling persecuted and paranoid to taking responsibility for their past actions and wanting to make reparation. It was most moving to hear about and to watch the video.

206   THE BUDDHA AND THE BABY

GM: Interesting. I don't know quite how or where we're going to apply all this. I do think one big distinction between psychoanalytic child psychotherapy and this way of working is that, as well as having to be a little bit more aware of bodily and nervous system issues, you also have to be prepared to be sometimes a bit more directive. I think that's a big challenge for a psychoanalytic psychotherapist.

MP: That's how you have to be with the NHS patients, as it is rare to be able to do pure psychoanalytic psychotherapy in the NHS. We have to adapt a lot and offer hands-on work by offering advices and practical suggestions, albeit they can still be psychoanalytically informed. It's the nature of our work with that specific clientele, nowadays.

GM: Absolutely, you have to give advice and I think that the neuroscience research for me is providing a bridge. There's new understanding now, of the autonomic nervous system for example, described in Polyvagal theory. It is Steven Porges's basic argument (2001) that there are two branches of the vagus nerve, a very primitive one, which we share with vertebrae and which is the most defensive last resort, consisting of complete metabolic shut down, freeze, floppy types of defence. Then we have the sympathetic nervous system with its fight/flight responses, shallow breathing, increased heart-rate etc. But if the parasympathetic nervous system is working well, the myelinated "smart" vagus nerve is firing. This goes from the brain stem, that is, the primitive brain, to facial muscles, heart, internal viscera, especially the stomach. The ventral vagus is full of oxytocin receptors that make us feel good; so when we feel good, relaxed, in love, comfortable, and happy, this vagus nerve fires away and people feel more at ease, have better wellbeing, and so on. This is what we see in long-term meditators. It can be measured by looking at heart rate variability. Traumatised people have limited heart variability and tend to be far less flexible. Dacher Keltner (2009) found that there are some people who have extraordinarily high vagal tone, great heart-rate variability, and he calls these "vagal superstars". He would count people like the Dalai Lama as such a vagal superstar! For example, those who have meditated a lot, maybe over ten thousand hours, seem unperturbed by stimuli

VAGAL SUPERSTARS 207

like very loud noises: their startle reflex does not respond even though their awareness is still completely present.

MP: Yes, there are fascinating researches on the effect of meditation on the brain.

GM: In a small way, I think, we want to try to bring some of that into our work with children.

MP: How do you bring that in the therapy room when you work with the traumatised, fostered children, whom, I understand, you have a lot of experience in treating? How is your knowledge of neurosciences affecting your clinical, therapeutic work with those children?

GM: I bring it in a lot with parents and carers, I would be very psychoeducational now, more than how I used to be, and I might say: "Look, when you have the kind of trauma that he has had, then there is a very primitive part of the brain that will fire up very easily and he will be very hyper-alert, with a very activated fight-flight response. When this happens he won't be able to take anything in, won't listen to you, won't be able to, he isn't just being stubborn. We can work together to try to find some way to calm him down". I use that kind of language quite a lot. When I am with kids in that state, sometimes I have to work hard to stay with myself, maybe trying to become aware of myself breathing and any tensions.

MP: Not if they're wrecking the place, presumably?

GM: No, if they're wrecking the place you've got to stop them. If they're very disregulated, you've got to go near enough to where they are and then try to bring them down. So a lot of it is to do with emotional regulation and it's not much to do with mindfulness at one level.

MP: Practically, what do you do?

GM: I just do what a lot of us do, which is try to speak at the same pitch they use and then try to slowly bring them down. That's emotional regulation not so much mindfulness, but there are one or two kids I have done some basic exercises with now, particularly helping them be a bit more aware of somatic states. Some are

208 THE BUDDHA AND THE BABY

terribly ungrounded—so just sitting for a few moments with their feet on the ground. This is easier with early to mid-late adolescents, I find, as they can sit and you can try to get them to be still, see what sensations they can fee and maybe take them through a body scan, sort of thing.

MP: You would do that in a session then, take them through a body scan?

GM: With a few I do that when I feel that my traditional way of working hasn't worked; if I feel that child psychotherapy is working with a kid, then I don't do anything else. Certainly I would try to get them into a place—by whatever means—whereby they're less sympathetically aroused and calmer, as I don't feel I can do any therapeutic work unless we get to that. I do find I now ask curious questions about the body, for example: "You seem a bit calmer now, what's happening with your breathing? How is your heart?", and those sort of things. That's less threatening; in fact it's a bit cognitive behavioural therapy-like.

MP: This seems essential before they can move more into thinking.

GM: Yes, although of course some kids think too much, so you have to bring them back.

MP: I call it hyperactivity of mind: butterfly mind as a child patient of mine called it.

GM: I agree, that's a nice description. There was an interesting book a few years ago called *The Mind Object* (Corrigan & Gordon, 1995), which was taking forward Winnicott's idea (1958b) of mind and its relation to the psyche-soma and argued that lots of children who do not have a reliable external object to identify with develop an over-reliance on their minds. Winnicott, I think, knew all this stuff that we're talking about today.

MP: Just like Freud, who had it all there in his thinking, and we now develop and expand on some basic points he had already made, in his time.

GM: Absolutely. In mindfulness, there is an experience which is a bit like what Winnicott describes as the psyche residing in the soma.

VAGAL SUPERSTARS   209

MP: They come together, don't they?

GM: Well, if you feel held as Winnicott says, or contained in the Bion sense, then psyche and soma are not separated in the way that we often see after trauma, stress, and anxiety.

MP: But in terms of origin, the mind and body are born together: the forming foetus in the womb, I believe, already has an emotional experience there, although it may be mentalised only much later on.

GM: Definitely. But I think the "butterfly mind", as you describe it, takes root when someone does not feel relaxed, at ease, or safe, when they have not been gathered up; then the mind goes off on its own track and there is less bodily self-awareness and less relaxation.

MP: Thinking of more theoretical issues such as attachment and non-attachment, ego and non-ego, and so on: how do you reconcile what appears to be on opposite ends in psychoanalysis and Buddhism?

GM: I don't know if I can reconcile them but I think we live in very different worlds to those where people are brought up in traditional Buddhist cultures. For example, in an interview with the Dalai Lama somebody asked about people who really don't like themselves, and he looked completely astonished and said that he couldn't believe that there were people who didn't like themselves. So, in a sense we live in another universe. I think that this attachment/non-attachment issue is very interesting because on one level they sound opposites, but you cannot move towards non-attachment, non-ego etc., those classic Buddhist trajectories, prematurely. First you need something good inside that you could rely on. The idea of non-attachment can, I think, be used as a kind of manic defence. I've seen it a lot in New Age circles and also in meditation retreats and in humanistic psychotherapy weekends; often when people seem very fragile, and ward off the unmanageable by ideas about non-attachment, that worries me. I suppose fundamentally what we try to do in child psychotherapy and in helping people to become parents, is for people to have this sense of feeling securely attached or having a good object inside,

210　THE BUDDHA AND THE BABY

whatever language you use, high vagal tone maybe. Only with that can we begin to think of these other spiritual things like non-attachment, otherwise, you're onto a hiding to nothing, I think. So, I don't really reconcile them but, I think in psychotherapy we're starting from a lower baseline than a lot of spiritual people and teachers. I think that the psychological health of many people starting on these paths is much more vulnerable than many who start spiritual paths, say, in the East. Some of these Eastern, meditation, spiritual centres in the West, will attract people who are very much on the fringe, are very fragile and desperately looking for a home. So, the psychological work/help has to be primary and there is a danger when meditation and spiritual ideas are used as a short-cut.

MP: I agree with you entirely and you meet rather troubled people in these monasteries and Eastern religion places. It can be very dangerous, indeed. So, a proper psychological attachment has to be there, before embracing the spiritual path of letting go.

GM: If you think of attachment theory or if you think of Winnicott, actually, once you feel secure inside yourself or you know your mother is there, then you can relax and you can let go; by the same token, we are not ready for these spiritual things until we feel secure inside ourselves.

MP: It's like the dummy: you can let go of it when you have a good mum inside you.

GM: Yes and another danger is that people become obsessed with ideas that are never really going to hold them together; we are back to the mind-object and butterfly mind. In both good therapy and in mindfulness, I see a movement towards feeling more at ease in oneself, being able to forget oneself a bit more. Many of the people—adults I'm thinking of—who come to us for therapy are incredibly self-obsessed as they've got so little good inside and as they become healthier, with luck, they become less narcissistic, less self-obsessed, and can let themselves go a little bit.

MP: Someone else has spoken about the over-attachment to one's ego being a narcissistic state of mind, i.e. a neurotic state, versus a more relaxed and humorous sense of oneself, free from the self-hatred that astonishes the Eastern people, as you've mentioned earlier on about the Dalai Lama.

GM: It's a bit of a superficial a way of understanding it but it's my way!

MP: I think it's a view shared by many people: Buddhism and psychoanalysis just give different meanings to the same words, to the same terms: even the Dalai Lama talks of the necessity of a healthy mother–child relationship. When they found him to be the reincarnation of the previous Lama and he was taken to live in the Potala, his parents also moved nearby, because he was only five or so, at that time. He has maintained the simplicity, the freshness and spontaneity of a child, yet his thinking is also highly sophisticated (Goleman, 2003).

GM: He's a remarkable person, indeed.

MP: On a more personal level, have you ever had any particular mystical or enlightened experience that you can share here with me and the readers?

GM: Not really, I had some experiences, which I think of as feeling blissful, I suppose, but I wouldn't claim great spiritual revelations or anywhere near an enlightenment or awakened state. I'm afraid not.

MP: There is a question, which is linked with letting go of the ego that is emptiness: how you see the idea of emptiness in your work?

GM: I find that I turn to Winnicott a lot, and also, as many people, to Bion. With Winnicott I think of that that lovely paper: on the capacity to be alone (Winnicott, 1958a). I have for a long time pondered what the different words mean; whether to stress the being, or the alone or the in the presence of, but I think he really understood about just being. That sense of being is the prerequisite for some of the things you've mentioned about the Dalai Lama: playfulness, openness, curiosity and an angst-free way of being. Obviously, when we are working in therapy and with children, of course, we are very aware of the transience of things, and that peculiar mixture of blissful cherishing but at the same time, aware of the emptiness of things. In my own way they come

212   THE BUDDHA AND THE BABY

together, but I have no way of thinking about how it translates into the language of therapy.

MP: Well, many thanks, Graham, for all this, and I enjoyed getting to know your thinking and your projects a little more.

References

Corrigan, E., & Gordon, P. -E. (1995). The mind object: precocity and pathology of self-sufficiency. 1–22. New Jersey: Aronson.

Goleman, D. (2003). *Destructive Emotions and How Can We Overcome Them: A Dialogue with the Dalai Lama*. London: Bloomsbury.

Kafka, F. (1917–1918). *Collected Aphorisms*. N. 103. Translated by M. Pasley. London: Penguin Books, 1973.

Keltner, D. (2009). *Born To Be Good: The Science of a Meaningful Life*. New York, London: W. W. Norton.

Porges, S. W. (2011). *The Polyvagal Theory: Neurophysiological Foundations of Emotions, Attachment, Communication, and Self-Regulation*. New York, London: W. W. Norton.

Vipassana Research Institute (1997). *Doing Time, Doing Vipassana*. www.prison.dhamma.org. DVD available at email address: bookstore@pariyatti.org.

Winnicott, D. W. (1958a). The capacity to be alone. In: *The Maturational Processes and the Facilitating Environment*. London: Karnac.

Winnicott, D. W. (1958b). Mind and its relation to the psyche-soma. In: *Through Pediatrics to Psychoanalysis: Collected Papers*. New York: Basic Books.

CHAPTER SIXTEEN

Jung and the Buddha

Dialogue with Jackie Van Roosmalen

Grant me the courage to change
that which can be changed
The strength to endure what cannot
be changed
And the wisdom to know the difference.

—Reinholt Niebuhr

MP: Jackie, I am delighted that we can talk on the phone and at such short notice just before Christmas. I am particularly intrigued by your experience as a meditator and one of the last child psychotherapists trained at the Society of Analytic Psychology i.e. the S.A.P., the Jungian training, just before it was discontinued.

JVR: Yes, I trained in the nineties and I qualified in 2006. My peers were Joanna Goldsmith and Alessandra Cavalli. And yes, I did have a Jungian analysis.

MP: I believe there is not a huge difference from the other training originated by Anna Freud and Melanie Klein, is that right?

214   THE BUDDHA AND THE BABY

JVR: The main difference is that Michael Fordham's model of the primary self is central. This is the idea that each individual is first and foremost a Primary Self, a psychosomatic unity, a whole. This Self relates to the environment and to others through a dynamic that Fordham termed "deintegration". Reintegration is the process whereby this experience is taken in and integrated. Through the dynamic of deintegration and reintegration an internal world that is based on experience develops; an ego and internal objects develop. An example is that of a baby, who feels hunger, cries as a way of signalling this hunger (deintegration) and the mother responds by feeding and soothing the baby. The baby reintegrates the experience of hunger being satiated and her needs being met as well as the experience of being soothed.

MP: It's fascinating.

JVR: Yes, it makes a lot of sense to me and it links for me with notions of the "unmanifested", what is not formed but, nevertheless, present. Meditation for me is the process of paying attention to what is present yet unformed, that is, what is before or behind a thought or a feeling, what is "pre-mind", if you like.

MP: Do tell me more on what comes to your mind about meditation and your work with children.

JVR: I suppose what is central to my mind and my meditation at the moment, is the relationship between the observer, the experience, and the "me" that is neither of these but something that comes before, a Self. Where is it located? In the body? In the mind? In both? In neither? For example, take the feeling of pain: there is a me, who can feel it and observe it and locate it in my body, and also let it go. But there is also something that is both of me and not of me that is present and not at the same level as this felt experience. So there is a relationship between the feeling, the one who feels it, and that which is present and not part of this duality. This awareness helps me to not identify with a particular thought or feeling.

MP: You are talking about the observing ego, aren't you, and how the meditation helps to develop that, presumably?

JVR: Yes, and it can be very useful to introduce this perspective to young people who are feeling overwhelmed by inner turmoil.

JUNG AND THE BUDDHA   215

MP: In therapy, our focal point is the understanding of the relationship with the other. But tell me, how long have you been meditating now?

JVR: I dipped in and out of it since I was a teenager but I did not have a disciplined, formal practice. More recently, about three or four years ago, I started again and now I practise every morning, although I'm not sure I do actually meditate, I try, I practise!

MP: How did it come that you started again?

JVR: I found I simply needed this contact in my day-to-day life. Contact with my Self, and with the simplicity of now. You know, there's much more to who we are as human beings than thinking and doing. It is what is "behind" this, "unmanifested", that is who we truly are. And I am coming to trust and rely on this more.

MP: Also your Jungian background with its spiritual stance seems to come together neatly with your meditative interest, doesn't it?

JVR: Yes, you know, I'm very interested in "the present moment". I don't interpret very much in an intellectual way. Meditation helps me to stay present in a feeling exchange, to be aware and notice in the moment what I'm feeling in myself and in the countertransference. As well as what the child might be feeling and to bring attention to that moment to moment exchange.

MP: Would you, then, describe to a child the feeling you have noticed he or she might be feeling?

JVR: What comes to mind is a seven-year-old boy I am working with, at the moment, and who suffers from a very rare disorder, which could end up being fatal. He has a history of self-harm and has been preoccupied with thoughts of death and dying.

MP: He's probably aware of his life and death precarious condition, isn't he?

JVR: Yes, and his parents, understandably, have really struggled to assert any kind of boundary and authority because his mother has been so terrified of losing him. He's ended up being very manipulative in the family and he overplays the role of victim.

MP: I'm thinking of the secondary handicap, term used and so clearly described by Valerie Sinason (2010) in her work with children

216   THE BUDDHA AND THE BABY

and adults with mental handicap where there the environment adds to the original physical handicap or disability, a secondary handicap, which is dictated by the uncontained emotional modality of relating to the primary physical condition.

JVR: That boy experiences me as "the illness", if you like, and he hates me. He relates to me as to his illness: he tries to manipulate me by hurting himself and being vial at times. I took a position, very early on, to be very clear about boundaries in the work and not to be flexible in the way that I am with other children I work with. For example, if other children want to come into the room with their mother, that might be fine; but with him, I said: "This is the way I work: You come into my room on your own. You don't have to work with me, it is your choice, but if you agree then this is the way we work." I took a very strong position because I felt he needed to know exactly where the boundaries were. I never changed and that meant that he kicked off and hated me. He screamed and shouted and swore at me, he punched himself repeatedly and refused to come into my room. But, he also showed curiosity about what I had in my room and whenever someone walked past him he stopped his tirades. Because of this I felt reasonably confident that to some extent he was choosing this position. Now we're beyond that: he doesn't hate me all the time; he's safe enough to fight me and he now knows from experience that no one is going to die from his anger and hatred. He and his "object" are not as fragile as he has feared.

MP: It's very interesting that you took such different position with this boy who's so ill.

JVR: I think it was because he tried to change the rules and move the goalpost and be the boss, and he needed to know I was the boss and was strong enough to take whatever he threw at me; he wasn't going to damage me and he wasn't going to die, nor was I. It's been a really difficult process, and it was hard to like him; now it's easier. In terms of meditation, what I was trying in my mind to be in touch with, was what is behind the behaviour, before the illness, his self that made him behave in this way, you know, he could have handled it in a totally different way; they say that *karma* is created by the way one responds to life's events.

JUNG AND THE BUDDHA 217

I constantly name things like: "Look what's happening now", and I talk aloud, wondering what it could be that made him behave in that way. In this way, it is important that he knows that I'm thinking about him and I am having a dialogue with myself in trying to make sense of his behaviour and what is driving it. For example, I would say: "You are here today because you agreed to meet with me, yet you absolutely hate me and that is because I'm not doing what you'd like me to do. You're so angry with me because I don't agree with you, and you really think that the more you hurt yourself, then I will agree with you and change my mind." I became the person that he loved to hate, and it seemed essential that he went through with this experience.

MP: It's interesting about your boundaries with him, and I even wonder whether, by you having decided to be inflexible with him, you had also taken up the position of reality, the reality of his illness, a reality that cannot be changed.

JVR: Yes, I think so and—I can't be sure—but I also felt that his behaviour was manipulative and just for the sake of it because he had learnt to get away with things to get what he wanted. So I felt that what he needed was an approach, which in a way was very behavioural.

MP: That's where I think we need to adapt our technique to the needs and predicaments of our individual patients: technique may also change, when things change due to the child's development and to the therapeutic process moving on. I surely have the experience with a seven-year-old boy, perverse, violent, and omnipotent, who is spurred onto further aggression by words and interpretations. I state over and over again that I am the boss in our sessions and he has to comply with certain rules; occasionally this has eventually fostered some symbolic play.

JVR: I think this is not a move away from thinking analytically; it's along side with it. I think it is analytic but we put it into practice rather than talking about it. When I work with adolescents, the value of meditation feels especially relevant, possibly because there are many more moments of stillness: they're not running around the room playing or acting like younger kids do; the adolescents talk more and reflect more.

218　THE BUDDHA AND THE BABY

MP: Do you find yourself talking with them about meditation or meditative things or doing it?

JVR: Yes, very much so. It depends on the person and how available they are to perceive in this way, but ordinarily it enters the relationship by me trusting the silence and being closely attuned to the quality of silence and how that changes; then giving it words and wondering in that silence if the young person is feeling something similar or different and tracking what's going on in their mind. I'm quite interested in what's coming up in someone's mind without censoring it. I may say: "It doesn't matter what it is, just notice what comes into your mind". That reminds me very much of the very early mother–baby relationship of noticing small things and putting them into words. I love that aspect of the work which is so important, I think.

MP: And do they follow you, do they tell you what comes to their mind?

JVR: I'm just thinking of a boy, he is thirteen, whom I've just finished assessing for psychotherapy. He comes from a very deprived family with a history of sexual abuse. So it's a very complicated situation and family. He's not showing any symptoms, he's well adjusted at school, has friends, but the request for therapy came from a specialist agency, which wanted him to have preventative work. So I offered an extended therapy assessment. He is predominately silent in the room; he is a very sweet boy and is likeable, but doesn't know what he feels or thinks or wants; he doesn't know who he is, and it's very difficult. He doesn't know what to do with the offer of time and space for himself. In one way, I feel pressurised to work on the sexual abuse, but actually it's just not present in the room, in his mind, between us. What we've agreed is that together we'll begin to get to know him by paying close attention to what comes into his mind and any sensations in his body. In this way, mindfulness has really been very useful. To notice if there are tensions and feelings anywhere in his body and if that may lead to thoughts. I think he thinks I'm completely mad, "what the hell are you doing?" type of projection. I do a lot of talking because he is so silent, and he's not silent in a withholding way, he's silent in an unformed kind of way.

MP: He seems to be a child with no identity, a perfect target of abuse, and a victim, doesn't he?

JVR: That's right, and he is the kind of child who communicates with his family by provoking feeling in them, for example, he will scare them by jumping out from behind the door. What I talk to him about is: "Perhaps you can notice what you can make them feel", in the hope that he may see what he generates in someone else. I say: "You may feel this seems crazy to pay such close attention to things that come into your mind or noticing your physical body, but I don't think as a baby anyone ever paid very close attention to you, your feelings and experience. Now here is a chance for you to begin to get to know yourself."

MP: He's going on with therapy, isn't he?

JVR: He's going on and has given his consent but it feels that he doesn't have much choice because everybody in the network wants him to have therapy. So it's tricky and part of my work is to help him have a voice and a choice including: "I don't want to do this any more". But we're not near that.

MP: I can see that and it may help him to say: "I don't want to be abused any more". Now, earlier on, you were talking about mothers and babies, can you say a bit more about it?

JVR: In my meditation and mindfulness practice, the idea is not to stop your thoughts but to bring the attention back to, say, for example, an awareness of your breathing. So when a thought comes into your mind, you just notice it and bring your focus back, and it can lead to an appreciation that thoughts come and go and the mind is racing and so on. In therapeutic work, I am interested in someone else being aware of their own thinking process or in their stillness. I've noticed with adolescents that some subtle movements or subtle exchanges of feelings, a gesture, an eye contact can be noticed and named. Paying close attention and responding to these nuances, as a mother does to her baby, can enable a young person to develop this capacity for tuning in to him- or herself.

MP: What would be the purpose of helping kids to develop that level of body and mind awareness?

220 THE BUDDHA AND THE BABY

JVR: That would help them have a sense of who they are or that they are; that that is me, and this is what I'm feeling, and this is my body in this moment; also that they have a sense of the moment coming and going and that nothing lasts. If you had a very bad experience or are in touch with overwhelming feelings, you know there is a beginning and an end. You can develop a relationship to it so that you learn not to identify with it. You can develop a sense of yourself outside of that feeling, you don't have to identify with a certain state of mind.

MP: That's the difficult task we have to master all through our life. Kids follow you in that, do they?

JVR: Yes, in my experience some do.

MP: Any other vignette that comes to your mind?

JVR: I've just finished working with a girl who recently turned 18 years old. She was referred for post traumatic stress disorder, obsessional traits and severe depression and self-harm. She was on a very high dose of anti-depressant medication. Within the therapeutic work we did some mindfulness practice. She was talking about the conflict in her mind—she had a very abusive relationship with her mother over many years—and although she did not have contact with her mother any more, that battle was being replayed internally, and with me in the therapy as well. That conflict was very present in her mind in one particular session and it was stressful for her, anxiety-provoking and that internal battle was all-consuming. She was able to recognise that there was only a battle because she chose to take up arms in response to that part of herself that was picking a fight. Once she could recognise that she was responsible for the battle raging within her she decided to put down her weapons symbolically and not to respond, because she could see that it takes two to fight. So she decided not to respond to that part of herself that was looking for a fight or continuing to fight. An image then came into her mind of a pond and she said that at the surface the waters were very choppy and stormy and if she just let herself drop down to the depths it was still. She had found peace. We used this image frequently over time whenever she found herself repeating a pattern of abuse or conflict with her internalised mother. "I'm in choppy water, I need to drop, let it go and sink to the bottom and be at peace in the pond." That really worked for her and it was very moving. It was amazing working with her. I only worked with her for eighteen months, but by the time our work came to an end she was able to experience a broader spectrum of feelings and was able to recover happiness after feeling fear, self doubt and pain. She was no longer a victim.

MP: That's fascinating: what a beautiful way of offering psychotherapy and meditation together. Jackie, have you used mindfulness in other context?

JVR: I have run a Mindfulness group for school nurses in the borough where I work. We have met once a month for five months. There is one group member who has a breathing difficulty and she was very nervous about paying attention to the breath as she feared that it would bring about an asthma attack. She was able to observe her fear as it emerged and the felt experience of this fear in her body (quickening of heart rate), the thoughts that followed: "I am going to have an asthma attack", etc. She was amazed when her sinuses cleared! She hadn't tried to do anything or change anything; she was simply in the present moment. This happened on two separate occasions.

MP: What's your thinking on attachment and non-attachment, Jackie?

JVR: My thoughts on this are simply not to attach to an outcome, or a future or a past. Paying attention to this moment is what matters; it is only in this moment that anything is real. We are constantly reinventing ourselves, getting to know ourselves, making sense of Life: the only true experience is Now. Ideas, theories, organisations are illusory, and to some extent so are our feelings and our thoughts. The paradox is that psychotherapeutic treatment is most valuable when it enables the patient to get to know the content of their own mind, what one feels and what one thinks. However, what is even more important than this is the ability to realise that even this is an illusion and in order to really get to know yourself you need to let go of your feelings and thoughts!

MP: Your take on this issue is very unique and embedded in the depth of your philosophical approach to life.

JVR: Well, meditation practice helps me to deepen my awareness and strengthen my capacity to observe, myself and others. I have noticed that simply by being aware, present in a moment, with a focus on being, rather than on doing, has a profound effect in itself. I am appreciating more and more that we are very limited in what we can do for someone else as therapists, we cannot heal or change or relieve suffering. But, by being with someone in their true expression, whether it is the expression of pain or rage or fear etc., can enable a transformation that comes from within that person and can enable the natural potential for healing that is in us all. Through meditative practice, I am more enabled in the consulting room to guide my adolescent patients, and parents in particular, to observe their thoughts, feelings, and responses as they arise in our relationship without judgement, without trying to control or change them, but simply to notice. In this way, we can begin to get to know "the true self".

MP: Well, on these hopeful notes, we can say goodbye now, with many thanks for this most enjoyable and interesting conversation.

Reference

Sinason, V. (2010). *Mental Handicap and the Human Condition*. London: Free Association Books.

CHAPTER SEVENTEEN

A Burmese noodle soup with Buddha

Dialogue with Aye Aye Yee

I have also realised that one must accept the thoughts that go on within oneself of their own accord as part of one's reality. The categories of true and false are, of course, always present but because they are not binding they take second place. The presence of thoughts is more important than our subjective judgment of them. But neither must these judgments be suppressed, for they are also existent thoughts which are part of our wholeness.

—The Vulnerable Saya U

MP: How unique it is to meet you to talk about Buddhism and your work as a child psychiatrist in a busy and stressful Child and Adolescent Mental Health Service in East London, while being kindly offered a delicious, original Burmese noodle and coconut soup at your home lovingly prepared by you. We are also surrounded by pictures of Buddhist monks walking with their alms bowl in Burma and by other inspiring Buddha images and statues: this is the home of a family with long standing Buddhist tradition, I understand. You have not converted to Buddhism as most of the people in this book. But tell me more about this

224 THE BUDDHA AND THE BABY

family spiritual tradition and how you decided to become a child psychiatrist.

AAY: People who underwent a conversion to Buddhism, as you call it—have more understanding, reading, and knowledge of what Buddhism is about. There are lots of family rituals and cultures that I've been born into, and for example, now my son, who's a very bright and knowledgeable young man, is querying some of the traditions that we have and has been asking me why we do and believe in certain things and the belief system itself. I often feel at a loss in trying to explain to him. I would only say that this was passed on for generations. This was not good enough for my son, who has started to study the Dharma in detail, and now when he says his prayers in Pali, he knows exactly what they are about and is not just reciting them.

MP: It's fascinating and now, through your son, you're having a chance to think more and to seek more for the meanings of the Buddhist rituals and prayers you say daily. I think this is not unlike what has happened in the Catholic tradition I come from and how I started to want to learn more about it when I entered adolescence.

AAY: I was noticing things. My son, whom I have observed since early on, I've noticed to be quite advanced. When he was about two, my mother would take him in front of the Buddha statue in her home shrine in Burma and would recite her prayers. He used to repeat them in his newly learned language while playing and pottering around grandmother. That's how we and he were raised. In my family, we don't eat pork or beef for religious, medical, and superstitious beliefs. My son wanted to learn the truth about the above practice, so I also read and learned to seek for more understanding. Research has also proved that a spiritual approach speeds up the recovery from mental illnesses.

MP: Where were you working when you first qualified?

AAY: In a huge Victorian hospital in St Albans, Napsbury. So for me, it was a medical model throughout: you know, you see the patients, you do the mental state, and then do the medication. At that time, I was doing my adult psychiatry rotation and dealing with psychotic patients, personality disorder; as a

A BURMESE NOODLE SOUP WITH BUDDHA 225

trainee, you are more prone to work with the bread and butter part of psychiatry, you know, which is full-blown psychotic cases. So I never got around to really having this very deep therapeutic relationship with patients. Using the medical model doesn't put the emotional aspect on the forefront because you are very detached from the patient.

MP: One needs a lot of meditation, then.

AAY: Yes, but, Maria, I didn't know that at the time. In 1994, I came here and started working as a staff-grade child psychiatrist at Loxford Hall from 1997. I found that child psychiatry is a total different ballgame. You're more in a one-to-one therapeutic relation with the child. We see them, do mental assessment, family assessment or other assessment, and after the assessment you recommend and provide treatment, which includes doing therapeutic work with the child as well. You cannot totally detach your own feelings from the child's sufferings.

MP: You don't get so involved with adults, do you? Here with children and families you do get more involved.

AAY: More involved and you can't just say medically. "That's it, I've done this, and I won't be concerned about this patient any more"; it doesn't work like this in child psychiatry. I do get affected sometimes by their stories, I do think about these young people who are in horrendous situations. There was one young girl I saw from an African country, who was self-harming to the extent that she wasn't manageable in the community and she was admitted to a specialist unit. Even there, they could not contain her. She was discharged back to the community and we had to take her back. I found myself feeling frustrated, anger, and all those emotions. So this is one example of one of my cases, which in the initial part of my life as a child psychiatrist I got really affected by and I kept thinking about it.

MP: So you're talking about a deep difference in your professional self when you started to see children and young people. Were you going on to say something about meditation, I think?

AAY: Meditation practice becomes very important, but also when I do my work and now in my everyday life and also to understand myself. "Is this my anxiety or is this the situation?" How

MP: do I take a step back and re-assess the situation and not get too worried and involved? So, to answer your question again, meditation is helping me to be more mindful, reflective in the whole process of everyday life and in my work as well.

MP: In your work with children, families, and youngsters, how do you bring in your Buddhism, apart from your attitude of being more mindful, more reflective? How is your Buddhist thinking affecting your work?

AAY: My formulation and interpretation of the case is not really affected by the ideas of Buddhism, but having said so, I'm always trying to bring in some cognitive and meditation work. In some cases of youngsters who are receptive and cognitively mature, such as sixteen- or seventeen-year-old kids who are deeply anxious, I would bring in a little bit of meditation by saying: "Well, this is a process", and I try to understand their thoughts in the here and now and ask them to write down their thoughts. I would say: "These are your thoughts, how dangerous are your thoughts to you?" I can think of a seventeen-year-old boy who's managed this well and is now able to go to college. When he first came to see me, he was very debilitated by his severe panic attacks; he was agoraphobic, rigid, and perfectionist, but was also a very talented young man. He recounted that the first time he had a panic attack, he was coming back to London via one of the tunnels and was with a friend and his family; he suddenly felt very worried that he'd got stuck in the tunnel. From then on, his panic has extended so that if he goes out on long journeys, the thought of going through that tunnel comes to his mind and he has a panic attack.

MP: Does it mean that he hyperventilates and feels he cannot breathe?

AAY: Yes, and also he has palpitations, gets shaky, feels like throwing up, and thinks he's going to lose consciousness.

MP: Poor kid, it sounds quite severe!

AAY: Yes, very severe, and what happened is that previously he was a very academic, able boy, was an accomplished professional judo player and a football player. He became very incapacitated to the point that he wasn't even able to go to school. Initially, because his anxieties were so profound, you couldn't talk to him and make any sense to him. He was always preoccupied with those thoughts. At one crisis point, he couldn't even sleep in his bed: he was shaking and crying.

MP: Like a terrified infant!

AAY: Yes, like a baby and was sleeping on a mattress on the kitchen floor. We had very intensive CBT therapy, and I tried to identify with him in that one-year-long treatment—weekly first then less frequently. He was very receptive to the idea of the mind–body link: whatever the body feels, the mind interprets as a catastrophe: increase in heart rate, increase in-breathing, and the mind would react in a fight-or-flight mode as if he were in great danger.

MP: Presumably in danger of dying?

AAY: Yes, dying during sleep. Then we spoke of how the mind plays up, you know, and how the mind is like a raging bull.

MP: Is the mind a raging bull a Buddhist metaphor?

AAY: Yes, and I said to him: "Well, listen, if you let the raging bull run amok, then it will, because you let it. How are we going to rein it in?" He responded very well to that analogy. It is a slow process because kids who are in that panicky state, cannot think, so you can only go very slowly. I say to them: "Do sit there and let's think about your thoughts", and that's how I introduce mindfulness.

MP: So, you do actual mindfulness practice in your work with kids?

AAY: Yes, I introduce the meditation but I cannot do it with every child.

MP: Did you ask him to sit on a chair, to close his eyes and focus on breathing as one does in meditation?

AAY: I asked him to relax and I talk him through the muscle relaxation.

MP: Is that like body-sweeping meditation? Isn't like what they do in yoga when they ask you to tense up each body organ then to release them with the outbreath?

228   THE BUDDHA AND THE BABY

AAY: Yes, yoga comes into it as well. I ask him to observe his thoughts and what sort of thoughts he has after doing the muscle relaxation.

MP: What thoughts did he share with you, Aye Aye?

AAY: He said that a lot of thoughts came to his mind, and I asked how he felt in his body when each thought comes to mind. He said: "When I have this thought, I panic and my temperature goes up and up." I say: "Don't try to get rid of it, stay with that." He did and after a while he said: "It's gone now", but then he had another thought and we repeated the same process, over and over again.

MP: Can you say some of the thoughts he might have had?

AAY: He worried about living away from home when he goes to uni, becoming sick and being alone. I do not offer any reassurance, because if I did that, it would only reinforce his worries. I need him to understand that the thoughts are irrational, that those thoughts do not stay and that, you know, they will come and go.

MP: In this respect, there is a strong link with Buddhist meditation and the notion of impermanence; that is also the friendly reminder you offer me when you see me at work fraught with issues related to institutional dynamics. It is a precious reminder that it is impermanent, and I need not to attach to the distress caused to me.

AAY: And I also appreciate having you in my life and understanding that extraordinary and scary experience I once had during meditation. Sometimes we need to be reminded. That young man would go home and practise both the muscle relaxation and mindfulness.

MP: Mindfulness consisting in becoming aware of his thoughts after the muscle relaxation and to let them pass, doesn't it?

AAY: Yes. This young man has now gone to university, is living in a hostel away from his parents; he still has panic attacks but he can manage them.

MP: He may need to go into psychoanalytic psychotherapy at some point, to help him understand the deep-seated root of the original panic attacks as he crossed the tunnel and of the other attacks, of course.

AAY: Yes, probably.

MP: It is very interesting the way you manage to marry the mindfulness you have acquired from your generations of Buddhists in your family with your work as a child psychiatrist. What an interesting journey it has been from your medical and somewhat mechanical style, as you've described it earlier, to a more people-oriented, spiritual, and philosophical one with body–mind–emotion connections. What about with younger children?

AAY: I don't think you can use that approach unless you've developed the cognitive ability, but you can help parents and carers to understand where the child is coming from.

MP: Yes, help the parents to help their youngest children, but sadly even the occasional under five, who used to come to me, will no longer be seen in our CAMHS clinic. To think more of the metaphor of the raging bull, do you rein it by observing it?

AAY: No, you don't observe the raging bull: you pull the raging bull and tie it around the post. In this way, you recognise the thought, you understand it, and you rein it: this is a thought, it won't be there for long; it comes, it goes.

MP: Does that mean that the thought does not affect your body state, does not agitate the body, as you just see the thought coming and going?

AAY: Yes, you just recognise it; you don't try to stop the thought because the more you try to do that, the more you get anxious and the more it gets back to you. You just let it come and go, and you go back to the breathing, and after practising that for a while, there will be a time when there will be stillness, and to recognise that stillness is transforming in itself.

MP: Very interesting; now how would you reconcile the idea of attachment to non-attachment in Buddhism?

AAY: I think when you say attachment; it may mean a different form of attachment. When we talk—as child psychiatrists—of

230 THE BUDDHA AND THE BABY

attachment between mother, child, father, peers, etc., we mean something. In Buddhism, this attachment may also be part of it, but it usually refers to attachment to this world: we want this, we want that, and so on, but then suffering comes with this sort of attachment. I don't think Buddhism teaches non-attachment as in the formal sense, what do you think?

MP: Not at all: Buddhism fosters healthy psychological attachment between children, parents, family members, peers, colleagues. It's the grasping, the holding on, and clinging type of attachment which is unwholesome and creates suffering, that Buddhism refers to, as I understand it.

AAY: To be attached and to be over-attached, I think there is a difference. This is just my view, but it may not be right as I haven't studied the Buddhist theory on this.

MP: There is no right or wrong view: it is just a view. How do you apply this Buddhist idea of non-attachment in your work, for example with the young man you mentioned above?

AAY: I help him not to dwell on his thoughts: that's more to be detached, but not to deny the thoughts.

MP: What about the sense of self: in your cultural background emphasis is placed more on the sense of community than on the individual as in Western societies. How do you manage this with the idea of helping kids grow a healthy sense of self?

AAY: It's not no-self; it's just that there is no: I and Me.

MP: This puzzles me; can you say a bit more?

AAY: You really go into the state of impermanence in meditation and into the molecular part of yourself that you are observing: galapa is the smallest atom, which the body is made of. Thinking of: "I" becomes a perception not a real "Me". I am just an aggregate of cells, of galapas, which take the shape of "Me". Every moment they disintegrate and, you know when you die, you become part of the other i.e. the earth.

MP: But there is a conventional self and a me, which is different from the real self, which is no-self, if I understand this correctly?

A BURMESE NOODLE SOUP WITH BUDDHA   231

AAY: Well, I also need to understand this better and, at the moment, I have nothing more to add.

MP: To move to a more personal level, did you ever have a mystical or a particularly striking, unusual experience in the context of your practice?

AAY: I had an experience of intense joy once during a retreat at the International Meditation Centre in Wiltshire. I was lying on the bed after lunch and a shower and was meditating when everything came to a still point: I wasn't thinking, I wasn't even aware that I was breathing, I wasn't asleep, it was complete stillness. I thought: "Oh dear, this is what death is going to be like?"

MP: Death, you said?

AAY: Yes, because it was so peaceful.

MP: And you loved that?

AAY: Well, that really shocked me.

MP: Do you think that is what death is really about?

AAY: It was very peaceful, so peaceful I have no other interpretation: you normally find peace in sleep after every day's struggle, you sleep and it completely goes away. I think meditation is when you get that mind stillness but death would be going one step further and that means that you're not bothered about the hassles of day-to-day life, which is suffering every single day, you know. I think that all religions prepare us for death and dying, the scariest things in life. Christianity, Buddhism, etc. give us comfort that when we die, it is a normal process, and for us to do more good things in this life, with the knowledge that there is an after death, is helpful.

MP: Do you believe in an afterlife, in reincarnation?

AAY: Yes, as a Buddhist, I do.

MP: Does it mean that when you die your energy will take another shape; hence you have to earn merits in this life to be reincarnated in a higher realm of existence?

AAY: The mind, the spirituality, the energy is what you carry with you.

MP: Is that what goes on to live, that is, a transformed energy? But what is left of us then if our soul is being reincarnated in a lower realm of existence such as the animal realm? Can you clarify this for me, Aye Aye?

AAY: I've been reading about mind and matter: the energy is like a carbon, which is being transported into another life, another being, and you wouldn't even know what's happening: it's just whatever you're going through is the interpretation of your past *karma*. That's all I can say so far, well now I am embracing this more also thanks to my son's influence. The child leading the parent! But now we need to get on with our Burmese soup to nourish the body after this talk.

MP: Yes, very pragmatically indeed: we need to feed the body after this spiritual feast. Many thanks: it really was a great privilege to be offered into the alms bowl of this book a taste of your life experience as a native Buddhist and a child psychiatrist: a unique encounter with you, Aye Aye, Sadu, Sadu, Sadu.

CHAPTER EIGHTEEN

From the cushion to the couch

Dialogue with Nicholas Carroll

Wisdom tells me I am nothing,
Love tells me I am everything.

—Nisargardatta Maharaj

MP: I understand that you are an adult counsellor and psychosexual psychotherapist and I'd like to ask about the impact your long-standing Buddhist meditation practice has had on your work with the adults you see, and in particular with reference to the child part inside your patients. Before that, I'd like to ask you if you come from a religious background and when you first became acquainted with Buddhism.

NC: I was bought up nominally as a Catholic. My father was an agnostic and my mother a non-practising Catholic who used to take me to church on Sundays because she felt it was the right thing to do. When my parents separated—I was about ten— my mother sent me to boarding school as she wanted me to be exposed to a male environment. This was very thoughtful and kind of her, but she didn't really quite know where she was sending me. It was a school run by Christian brothers, before the

233

234   THE BUDDHA AND THE BABY

II Vatican Council, which I experienced as a pretty brutal place with corporal punishment and not very much to do with Jesus' love for fellow man. This experience obviously informed me in many ways. There was compulsory mass every morning, whilst on Sundays we had mass as well as benediction in the afternoon, as well as regular religious education during the week. The message was that the Catholic faith was the only true faith. I took it on trust and tried to establish a relationship with God, but after trying, probably until around the age of twelve, I realised that my prayers were not going to be answered. I was waiting for God to say "Hello" in response to my prayers to him! But it never came. I was quite shocked to discover that there was a proscribed list of books we weren't allowed to read if Catholic. I was outraged at the thought that somebody could dictate what we were allowed to read, books that were actually in print. I increasingly grew to understand that the school was abusive and that the brothers were not really that well sorted out, and decided that Christianity was not for me. At the same time, there were aspects in communal living that I quite enjoyed, even including some aspects of the collective celebration of the Mass, although I didn't understand its significance. I disliked the long boring services that were also quite painful when having to kneel for long periods of time, a test of stamina. There was an organ in the school chapel and one of the brothers, who was very musical, was one of the organists. During Benediction, he would play the appropriate music and then, during intervals, he would quietly play some improvisations into which he would occasionally introduce a theme from one of the current pop songs, either by the Beatles or the Beach Boys, some of which are very melodic. None of the brothers would recognise these short riffs; but as you can imagine, many of the boys did. We would nudge each other whilst trying to keep a straight face, enjoying the incongruence.

MP: He was not censored like the books!

NC: No, that's right. In trying to establish a connection with God, I remember going to the school chapel and praying, listening out and just hearing the silence, which only much later in life did I realise may have been the real answer. The stories in the Bible made me hope that there would be a manifestation of some kind:

FROM THE CUSHION TO THE COUCH   235

a burning bush, perhaps, or an angel or something, but nothing of the sort ever occurred. So I lost my faith. But I believe I absorbed many of the moral injunctions from the tradition.

MP: What about Buddhism, then?

NC: That came much later, I was in my very early twenties; it was a time in my life when I was a very confused young man. I was travelling on the Moscow-Vienna sleeper that I had boarded in Warsaw, where I have family (my mother is Polish). I shared a compartment with an elderly Austrian professor, who was living in China teaching anthropology when the Communist revolution took place in 1948. He had been given the choice of either leaving or staying in China with his Chinese wife and family, but if he stayed it was only on condition that he gave up teaching anthropology, which was regarded as a bourgeois subject, and agreed to teach German. He had chosen the latter and was making his second visit home to Vienna when we met. I found what he had to say quite fascinating and asked him hundreds of questions throughout the journey about his life and experiences in China, which even then was regarded very much as an exotic country. He wondered if I was a journalist having kept him up all night asking so many questions. I found what he'd said so interesting that I resolved to learn Chinese in order to get to know the culture better, and on returning to London I enrolled for an evening course in Mandarin at the City Literary Institute in Holborn. For a nominal additional sum it was then possible to take an additional subject, and I chose Chinese philosophy. The teacher was a Chinese whom I found most inspiring. He was knowledgeable in both Taoist and Buddhist philosophy as well as being familiar with Western thought and, fortunately for his Western audience, very articulate in English. Although I had done a fair amount of reading in a very amateurish and random way on philosophy, religion, and psychology, I was quite overwhelmed by his presentation. He seemed to both know and embody what he taught. This exposure to Taoist and Buddhist philosophy and teachings led me to start practising them, and the two traditions coexisted within me for many years. I was inspired by both of them but found it difficult to reconcile their different emphasis. Taoism was to me very much about cultivating and developing one's energy,

236   THE BUDDHA AND THE BABY

ideally allowing it to circulate in the body and harmonising with the Tao. The Buddhist path appeared to be more cognitive and seemed to have a less friendly relationship to the body. It was a more reflective tradition, and appeared not so body-oriented, although in practice it is actually very much body-orientated, but differently.

MP: Did you start practising meditation then?

NC: Yes, I was about twenty-two, so I've been at it for many years. Initially, I taught myself from what I read in translations by Lu Kuan Yu of Ch'an on Zen teachings, but later I practised in various group settings where there was some guidance and structure that can be so helpful in getting one through the difficult initial stages of practice. When I started the courses at the City Lit, I found myself on a rollercoaster, moving from great excitement at the discovery of these teachings, to feeling very downhearted at the realisation of my shortcomings compared to all the masters whom I was reading about.

MP: Did you go to therapy then?

NC: No, I didn't get into therapy until many years later; starting my training as a marriage guidance counsellor when I was in my thirties. But it was about the same time that I started learning Mandarin that I began to work on myself. As a result of a dream I took up training as a woodworker, initially as a carpenter and joiner, and then later as furniture maker and designer. This eventually resulted in my running a workshop and then managing a small refurbishment company, which despite the pressure and time commitment that it required on top of my "spiritual" seeking, provided me with the income to maintain my family, and later the flexibility to train as a counsellor and therapist. It was a very challenging period of my life. Working as a woodworker on the tools was a "foundation" training, for unlike a paper-pushing job, there is an immediacy about physical work because of the almost instant feedback one gets. If you don't do anything, nothing happens; if you make a mistake, you find out very quickly; and if you do something well, you see the good result. There is a very clear causal connection between intention, action, and result. It was a tough discipline, which is what I needed as I was rather

FROM THE CUSHION TO THE COUCH   237

dreamy, not to mention lazy. So my woodworking was a form of training through which, I now realise, I was developing on many levels, physically, emotionally, and indeed mentally.

MP: A self-made man, in other words.

NC: In a sense, and looking back, it was hard work. My eventual personal therapy was with a Jungian, an open-minded and very fine elderly lady who was, as all good therapists are, a very good listener. As it is for many, it was initially an unfamiliar experience to share my inner life in such detail with someone. Coming from a mixed European background and speaking three languages, my life had been very rich, but it had also been a very solitary experience in that I had been unable to identify fully with any one group, always being aware of how the same event could be interpreted from many perspectives, all of them different but all of them also "correct".

MP: How does Buddhism affect you in your work as a therapist?

NC: What the Buddhist tradition has offered me is an all encompassing context or framework of reference, which together with my therapy training and practice as well as my life experiences, has helped me make some sense of life. It allows me to deal better both cognitively and emotionally with the complexity, confusion and despair that clients bring. It helps provide a reference point and context for what I hear and experience. Having had to experience, process and make sense of my own suffering helps me process the suffering of my clients. Interestingly, I find that this processing of the client's suffering often parallels and mirrors the client's process. It makes me better able to fully engage in what is nowadays increasingly referred to as the process of rupture and repair, but seeing it also as part of a bigger process. Sometimes the repair or resolution is not necessarily a change in circumstances *per se*, but a change in perception, a change in relationship to the circumstances, a movement towards greater acceptance.

MP: It's called projective identification, where the therapist allows him- or herself to fully experience the emotional impact of the patient and almost becomes the patient temporarily, such that the unity of experience can be felt in body and mind. Then a

238 THE BUDDHA AND THE BABY

progressive digestion and a separation from the patient and the emotional impact occur within the therapist, who then tries to either speak or keep it inside in a way that already and silently modifies the patient or the relationship patient–therapist.

NC: Correct; even if you don't comment explicitly, the way one processes one's own experience of the process, this is unconsciously and subliminally communicated to the patient in a way that parallels, or perhaps helps amplify and facilitate, the process they find themselves in. In that sense, one is a fellow traveller, at least for part of their journey, perhaps better equipped than the patient, though of course not always. In this, my experience of meditation has been immensely helpful, for in sustained meditation practice one is exposed to one's inner "hells" very directly, and because of the more solitary nature of meditation, perhaps more so than that in therapy. It can be the making or breaking of one. It was as a result of my meditation experiences that I was drawn to counselling and therapy, which eventually provided me with a vehicle to work through my own reparative process through helping others. The experiences gave me a greater resilience and capacity to cope. My meditation experiences were very significant, a re-birth experience. I was thirty-three years old at the time.

MP: Can you say a bit more of what happened to you in this re-birth experience?

NC: Somewhat reluctantly if I am to be truthful. I haven't shared them very much. They are very personal and I'm not sure how helpful it is to share them in detail. It is best to make one's own journey rather than hear others' experiences. It has taken me many years to get over them for there is always the temptation to make something of them, to identify with them, whereas all they are in fact is a series of experiences which remain as memories, which whilst immensely significant and informative, one has to eventually let go of.

MP: Physically and emotionally painful, by the sound of it!

NC: Yes, as in any deeper enquiry into one's psyche, there is a lot of pain, and it is physical as well as mental. If one perseveres and if one is fortunate in navigating the dangers successfully, it can result in some very wonderful experiences that inform one on the relationship between consciousness and phenomena. One has a direct experience of the intimate and inseparable relationship between physical and mental phenomena, that we are indeed a mind body manifestation. More importantly, seeing the conditioned nature of all phenomena and its transience can lead to an ongoing and very profound enquiry into the nature of existence itself. In my case, it came about through an increasingly deeper stillness accompanied by a corresponding movement of energy in the body, which eventually manifested as a strong heat. Sustaining stillness of attention, maintaining a non-reactive presence, was essential, for that was what allowed a natural process to take place, allowing the energy in the form of heat to move and circulate more freely in the body.

MP: You mean, you felt a burning heat?

NC: The physical sensation was that of heat, which it is so tempting to react to, to engage with, with a desire to will it on, to help it move on. But any active wilful mental engagement has quite the opposite effect, it slows the process down or it stops altogether.

MP: Perhaps like an orgasm that doesn't come?

NC: Yes, perhaps. As the mind returns to stillness, the energy gradually does move again, only to get stuck again further on in the body when one engages with it, so again one has to let go, which again frees the process up. It's an absorbing process and if successful, eventually leads to a loss of identification with one's sense of self, which then results in an experience which can only be described as a sudden expansion of consciousness, where one is in effect consciousness itself expanding into space, ending in what can only be described as a going beyond, about which and of which nothing can be said. This was followed by a gradual contraction of consciousness and a return to the body, which is experienced as a completely integrated mind–body unity, a unified and interconnected embodiment, with a sense of oneness with everything. Naively, I thought I was enlightened, but gradually I came to understand that it was simply a powerful "peak" experience, or as Buddhist psychology would describe it, an experience of the

240   THE BUDDHA AND THE BABY

absorptions; enlightenment itself, in the Buddhist understanding at least, being something else.

MP: I am thinking of Epstein's *Thoughts without a Thinker*. Well, this is very interesting because I usually ask people at the end of these dialogues, whether they ever had any mystical experience, and you started by telling me that.

NC: The powerful effects of this experience stayed for many months and, a year or so later, were followed by what I would describe as an "after-shock". The analogy that comes to mind is that of being in a dark room all one's life, then suddenly having the room illuminated, brightly revealing the contents of the room. The illumination is wonderful—one is no longer in darkness. But what is revealed is not pretty. This is the after-shock. It is being confronted with one's individual shortcomings, one's selfishness, everything that one had a sense of but didn't really want to know. A total exposure to what in Jungian terms would be called the shadow. A profoundly, totally despairing realisation of one's imperfection, so completely humbling, and with no escaping its truth.

Having reached the full depth of despair, there followed, quite unexpectedly, a blissful stream of an all accepting and forgiving love, an extraordinary sense of being completely and unconditionally accepted just as one is, a complete melting and dissolving, giving rise to tears and of feeling blessed. This experience put me at a crossroads. It was so tempting to put it down to an experience of God, as these experiences often are. The problem was that I didn't believe in God and I wanted to be able to square the experience and understand it fully in non-theistic terms. I struggled with this question for some time and eventually decided to leave the question unanswered. I simply didn't know.

It was a good move. It has taken me the rest of my life to make sense of what happened, and to understand the experience better, both cognitively and experientially, knowing that ultimately the heart of it is beyond words, an ineffable mystery which can only be "known" indirectly. This was an understanding and experience that I have been digesting ever since. Any cognitive or belief-based understanding is essentially a re-presentation, and as such it is one removed from the "nameless". With this type of experience, what seems to happen to many is that they confuse the re-presentation, that is, their ideas or beliefs about their experience with the direct and immediate experience itself. After a few years, which were a form of recovery and reorientation, I became interested in the world of counselling and therapy, and embarked on a new journey into counselling, psychosexual therapy, and trauma therapy. I never felt able to share my meditation experiences, partly because I didn't know how to articulate or present them, and also because I didn't feel sufficiently detached from them; I hadn't integrated them sufficiently; and partly because it wasn't the done thing to do in my professional world, at least not in the largely psychodynamic and psychoanalytically informed world I found myself in, though it might have been better received in Jungian circles and, of course, transpersonal ones.

MP: I recently went to a Jungian meeting at what was then called the British Association of Psychotherapy—now it's the Federation— and people were talking freely about mysticism and spirituality. It was a real treat for me.

NC: My experiences are, of course, not unique. What they do, though, is profoundly inform and affect one's perception of life and of oneself. What I have learned is that we end up better able to manage and live life in the world if we allow ourselves to be open to the world, and accept everything we experience, both pleasant and unpleasant, whether it be on the cushion, on the couch, or indeed our daily lives. If we want to have a taste of real peace, we have to allow ourselves to know the horrors as well as the beauty of the way things are.

MP: Last night I went to listen to Jon Kabat-Zinn's talk on mindfulness, and he said something along the same lines, that is, that you sit on the cushion and you meditate and you think you're getting into a nice relaxed state but then your hell begins; you experience the whole universe on the cushion: the Buddha, the bad, and the hell. My hells, I experienced them on the couch, which of course paralleled my life at that time, more than on the cushion; even though what popped up on the cushion was also difficult, but it was more healing for me and clearly on a different dimension.

NC: It's a very individual journey. Personally I see no conflict between Buddhist teachings and therapy. Buddhism is much clearer in its

242   THE BUDDHA AND THE BABY

injunctions and in the importance it gives to ethics and morality as a basis for practice and enquiry. Buddhism is also the prime source of inspiration for the current popularity of mindfulness practice, which is now found in so many therapeutic modalities. Buddhism has a clear sense of purpose and direction, whose ultimate aim is realisation. Western therapies are much more diverse, with many different aims and methodologies. What Western psychotherapy does have is a very good understanding of the developmental process and of attachment styles and their effects on the individual. Both Buddhism and Western psychological perspectives, in principle at least, have a similar open-minded spirit of enquiry as well as a shared aim in alleviating suffering. The two "traditions", if one can call them that, complement each other very well. The Western therapies have a very good understanding of the relational process. The Buddhist approach, though relational in many ways, is essentially more individual. Both "traditions" have different but complementary skills sets, which now appear to be increasingly informing each other. For myself, I feel I have managed to gradually integrate my understanding and practice of Buddhist perspectives with Western psychological therapeutic ones. I find the combination offers a pretty comprehensive overview or framework within which to live and work.

MP: You know Nina Coltart; she felt very much the same: no conflict between the two traditions. Well, thinking of the issue of attachment and the fact that we have to be well attached to many people and many things in life to be able to function well as human beings, yet Buddhism encourages non-attachment.

NC: I think it's important to understand that Buddhist teachings, the core ones, are directed primarily at mature adults; it's not an injunction for small children to detach themselves from their parents! The idea of leaving the world to take up a monastic life, to become a *sannyasin* or *samana* (renunciant/homeless one), is done at a higher order of maturity.

MP: But it also transcends the ordinary life, because you can be a Buddhist and still lead an ordinary lay life without joining the order, can't you?

NC: We are talking about the classical tradition because there is no doubt that the ideal life presented in Buddhist teaching is the so-called "holy" life, which is the monastic life; a life of relinquishment. Relinquishment can be practised in lay life, of course, but the challenge in being a lay practitioner is that one is constantly confronted with one's attachments; so if one is married, has a family and a job, then of course one has attachments and engagement with all of that. There's something more extreme in a monastic life because there is the formal relinquishment of all worldly engagement when one takes the precepts, the equivalent in Christian monasticism being the taking of the vows of poverty, chastity, and obedience. The spirit and emphasis in Buddhist monastic training, and indeed lay practice, is that it is undertaken voluntarily; it's an act of choice. Taking the monastic precepts is a conscious expression of intentions. Whereas for Christian monks and nuns, for example, there is often a lifelong commitment of unquestioning obedience to one's superior, in the Buddhist monastic tradition one goes through a period of basic training of seven years or so, but after that one is an independent agent, one can go from one monastery to another, or indeed choose to go into a reclusive life, for instance. There appears to be much more of a choice, but it is important to remember that at all times the monastic is dependent on lay support, or at least that is the case in the oldest traditions such as Theravada. But in talking about the core of Buddhist practice of non-attachment we are not just talking of non-attachment to physical materials and possessions, we are really talking about non-attachment to emotions and states of mind; of being able to let go of everything that arises in consciousness, be it physical phenomena, emotional, or mental. Now this applies to practice in lay life too: it's about letting go, not so much of what is arising or happening in our consciousness in itself, but to the relationship that we have to what is arising or happening, that is, our attachment or aversion towards it; for in Buddhist thought, the root of suffering is seen as attachment, or craving. One can become very extreme in the practice of non-attachment, and the emphasis in Buddhist teaching is on practising the Middle Way: of not going to either extreme, either that of excessive asceticism or of over-indulgence. It always tries to strike the middle, not some sort of poor compromise, but getting the balance right, and each of us has to find this balance for ourselves.

In Buddhist practice, non-attachment is essentially non-reactivity, and by that I do not mean not having a reaction *per*

244   THE BUDDHA AND THE BABY

se, for that is impossible, but literally not re-acting, not acting impulsively to stimuli, stimuli that might be pleasant, unpleasant, or neutral. Being aware, not reacting, but preferably responding as best one can. It's noticing our preferences: I like this, I don't like that; I want this, I don't want that. It's not denying that this is what we feel, it's more about developing a more spacious relationship to that instinctive: I like, I don't like, towards this reactivity moving towards something or moving away from something. It's what Freud touched on when he spoke about the pleasure and pain principle: we're attracted towards pleasure and we avoid pain. It's an insight that Buddha had, an insight that Freud had. One can see it psychologically in terms of the maturity of the person and the capacity for deferred gratification. The same principle applies to spiritual practice; it's about learning to defer short-term rewards in order to enable longer-term rewards, which in the Buddhist tradition is ultimately enlightenment, or realisation. Mark Epstein is excellent in highlighting the themes common to both Buddhism and Freudian thought; worth reading. Of course neither of these thinkers, Buddha or Freud, can claim ownership to that understanding because essentially it's a recognition of a universal principle common to all life: the aversion towards what is dangerous, and of being drawn to what is pleasurable. From the earliest stages of life as it has evolved, it's a question of survival: it's a movement towards what you need to eat and what enables reproduction, and a movement away from any threat to existence. We all have this instinctive layer of reactivity, and all subsequent more evolved levels of development operate on the same core principles of like and dislike; "towards" and "away from". From a child's perspective, it's about making sense of the world, initially all based on the experience of the senses; going towards food, warmth and safety, and feeling averse to feelings of hunger, cold, and threat; and all the while trying to put two and two together as it were, trying to make sense of the world. Not knowing can be terrifying for children and indeed for adults; that experience of Bion's "nameless dread". We are closer to that whenever we experience a threat to our existence, physically or emotionally. What happens in Buddhist practice, indeed in any deep meditation or contemplative practice, is that one is, in a sense, letting go of safe and familiar reference points, and of course some people have difficult experiences in meditation: they can get lost, they can have panic attacks. Loss of identity is quite terrifying because our sense of identity is the construct through which we make meaning of this individual body in a world full of threats. This takes us to the sense of self: we all need a sense of self to survive. There are many misapprehensions around the concept of no-self (*anatta*), one of the key teachings of the Buddha. His was a very absolute statement, one which we can objectively agree to be true in the light of Western psychology and indeed science, which is increasingly pointing to that: we create a construct. Of course, not everyone agrees with that! Too frightening.

MP: Winnicott's false self perhaps?

NC: That's a very good one because that shows that we create a construct, we create a personality that allows us to relate in the world, but it can override our intuitive and felt sense of who we are and how we function; but it has a different meaning to that used by Winnicott.

MP: Yes, he believed there is a true self which is different from the no-self.

NC: Indeed, his "true self" is not the same as the Buddhist no-self. Much better explanatory models can be found in formulations such as ego states or sub personalities that help identify different parts of the psyche. They are very useful models because they're so close to the Buddhist concept of "no-self". We are a dynamic psychobiological process that develops in complexity over time, an interplay of experiences and meaning-giving in response to environmental input of information. We develop a number of "identities" or worldviews, not just on an intellectual level of understanding, but in how we experience ourselves in relation to the world, and these are constantly being rebuilt or reconstructed with the input of new information. We can talk of our different parts, for example the child part or the adult part and so on, different parts of ourselves coming into "being", as it were, depending on the context and all the associations that arise in that context. A very simple example might be of us as an adult functioning perfectly, or reasonably well in life and in relationships, but when our mother comes to visit, there is an immediate regression; what is associated with the mother suddenly comes to life and overrides and undermines one's more mature development. The "child" in us emerges at that point and we might become irrational, irritable, angry, frustrated, or just reactive. On the positive side, we may of course perhaps become very loving and kind, but there will generally be a greater degree of emotionality and a corresponding increase in irrationality, or indeed perhaps a shutting down, all triggered by the embodied associations that we have with our mothers.

In many ways, I find the body-based psychotherapies, ones that use mindfulness and body awareness, to be superior to talking therapies in accessing these states, especially in bringing about change on those instinctive levels, the ones that are affected, for example, by trauma. In sensorimotor psychotherapy, for instance, one focuses on the instinctive motor movements, which are our survival response to the experience of an immediate threat. If unprocessed, they remain literally in the body and often sabotage higher areas of our functioning. What needs addressing is this basic level of trauma around which patterns of reactivity constellate. By talking, one is often working very far away from the location of the trauma in the body. These body-orientated therapies, and EMDR is another one, use mindfulness, or body awareness, which helps access the implicit or unconscious physiological responses to threat associated with trauma and helps bring them into consciousness and thus eventual resolution. The outcomes can be extraordinary: I have found that individuals who meditate and have the capacity for deeper reflective body awareness and the ability to be silent and notice, are the ones who experience the fastest recovery from trauma: it's quite remarkable how quickly and well.

In some cases, it is possible to access the core trauma in a few sessions using body-oriented therapies, whilst in similar cases I might have spent perhaps many months engaged in talking therapy. We now know from much of the evidence that talking therapies do not change the traumatic response as effectively as body-orientated therapies do, something I can now vouch for from my own experience. What I find exciting is that in recent years these two therapeutic modalities, the body-orientated and the talking-orientated ones, are coming together and informing one another and even integrating, which is a reflection of the

FROM THE CUSHION TO THE COUCH   247

fact that we are a body–mind organism; and that the successful outcomes of these modalities are now being supported by hard evidence from RCTs, as in the case of mindfulness and EMDR.

MP: And the neurosciences are putting the body much more into the picture.

NC: Very much so. Procedural learning is what we learn when we're young, in relationship with the primary carer during our early and most formative years. Most is learnt unconsciously; it's what we grow up with, it's the environment that we internalise and which becomes our inner world. There are many small traumas that affect our development: the many fears and anxieties, and we now also know that we are learning even in the womb by the way the mother manages her own fears and anxieties. We also know from Allan Schore's work how the mother regulates the infant's affect level by how she herself manages her own affect in response to her experiences of life and indeed that of her baby's, and the baby picks that up through the way the mother is, how she looks at her, speaks, touches her, and so on.

MP: In that way, the baby develops a healthy ego if things go well.

NC: Yes, that dictates the health of the ego: so the genetic givens of the child are affected by environmental input. We now know the effect cortisol has, for example, which is produced in situations of emotional or physical stress, and how it affects the chemistry of the child's body and indeed the emotional "chemistry" of the relationship between infant and mother. In the very early stages of life, all these experiences are recorded in the unconscious, which thanks to neuroscience we now know is primarily in the right hemisphere of the brain, where very early brain development takes place, and which has the earliest and most direct connectivity with the body.

MP: What about the letting go and the non-ego in children or in the child part of your adult patients; how are these non-attachment, no-self ideas compatible with the development of a child personality?

NC: Well, to develop a reflective sense of one's ego, one needs to have a higher order of development than a child has. The child in the

248   THE BUDDHA AND THE BABY

adult, well, I'm thinking of an example of an adult who was sexually abused over several years as an infant and young girl. This became apparent whilst having a body massage treatment in a spa as an adult, when a deep somatic memory of sexual abuse was triggered, accompanied by the powerful visual image of the abuser. This was a terrifying and totally unexpected experience, as it was indeed also for the masseur, who had the shock of her life when her client's primal scream of terror burst the silence of the treatment room. Initially, the patient could not accept her experience, only further flashbacks began to convince her that she had been seriously abused. When she shared this with her closer family, it was vehemently denied by everyone because of its implications, as is unfortunately so often the case. This denial, of course, effectively reinforced the original abuse even more. I found that I was working with an adult in the consulting room as well as with the abused baby infant, but this infant was dissociated from the adult, she had a separate identity. The task was to help this very sensitive individual to somehow integrate this dissociated part of her, a part which for many months stayed in a closed cupboard in my consulting room where she felt safe. Befriending and reassuring her that it was safe to come out was a long and painstaking process. All the forgotten terrible experiences, which were remembered by her body with all the associated emotional and physical pain, had broken through into consciousness, where she "knew" that something was not right. The challenge was to go through a reparative process of re-integrating this terrified infant with my help, a therapist who happened to be male, and as such a potential abuser himself. So it can be a strange and moving experience in the consulting room: sometimes talking to the adult; sometimes reassuring the infant, who is mediated through the adult. It has been a real learning curve to develop and manage the relationship required, to attune to the different strands and dimensions of this complex mix of different ego-parts.

MP: The psychotherapeutic work with babies and small children is so fundamental to getting hold of these traumas before they become entrenched and affect the whole life of a person, producing so much deep suffering! Perhaps this is the place where meditation,

FROM THE CUSHION TO THE COUCH   249

with its emphasis on the physical body, the child and the adult come together somehow.

NC: I believe there is a connection: the emphasis on noticing sensations is one of the basic foundations of meditation, and the credit for recognising the relationship of sensations to the content of one's personal emotional and psychological life in a therapeutic setting, to my mind, has to go to Eugene Gendlin, whereas the credit for the spread of mindfulness practice in medical and therapeutic settings has to be Jon Kabat-Zinn's. Gendlin, a philosopher and psychologist based in Chicago, developed his therapeutic model on what he had learned from his own practice of meditation, using what he calls focusing, where the patient is encouraged to pay attention and stay with the sensations that arise whilst attending to his or her issues, without initially saying anything, in order to capture the pre-verbal "felt-sense" of the problem. He found that if the patient stayed with the sensations long enough, it enabled a natural resolution of the problem. It's as if the emotional issues were communicated through the sensations, and their meaning was then put into words afterwards.

MP: How do the emotions communicate that?

NC: Once the patient has identified the problem they wish to address, the therapist might suggest, for example: "Notice the sensation you're having at this moment and stay with that sensation without saying anything, just allow yourself to experience the sensation and then notice what comes up; notice what happens when you stay with the sensation". This helps the patient to find what Gendlin called the "felt-sense" or meaning of an issue before verbalising it. This is basically a form of mindfulness in relational therapy.

MP: Notice what happens when you stay with the sensations but presumably also in terms of noticing the thoughts?

NC: Well thoughts will arise but there is an injunction: don't go into thinking about it before you've allowed yourself to experience the "whole" of all the sensations, because the sensations are true and immediate indicators of what the problem is really about. But, and this is important, by staying with the sensations long enough,

250   THE BUDDHA AND THE BABY

you allow them to go through a process towards resolution. We generally prevent this process of resolution taking place because we subliminally and unconsciously avoid what is unpleasant and, all too quickly and easily, get caught up in thinking, without being fully aware of the underlying sensations and processes that inform the thinking. This is where mindfulness in the relational therapeutic context is used differently than in the practice of meditation, whether it be calming meditation (*samatha* in Pali), which is about inducing a state of calmness, or insight meditation (*vipassana* in Pali) which is more focused on recognising universal principles of the nature of phenomena *per se*, rather than resolving one's individual problems.

MP: Impermanence, suffering, etc.?

NC: Yes, the changing nature of all phenomena, insight into which, with all its implications, is actually one of the keys to real wisdom as understood in the Buddhist tradition. Mindfulness as exemplified by Gendlin's focusing method is, as far as I know, the first explicit application of mindfulness on sensations as part of a relational psychotherapeutic process. He developed what he calls focus-orientated psychotherapy, which he describes as an experiential method, one that also includes the interpretation of dreams, for which he also uses focusing and the "felt-sense" as it arises, in order to understand the dreams. He developed this form of psychotherapy with his graduate students. Jon Kabat-Zinn, based on his own experience of Buddhist-informed meditation, started to apply mindfulness to the patients in his care at the University of Massachusetts Medical Centre, where he was the director. He looked at how mindfulness practice could be taught in a structured way to groups of patients to help bring about healing. He carried out some empirical research using this approach on psoriasis, chronic pains, and depression. He designed the model on which MBSR (mindfulness-based stress reduction) is based, and which is now approved by NICE and used in the NHS.

MP: That's very positive, isn't it?

NC: Indeed, it's wonderful. This has been taken further and applied to mindfulness based cognitive behavioural therapy by Mark Williams based in Oxford, and others, with wonderful results.

FROM THE CUSHION TO THE COUCH   251

Mindfulness is now even being introduced into schools, again with excellent results in terms of enhanced learning, calmer and more co-operative behaviour, and without any loss of spontaneity.

MP: I recently went to a conference on mindfulness in schools with Jon Kabat-Zinn and others, and it was most heartening and illuminating. They had children from some primary and secondary schools talking about their experience of learning and practising mindfulness, and the effects of it. It was most fascinating.

NC: It's wonderful: it's good for mental health as well as for physical health. It has introduced many people to the world of meditation and potentially to a deeper enquiry into themselves and the values of our society. I am thinking of another patient who came following the end of a long platonic relationship in which she had been unable to declare her love. After many years of struggle, she had finally mustered up her courage and declared her feelings, only to be rejected. She came with what she described as a "broken heart". As we worked, we increasingly focused on what felt like her innate inability to make things explicit and express her feelings. Her family had been ruled by fear of a drunken and violent father. She would curl up in bed when her father returned home at night and listen as her mother and older siblings were beaten up in turn by the father. She herself was spared the beatings. She would go into a state of hyper-arousal and then into a state of hypo-arousal, where she would freeze and shut down, barely hearing what was happening. The current model of trauma describes the instinctive protective physiological mechanisms that kick in when we are exposed to threat. The first response is to look for safety with another, it's a social response, that is, get help from someone. If that fails, we fight or run away. If that fails, we freeze or faint, or we dissociate. This sequence is very interestingly explained by Stephen Porges in his polyvagal theory, a model that has become increasingly well known in the field of trauma. In sensorimotor psychotherapy, as developed by Pat Ogden, the aim is to identify the unfinished or uncompleted motor movement associated with the trauma, which when released leads to an "act of triumph" and resolution of the trauma. The unfinished or uncompleted motor movement is understood to be the core level of our disrupted or

252   THE BUDDHA AND THE BABY

"traumatised" higher emotional and psychological functioning. Having failed to make much progress through listening and talking about her experiences, we changed tack, and I decided to use the sensorimotor approach to access her early trauma. I asked her if she was willing to try an experiment, one that she could stop at any time, and re-enact what she did as a terrified young child.

I invited her to do so with her body in the consulting room. She agreed and tentatively went into a foetal position on the couch, which I mirrored as best I could in my chair. We stayed there for a while, and then I asked her to remember that traumatic situation by engaging all her senses, of sight, sound, smell, taste, and touch; effectively to re-live what it was like for her as a little terrified girl, frozen with fear in her bed at night. She closed her eyes whilst curled up in her foetal position. I asked her how she felt; she said "safe, secure, and protected". I said, "That's fine, good, enjoy feeling safe". This lasted for a long while, whilst I occasionally checked in on how she was, keeping her company, as it were. When it felt right I then quietly asked her with a tone of curiosity, what the disadvantages might be of remaining in that position. She replied that it was feeling trapped and unable to move. So I then asked, "If your body were to move or wanted to move, what would it do?" She replied: "I'd open my eyes". I invited her to do so very slowly, taking her time, which she did when ready. Having opened her eyes, she began to look around very slowly. I then invited her, again with a note of curiosity in my voice, to explore the rest of her body to see what it might want to do. Very slowly she began to move out of the foetal position, gradually re-orientating herself in the safety of the consulting room, in the here and now. It took her around thirty minutes to emerge from the foetal state, guided by her sense of the body, and not of her thinking, and then, from sitting upright she went into standing up and began stretching her arms out, then her legs and then her body, feeling free. The trauma was quite remarkably resolved: she emerged a different person. At the end of our session, which was longer than the traditional therapeutic hour, I checked her SUD levels (subjective units of disturbance) and they were negligible. Six months later, in a follow-up session, she was still fine. What had been released on the motor level was her frozenness. This freezing on the core sensory-motor level had impacted on her later developmental

FROM THE CUSHION TO THE COUCH **253**

stages, which included her ability to communicate her feelings to someone significant, the person she was in love with. This happened in one session, but obviously there was a context, a lead up. There was a good therapeutic relationship with the necessary trust, but the turning around of her long-term childhood trauma, that essentially happened in one session. She is a different person now, far better able to communicate her emotions, freed from her emotional and sensory motor "imprisonment".

MP: It's fascinating, and I was thinking of the re-birth experience practised by many therapists. I have personally witnessed a woman with a noticeable physical impairment that was the result of a birth trauma she was aware of, becoming unlocked through a somatic therapy using the re-birthing technique. This was done in one of Roger Wolger's weekends on past lives.

NC: Well, in a sense it is a form of re-birth; my patient's experience of being trapped in a traumatic response to threat was resolved by addressing it through the body, "using" mindfulness of an adult, her ability to be aware of what was happening in a safe context. These extraordinarily effective results are not uncommon in sensory motor-based psychotherapy or in EMDR.

MP: But you need to get to the details of early history to be able to get so fast to the major trauma in somebody's life, don't you?

NC: You do need the history, but interestingly you don't need to have the full history; you don't actually need to know the full details of the trauma that might be difficult for the patient to share. EMDR works with children equally well, where the bilateral stimulation (be it visual, auditory, or tactile) seems to activate a similar process of resolution. I personally see EMDR as a form of facilitated meditation. In this eight-phase protocol-based therapy, having identified the worst part of the trauma, one establishes the negative and positive self views that the trauma elicits in the patient, the corresponding emotions it gives rise to, and then the level of disturbance experienced. This is followed by sets of bilateral stimulation; with pauses in between during which the patient pauses, as it were, taking a breath, and seeing what comes up for them. What comes up could be a thought, a physical sensation, an associated memory, or even something completely random and

254 THE BUDDHA AND THE BABY

apparently unconnected, a process of free association. The patient is able to find a resolution to their trauma through a somatically integrated reflective process in what Francine Shapiro, the discoverer of EMDR, calls the AIP or the Adaptive Information Process.

MP: Both right and left brain hemisphere are involved!

NC: I would think so, and that "dialogue" between the hemispheres seems to promote a resolution of the trauma. There are a number of theories as to what might be happening, including one to do with working memory and another to do with a possible replication of REM sleep, although exact details of what is happening are still not understood. What is interesting is that in the process of bilateral stimulation itself there are few, if any, prompts from the therapist. There are no interpretations, there is no analysis: it's just whatever comes up for the client followed by a "let's just go with that". Some individuals process their trauma somatically, as my abused patient did, others cognitively, and some with a combination of the two; each person is different. The interpretations that people come up with about their own situations are often classic textbook interpretations, and they don't come from the therapist; that's the extraordinary aspect to this treatment. What comes up is a genuine heartfelt "self" insight, not just an intellectual understanding. I am often in awe of the innate wisdom human beings have and our capacity to reorganise and make sense of all the information that each of us carries. One also realises that the therapist is only a facilitator and not the "knower" of everything. It undermines any tendency we may have towards omnipotence; the therapist really has to get out of the way.

MP: It's a very good example of letting go of one's ego.

NC: Yes, letting go of our importance. It's an insight into our ego to know what it, the ego, is. That's why I'm so keen on these somatic modalities and integrating them with talking therapy because the combination is just so much more effective.

MP: And they are so akin to meditation apparently.

NC: That's right; they value the crucial importance of the physical level, and the two are best integrated. I find that sensorimotor psychotherapy and EMDR in their own ways integrate the verbal

FROM THE CUSHION TO THE COUCH   255

and reflective, the conceptual and interpretive together with the somatic, the feeling and the emotional.

MP: How does your Buddhist practice come into here, if at all?

NC: I think it's about—as I mentioned earlier in our dialogue—having gone through the hell of one's own suffering as an individual, having survived it and developed a greater capacity to tolerate the worst experiences. Knowing that there is an internal resource allows one to absorb almost anything, and that of course, is the containment in the therapeutic process. That, for me, has come through my meditation experience and my personal life. Where Buddhist teachings and insights have helped, is that they provide a model of life that is seen as a series of conditions arising and ceasing and that this applies to all phenomena, without exception. There is an emergent arising on the basis of certain conditions; and because these conditions arise as a result of conditions, they also fall apart and dissolve as conditions change; it's a process of conditions informing subsequent conditions; a causal process. In meditation experiences, one can see this happening in a timeless moment of the present, and one can then also see that this applies to all of one's life; it's true all of the time. This reveals that there's nothing fixed, there's nothing absolute about any of these experiences: they're all happening in a bigger timeless context. When one has intuited that bigger context, one effectively finds an ever-present, ultimately ineffable, and absolute refuge.

MP: Say a bit more about things all happening in the timeless moment of the present.

NC: Everything happens in the moment and the present moment is timeless. Time arises in the moment and passes in the moment. We only string our experiences together into the concept of time and space thanks to our memory of the past and imagination about the future. If you look at phenomena in the moment or look for the present moment: where or when is the moment? It's an infinite point; it's timeless. In fact, interestingly, we are living in the past all of the time because our conscious apprehension of what we experience always takes place a fraction of a second after the event, and we know this for a fact from neuroscience.

256   THE BUDDHA AND THE BABY

MP: You mean that by the time we become conscious of the present, the present has already happened and gone?

NC: Yes, so truly speaking, we're always living in the past; we might be living in present awareness, but present awareness is as close as we can get consciously to that ineffable a priori moment of reality, which is actually before it even manifests in consciousness. This can only be intuited, or known intuitively, but it can be "known" subjectively as an absolute certainty, the ultimate reference point: but it's a mystery. I find it incredible, for example, to know that my intention to pick up this cup, and to put it down, took place before I was even conscious that I was going to do that; my body and brain, or mind–body were already going to make that movement before "I" was even aware of that. That intention to pick that cup up was made before I was even aware that I had the intention to pick up that cup. Well, so where is the self in all this? Where is the agency?

MP: It's scary! But the agency is there because your agency was to "wanting to pick up that cup".

NC: Scary, but also potentially liberating and yes, the sense of agency is there but actually how real is it? My body–mind decided that before, so where is the agency? Is it "my" agency?

MP: Your body had already decided to pick up the cup so the agency is in your body!

NC: Perhaps, but where is the agency in the body, where is "me"? When the body falls apart where's the "me", where is the agency?

MP: I'm thinking of the body that is here in this room and you identify with.

NC: That's our confusion: we identify with this body but we know that the body is not self. This is true: this body is the coming together of conditions; it's not "my" body and the "I" that I think I have is essentially an illusion, in that it is a construct. The sense of an "I" is truer than the thought of "I". It's the identification with this body with a whole set of parameters that gives us "I", but there is no "I"; it's a functional construct and that's what is meant by no-self. It's a construct, a coming together of what in Buddhist psychology is referred to as the five *khandas*, or the five aggregates: a body, with sensations, perceptions, thought process-es, and consciousness, which when they come together form the body and mind; it's a very simple model, but it captures the key elements. When these aggregates are together, we have a body and mind; but start taking any of those elements away and "you" are not as you were. So what is that you? It's a constant coming together and a falling apart, a complexity of elements, until it all falls apart altogether. But our emotional attachment to that con-struct gives us a sense of identity, and when we are threatened it's not just our physical form that is threatened but it's also our sense of identity that is threatened; which we protect so desperately.

So, where Buddhism goes far further than any psychothera-peutic model is that it points to the essentially transient nature of the self, in essence no-self. The self, at the same time exists but also doesn't exist: out of this come these beautiful formulations "neither existence nor non-existence" or "form is emptiness and emptiness is form". These don't make sense conceptually because our thinking mind wants something concrete, but there is nothing concrete to grasp. And there you have a core Buddhist teaching in a nutshell: one not to be understood just intellectually but to be experienced intuitively, "known" to be true, through insight. That's where we can find a re-uniting, or a coming together, of felt understanding together with intellectual understanding. This is so incredibly difficult to communicate because it is an intuitive insight not only an intellectual insight. It's mind-blowing because it's a radical reappraisal, a complete shift in perspective; because instead of having one's core operating principle in our sense of identity, one suddenly realises there's something bigger, which in the Zen tradition is called: our "original face before you were born"; an *a priori* state which one could call an "un-become" state, which we emerge from and return to in the same moment.

MP: I was thinking of Jung's collective unconscious.

NC: There is almost certainly I would guess, a link between the collective unconscious and this *a priori* experience, which we apprehend through our right hemisphere about which Iain McGilchrist writes so lucidly. I feel that by meditative

258   THE BUDDHA AND THE BABY

introspection we move into that intuitive, unconscious part of ourselves, which is the right direction to move into, in order to have some sense of what is behind what we think is real. To do that, we go through our unconscious and this means going through all the inherent, procedurally learnt, implicit memories; these include our fears, our anxieties, our emotional, intuitive, unconscious frameworks of reference and associations, our traumas, all of which are embodied. We have to go through all that material, a process that Schore describes in the context of therapy, and I paraphrase, as a "reorganisation of the right hemisphere". The resolution of these emotional complexes allows for greater integration in a better wellbeing, through which, as it were, we can get to the heart of the matter, the underlying ground of our existence.

MP: You're still talking about the person, the ego, the unconscious, aren't you?

NC: No, no, I'm talking about an organism, us, which is an expression of something "bigger", which through its unconscious has access to the "whole", because what we do know, is that the unconscious—although not fully understood or known consciously—connects with the "whole". Through our collective unconscious we connect on an energetic level with all of conditioned and subtle phenomena. This can be experienced in meditation when our left brain quietens down; when we simply witness what we are experiencing when not engaging in cognitive mentation. It's then that there is a letting go of our sense of a separate identity, and the energy that is engaged in maintaining the sense of identity in relationship to what we experience, the subject–object relationship starts freeing up. The energy that was required to sustain this sense of identity is released and starts flowing in a way that integrates and connects. All this happens when we go into deeper states of meditation, which is where we experience the correlate of that process, a corresponding state of bliss in the coming together.

MP: Being at unison with the universe, I feel …

NC: In the early stages of absorption, as described in Buddhist psychology and verified by countless meditators, we can still think reflectively about what we are experiencing, but as we go deeper into the absorptions, gradually our thinking processes slow down and eventually stop; we feel increasingly blissful; then the bliss and the pleasant states begin to fade, leaving a state of perfect equanimity or dynamic stillness, which allows us to "enter" into what Buddhist psychology describes as the formless realms.

MP: Is that beyond samadhi?

NC: No, just very deep states of *samadhi*, where there is no personality, no cognitive functioning; the formless realms, ever deepening states described as boundless space, boundless consciousness, nothingness through to neither perception nor non-perception, which is as far as we can go in a meditative state; where there is the "experience" of, to use a different construct altogether, the Mystery of Mysteries, a realisation of the Ultimate, which is what essentially all Buddhist practice is pointing and leading to and about which nothing can truly be said. In Buddhist thought, none of these experiences are in themselves realisation of insight: but they allow for insight. Essentially, it's an experience of the dissolution of the ego, which then, as it were, re-forms when one comes out of those states back into time and space; but with a memory of the experience. The effects of such experiences cannot but change our relationship to our "selves". We can see through our ego; we no longer see our "self" as we did, because these experiences are transformative. The experiences are so immediate and so real that one cannot deny their truth or validity; but nonetheless, they're still experiences and the moment they are experiences there is a subject–object relationship between the subject and the object and, paradoxical as it may sound, ultimately the "Ultimate" is absolute subjectivity. These experiences lead to a new take on life.

MP: My questions lose their meaning now in view of this bigger perspective on experience of existence and beyond existence somehow!

NC: The beautiful thing about all this, from a Buddhist perspective at least, is that we don't have to believe in anything, any of it. One just has to have an enquiring and an open mind, and be willing to be still and notice; the injunction is "be still", that is, non-attached, which is found in other mystical traditions, as well as in the Psalms: "Be still and know that I am God". What we need to do is to let go of the conceptual frameworks we might have of God

260   THE BUDDHA AND THE BABY

or the Ultimate, and just go into a state of stillness; not reacting to what we experience to the best of our ability; just coming back again and again to observing and witnessing this process of life with the enquiring disposition of: "what is this?", an attitude of curiosity and interest, but without reactivity. The mind will do its stuff: it will do its jumps and somersaults, it will run on journeys, in circles; it will explore this and that; and every time we get caught up in the contents of this activity, we lose the plot. One wants to observe that point of contact between consciousness and the phenomena as it arises in consciousness; and come back again and again to noticing that one is noticing; noticing that one is aware; conscious of consciousness, being aware of awareness which keeps bringing us to that point of contact between the "witness" position and that which is being witnessed. With perseverance, bit by bit, everything is eventually revealed. That's the heart of practice. Everything else is essentially superfluous: whether it's bells or candles, chants or bowing; that's not the point or the purpose; potentially very supportive of course for many, but equally it can also be obstructive; they're all conventions, external forms. The key is a sense of enquiry, non-reactivity, non-attachment; observing the reaction but not buying into it, not taking it further; noticing the arising of thoughts and letting go of the thoughts, not holding on to them. There is inevitably a reflective process at certain stages, but it's important not to get overly lost in reflection as a substitute for enquiry, so that the reflective process enhances the spirit of enquiry rather than hindering it. Significantly Buddhism places great emphasis on the benefit of having a moral or ethical framework within which to practise, where the injunction is essentially to "do good". This supports meditative enquiry, because being dishonest, manipulative, untruthful, and so on, generates whole complex patterns of reactivity, of attachment to outcomes at the expenses of others, all of which emphasise one's sense of separation. A life based on truthfulness, on respect, and on kindness creates a fertile ground for deeper enquiry, because it doesn't add any more mess to the mess we already find ourselves in. It allows for a less complicated lifestyle that allows one to sleep well at night, where one doesn't walk around with a guilty conscience. Morality allows for deeper meditation, and good meditation allows for better morality.

FROM THE CUSHION TO THE COUCH   261

MP: Psychotherapy, too, is an ethical journey.

NC: Essentially yes, but it's not always stated so explicitly because you have the so-called non-judgemental stance that therapists often take up; but actually one does need to have some sort of stance; it's a question of not imposing it on others, but at the same time being very clear about it for oneself. One's own experiences as an individual inform the process of psychotherapy, so all the time one is communicating something subliminally, unconsciously, and if there is that dimension to ones being, that itself affects and informs the process. Being okay within oneself also allows one's own mind to move around more freely, since once the meta-perspective has been recognised or known, it is there, the ground of all one's database of experience and knowledge, as it were, and it can be accessed intuitively, spontaneously. This allows one to be more intuitive, creative and attuned to the therapeutic process; one has access to more resources.

MP: So, sometimes you don't really know how your Buddhism influences your practice but it definitely does.

NC: Yes, but it's not Buddhism as such; it's the experiences that practising within a Buddhist framework have enabled or facilitated, and it's the outcome of that that comes into the therapy; not Buddhism *per se*. Buddhism is essentially a vehicle that enables one to live life more fully and meaningfully. The injunctions to be moral and ethical are for reflection and consideration, they are not a revealed truth or a commandment as they are in the Christian tradition; you're not told to believe them; they're there to think about, to relate to; offering a reference point in relation to which one can examine and deal with the situations one finds oneself in. Buddhism points to something beyond the self and indeed beyond itself. It's not anything ultimate itself—unlike claims made by theistic traditions for themselves. That's why Buddhism generally resonates quite well with the Western secular, empirical perspectives. It's a path based more on enquiry, which is where science also gets its strength. Today, we find many have an aversion towards dogmatic religions, whilst at the same time it is also true that many others are drawn towards them, largely because of the emotional and moral vacuum created by our materially and

262 THE BUDDHA AND THE BABY

pleasure obsessed society, so people look to religions for support; hence for example, the growth of religions such as Islam in the West. I believe Buddhist teachings potentially offer a framework of reference that allows us to experience the fruits of meditation outside of a traditional "religious" context. It is interesting to note the rise of secular Buddhism in the West, which rejects most, if not all, of the traditional institutionalised practices and beliefs; it is very practical, down to earth, interestingly expounded by people like Stephen Bachelor, who by the way, is also worth reading. I do feel though, that secular Buddhism runs the risk of becoming too reductionist, downplaying what might be called the "subtle" realms of meditative experience which cannot be categorised or understood empirically. Having an understanding based on experience of the "subtle" or transliminal experiences in the "field" that exists beyond the physically explicit is very important, otherwise we run the risk pathologising or dismissing "mystical" states as forms of psychosis, which would be very sad.

MP: It's also important in the Eastern psyche, isn't it?

NC: From what I have read, heard, as well as seen a little of myself in the East, unfortunately a lot of Buddhist practice has been downgraded. In many places, it has become a belief-based ritualistic system, where the emphasis for many is more about gaining merit rather than meditating; it's often more about performing ceremonial rites and rituals and taking vows and precepts, rather than really practising. It has lost its original focus, but then that appears to be the fate of most institutionalised and well-established religions. Over the course of time, Buddhist teachings in Far Eastern countries have permeated society differently than here, where Buddhism is still relatively new.

MP: Well, from children to adults, to mindfulness, to society, to mysticism: we have covered a lot, Nick, thank you very much for this most illuminating conversation.

References

Batchelor, S. (1997). *Buddhism without Beliefs: A Contemporary Guide to Awakening*. New York: Riverside Books.

Epstein, M. (1995). *Thoughts without a Thinker*. New York: Basic Books.

Epstein, M. (2008). *Psychotherapy without the Self*. New Haven: Yale University Press.

Freud, S. (1920g). *Beyond the Pleasure Principle*. The International Psycho-Analytical Library, edited by Ernest Jones.

Gendlin, E. T. (1978). *Focusing*. New York: Bantam New Age Books.

Gendlin, E. T. (1996). *Focusing-Orientated Psychotherapy: A Manual of the Experiential Method*. New York: Guilford.

Kabat-Zin, J. (1990). *Full Catastrophe Living*. London: Piatkus.

McGilchrist, I. (2009). *The Master and His Emissary: The Divided Brain and the Making of the Western World*. New Haven: Yale University Press.

Ogden, P., Minton, K., & Pain, C. (2006). *Trauma and the Body: A Sensorimotor Approach to Psychotherapy*. New York: W. W. Norton.

Porges, S. W. (2011). *The Polyvagal Theory: Neurophysiological Foundations of Emotions, Attachment, Communication, Self-Regulation*. New York, London: Norton Series on Neurobiology.

Rahula, W. (2007). *What the Buddha Taught*. London: Grove Press.

Schore, A. N. (2003). *Affect Regulation and the Repair of the Self*. London: W. W. Norton.

Shapiro, F. (2001). *Eye Movement Desensitization and Reprocessing*. New York: Guilford.

The Bible. Psalm 46:10, King James "Authorised Version", Oxford University Press, 1997.

Williams, M., & Penman, D. (2011). *Mindfulness: A Practical Guide to Finding Peace in the World*. London: Piatkus.

CHAPTER NINETEEN

The child in the adult: psychotherapy informed by Buddhism

Dialogue with Steven Mendoza

Parents are very kind,
But I am too young to appreciate it.
The highland mountains and valleys are beautiful,
But having never seen the lowlands, I am stupid.

—Chogyam Trungpa, *The Myth of Freedom*

MP: Thanks, Steven, for agreeing to contribute to this project from your perspective of an adult psychoanalytic psychotherapist. I think the focus should be on your thinking about the child part in adult patients and how your Buddhist practice has influenced you in your professional work. Just a word to explain that I've always been impressed by how deeply you seem to be using the idea of "refuge" in the Dharma i.e. in the teaching of the Buddha, in your work. You are unique in this way of integrating the two. So, I'd like to hear more and also how you came to be a psychotherapist and a Buddhist.

SM: Yes, well, I think I was really hand reared as a psychotherapist. My mother always wanted to be a marriage guidance counsellor and was always interested in psychotherapy even though she never read any books nor had experience until she trained as a marriage guidance counsellor. When I was a child she was bringing Klein and Bowlby into the house. So I was brought up on it. Most significantly, both my parents were devoted and very sincere parents, but both had tremendous emotional problems of their own, but stop me if you heard this before!

MP: This is very interesting about your mother and, of course, most of us psychotherapists come from families thriving with emotional issues and possibly with an awareness of that in some family members.

SM: Yes, we're doing their therapy.

MP: I remember John Steiner quoting, I believe Henri Rey, who said that what patients bring to analysis are their own parents to be repaired, internally, of course.

SM: That makes perfect sense. So, I think I was made a psychotherapist. You know, as a very confused student of psychology, already in psychotherapy, I would make endless lists of possible careers and the one which was always on the list, was psychotherapy. At that time I hated and despised psychoanalysis and was interested in experimental psychology.

MP: Was that for political reasons, as psychoanalysis was not sound enough?

SM: Yes, I thought they were political at the time. Psychoanalysis was seen as normative and as exerting power over the patient by the analyst, as promulgating a culture of antiquated gender issues and so on. In the middle of all this, I found myself so disturbed, especially by my mother's death, that I went into psychotherapy, while continuing to despise psychoanalysis!

MP: How old were you when she died?

SM: Twenty-four, so it was a bit of a shock. I've been trying to remember when I first heard about Buddhism. My father had a friend who might have been a Buddhist. He certainly gave me a big sheet of large Chinese characters to be copied, and I was fascinated by them. But certainly, when I was fourteen, we had to do a project

THE CHILD IN THE ADULT   267

in Religious Knowledge class at school and I chose Buddhism, probably because I already wanted to know what it was and I had probably already heard very good and touching reports on the conduct of Buddhists. I grew up with the feeling that the only comments you ever heard about Buddhists were wondering comments on how unfailingly good and wise they were. I thought: everybody has such good things to say about Buddhism, but then actually nobody bothered to find out more about it. Then we all started to take drugs. It was 1968 and if you were cool, you smoked hashish and that was it. I read about Aldous Huxley: I read *Heaven and Hell*, and read about experiments with mescaline and, indeed, I took mescaline in a controlled experiment by the biochemical department at Trinity College in Dublin.

MP: Dublin?

SM: Yes, I failed my A levels and I got into biology in Dublin where the course repeated the A-level syllabus. But I was very depressed at the time and unable to comprehend that my mother was dying very slowly from leukaemia. We were told that they'd discover a cure. We were watching her dying, but nobody could actually address the reality that she was dying. I was an anxious child, anyway, and I became depressed and confused. I started psychology at Brunel and read Carlos Castaneda and discovered weirdness and the low numbers of Dewey's decimal system. Basically all the weird, philosophical, mystical books in the library had numbers beginning with lots of zeros, and I discovered that if you went down the stacks in that part of the library, you started digging up all kinds of strange books and among them books about Buddhism. I read all the things they didn't teach on my degree course: we were just such a stroppy generation! We thought we obviously knew better than them, and I ended up with a little Pelican book of ancient Buddhist texts and eventually discovered the differences between Mahayana and Theravada Buddhism. I discovered finally this idea of becoming enlightened: that the obvious thing you do when you're enlightened is to lead everybody else to become enlightened. What else would a Buddha do? That was it. But I never became a Buddhist until my first wife got a letter from her first husband saying he was going to evaporate. He meant he

268   THE BUDDHA AND THE BABY

was going to live in a Tibetan Buddhist community in the Lake District, with the Gelugpa Order. He had the teaching I'd been looking for, so I became the disciple of the first husband of my first wife!

MP: Life is funny!

SM: Life is wonderful and he was a brilliant teacher. He's now abandoned his robes and married an American woman, but that's what happens. But he taught me Dharma. What shocked me about his Dharma teaching was that it was very emotional and very practice-based. I'd always thought that Buddhism was very intellectual, and that you just sat there and meditated and that's it. They had all these recitations, which were full of emotions and faith, and they turned me around, really, to somebody who had to think about love, compassion, and giving and to emotional things rather than what I thought was the pure intellectuality of enlightenment.

MP: I think all strands of Buddhism are like that; even Zen, which may appear based on intellectual, non-sensical questions, the koans, is highly practical, common-sense, and leads to emotional realisations.

SM: Yes, I was only reading at the time not practising. So, I began to sit down with people and practise at Manjushri Dharma Centre and they turned out to be the founder members of Geshe Kelsang Gyatso's New Kadampa Tradition. Geshe Kelsang said that it was not Tibetan Buddhism, that it was the Dharma of Shakyamuni Buddha. It's the same Dharma that was brought from India into Tibet. The same Dharma that now comes out of Tibet to the West. It's just Buddhism, it's not Tibetan Buddhism, and he was very insistent on that. I was very affected by the devotional prayers and *pujas* being recited. I had always skipped them in my reading, as I had felt they were just religious rubbish. I was very emotionally affected just by hearing the way these people were reciting, so much that I would go into the *gompa*, as they call a shrine room, at the Madhyamaka Centre in north Yorkshire, in the early morning to go through these texts and try to work out why they would make me feel emotional. I found there what I've always been looking for and without going to Tibet. It came to me.

MP: This is life, isn't it? When you are open, things come to you.

SM: I know it's crazy how things happen.

MP: What did you find then?

SM: I found something that turned me on, you know. I would go into a state of mind which felt good, where I felt well-disposed towards other people, where I didn't feel other people to be critical of me. I felt moved to feelings of reverence, I felt inspired by the idea of emptiness and the structure of the Dharma.

MP: It sounds that you were turned towards the forces of life rather than depression with the death of your mother in the background and more negative stuff, perhaps?

SM: Yes, I discovered the concept of the Buddha Nature, of compassion and wisdom, which had been there inside me but had been obscured by what I'd now call delusions. Compassion and wisdom were characterised by Chenrezi and Manjushri. They did it with imagery. They had big pictures of these people in the shrine where you sat. Chenrezi has a thousand arms reaching out in compassion to people and weeps tears of compassion. Manjushri has a sword to sever the true from the false. These two Buddhas are the two aspects of Buddha himself. This teaching seemed to me to reconcile wisdom and compassion as Bion (1962) reconciled intellect and emotion in container/contained. I was struck by this example of how much these thousand-year-old teachings anticipated recent developments in psychoanalysis. I sat in the gompa hearing teachings and in my excitement I wanted to show how the Dharma could anticipate psychoanalysis. It seemed to me that if it could anticipate European culture by a millennium it might also go beyond it. I thought that psychotherapists might have things to learn from the Dharma that are not in our own canon. I also thought that it would be salutary to have to acknowledge the primacy of the Dharma's formulations over the West's as Mendel's primacy had to be recognised in genetics. I think there is still a smugness that believes the intellect was invented by white men in Greece. This showed me that the two sides of me: the emotional and the intellectual could be brought into balance. In the Gelugpa tradition, we had fun and were playful and enjoyed life and acted naturally, sitting drinking tea and chatting without reference to how revolutionary our practice had been. I remember one newly ordained monk bursting into the conversation to say how mind-blowing the teachings had been. No one responded to this. It's the Gelugpa way to appear ordinary. They say you should not gather disciples by showing miracle powers but by the quality of your teaching itself. Of course, not all Gelugpa have miracle powers anyway! Thinking of this interview, I saw Dharma as cultivating what feels to me like the child in everyone. I found this in a book by a German called Lama Anagarika Govinda, who wrote a serious philosophical kind of Buddhism. He said people with very high Buddhist accomplishment are like children. They have an absolute innocence, immediacy, and playfulness that characterises children. He asked why you then have to go through the business of studying Dharma instead of just regressing. It's because there has to be a developmental process. You have to return to childhood having gone to the extreme of adult development and it's when the two interrelate, when you can integrate the very sophisticated periphery of differentiation and the unitary centre of pure single-pointed consciousness in which infancy begins. At the centre of our origin, our consciousness is essentially a single point of being, one pointedness. You simply are; there's simply the fact of your being. In the practice of mindfulness, *samata* or *Samadhi*, we observe the arising and the departure of objects of consciousness. We recognise that we have been drawn into fantasy and return to the observation of the mind, and gradually those who persist in this arduous practice find that the mind, not my mind, unfortunately, becomes still and empty. This they call quiet abiding, and it gives skilled meditators a physical as well as a mental suppleness and stillness. The practice of free association is anticipated, although without the contribution of the analyst. For me, good practice as a psychotherapist has the discipline of the practice of mindfulness. I recall my mind to the communications of the patient and my associations to them. The shadows move across the floor as the session proceeds. It seems to me that the attention of the child psychotherapist has to be the same as that of the adult therapist and that both make the effort of concentration and enjoy the meditative state that engenders. I am trying to write about all this and have begun with a first paper.

THE CHILD IN THE ADULT   271

MP: The child lives in the here and now. Beyond the sophisticated and hard aspects of Buddhism, one basic aspect of the practice is to live in the present. Perhaps that's the link with the child side of these highly enlightened people?

SM: Yes, I think so, yes, but it's that hard for us to get back to that child state. We have to go out to the periphery of the elaboration of the adult world of discrimination before we can return to the unity of the child or even infant.

MP: It's very interesting this observation of Lama Govinda. I agree that the more enlightened people are, the more in touch they are with the child inside them, and I'm thinking of the Dalai Lama as well as other spiritual leaders, who have preserved or cultivated or rediscovered the pure, joyful, simple, innocent, refreshing aspects, which are the healthy prerogatives of the child. Even in Christianity we find that: Jesus saying …

SM: I think these are the words "Unless ye become as a little child, ye shall not enter the kingdom of Heaven".

MP: This is the depth of this thinking and what a splendid, so far un-thought-of connection between Buddhism and childhood. But, how do you think this deep thought links to your work with the child side in your adult patients, and vice versa?

SM: I remember one of my Dharma teachers once asking me what my colleagues would think of Buddhism. I said they'd think it is a manic denial of death, because they talk so much about re-birth and they think so much that in your Dharma study (my teacher was believed to have had a preconception of the Tibetan language; of course, he was also very bright!) you continue from your previous life and that you may continue in the future life, if you're fortunate enough to be reborn in a human body in a place where the Dharma is taught, what they call a perfect human rebirth. I think that being a psychotherapist made what I was talking about in the Dharma very real to me, although they didn't talk at all in terms of the unconscious and do not know such a concept at all in their ordinary psychological writing, but a lot of what I was taught makes a great deal of sense because I had already been into it as a psychotherapist. The practice of taking and giving that

272   THE BUDDHA AND THE BABY

they talk about: bringing out all the negativity as black smoke and visualising yourself as more and more clean and pure and made of light and breathing in the light, is very psychological. Then they reverse it and they teach you to take in all the negativity of other people and breathing in the black smoke and to purify it inside you and breathe out a clear, white light in your visualisation. This is so like Bion's (1962) idea of the mother's capacity to contain and to transform in her alpha process the thoughts the infant cannot bear. I'm working with a highly successful and gifted man, whom I show more and more to identify himself as a boy who is not manly enough and is unloved and angry. The sadness of this child began the analysis, and I tell the man that the child will continue to obtrude until we understand and attend to his needs. It's really a classical Oedipal scenario. Buddhism instructs us in compassion for what in a patient might make us angry. It counsels the merit of fulfilling wishes, giving people what they want, where the Protestant and Jewish ethics believe privilege must be earned.

MP: This is a fantastic connection. We, as psychotherapists, perform the maternal function of "breathing" in the bad stuff or projections from the infant, that is, the outside world, and transforming this bad stuff into something good, the "light", and offering it back to the infant, that is, the outside person or world. Such a striking parallel between this Buddhist practice and the psychoanalytic practice!

SM: Just sitting on the floor and studying Buddhism part-time for about ten years, I would constantly think that I knew the equivalent of such practice in psychoanalysis, and I wanted so much to describe Buddhism to psychotherapists and say that thousands years ago people came to the same understanding of the mind by a completely different process. Such wisdom achieves the same knowledge more simply, beautifully, and earlier. Psychoanalysis should show some humility in the face of all this. Psychoanalysis owes it to itself, as a scientific process, to acknowledge the primacy of the Buddhist understanding of the mind which is so sophisticated. It is fascinating to see that people who didn't have a Western European culture had such a spiritual and philosophical understanding. In my racist, colonial way, I found it hard to believe that they were as good as us and, of course, if anything,

THE CHILD IN THE ADULT   273

they're better. Philosophically, there's a tremendous corroboration of psychoanalysis in Buddhism. In research methods, they call it a convergent operation. If you can construct a completely different experiment on different premises and both converge on the same finding, then there's a tremendous added validity in that convergence. Hearing Dharma confirmed what I knew as a psychotherapist, made psychotherapy much more convincing, valid, and believable; it was almost like a proof.

MP: I totally agree with this.

SM: Another link to childhood is in the central practice of the Lam Rim, that is, the stages of the path to enlightenment: a series of visualisations and teachings starting from suffering and leading to enlightenment. One of these is to visualise yourself as a multi-coloured crystal, with a different colour on each face. This is called the wish-granting jewel, and you visualise yourself granting wishes of all sentient beings, which for me—with my very English attitude—I believed that people's wishes should not be granted at all, you jolly well have to earn it. Well, it was quite a remarkable practice that wishes are for being granted, so as a practice, it changed my whole outlook really, to something which might sound obvious to anyone else. That gave me a completely different attitude to, amongst other people, patients. Similarly, when they speak of rebirth and of the different worlds into which we are reborn, they speak of the world of animals, who are creatures that suffer fear all the time and what you need to do is to protect them: animals need protection, you know, so that their wishes are granted, the vulnerable are protected. It sounds obvious when you say it, but I found it quite remarkable as a practice, and the virtue of protection gives me a very different attitude to the patient.

MP: And it's a very parental attitude, isn't it? You do not make a baby earn his milk, or have his nappy changed, do you? It's natural and instinctive to give a baby care, protection, and love, to grant his or her wishes and needs.

SM: Indeed. Now, to go back to the question: how do I relate to the child in the patient as a Buddhist therapist, it's a hell of an intriguing question. The giving and taking has its equivalent in

274 THE BUDDHA AND THE BABY

container/contained. I would call it as much a Buddhist process as a psychoanalytic one, and it relates as much to the child and even the infant in the patient as to the adult. I think of my psychoanalytic practice as Buddhist, but I find it quite hard to justify that assertion. What I thought of was that, for me, the main force in Buddhism is emptiness. Wisdom consists of the understanding that things exist for us only in the way we see them.

MP: So there is no absence?

SM: The true nature of existence is beyond us. The Dharma says that all the objects of our perception are constructions of our own mind: they have no inherent existence, they're empty of inherent existence; it's what we would call phenomenological; this is not very different from Plato or Kant, except that they practise it as well as write about it. So emptiness is the emptiness of phenomena of inherent existence. I think of the emptiness of the mind as well. In the meditation on the mind, the pointing out instructions are three; as best I remember them, they are that the mind is vast like the ocean, clear and cognising objects. But the actual doctrine is the emptiness of mental phenomena of inherent existence. It is not the emptiness of the external world. That, as I understand it, does exist inherently but for us it is only what Bion calls "O" (1959). They try to acquire an actual experience of emptiness, what they call the dual view. Emptiness is such an essential concept for psychoanalysis because the whole point of psychoanalysis is to realise how much of what troubles us is fantasy, is not only fantasy but delusion. I thought more and more about identity and identification and identity is what we are and to identify is what we do; but actually I never reach my identity: I'm always making an identification and am always trying to do the being of somebody I identify as. Sartre calls this good and bad faith in *Being and Nothingness* (1943). He writes of the difference between being and doing. He writes of a self-conscious waiter, who is doing the being of a waiter, trying to act like a waiter. He contrasts this with the good faith of a waiter who is just waiting on tables. He is being a waiter not doing the being of a waiter. In psychotherapy, I feel under pressure to interpret to prove to myself that I am a psychotherapist. But I am much more a psychotherapist when I am just staying with my own transferential and countertransferential

THE CHILD IN THE ADULT   275

responses to what is happening in the consulting room. Most of the time in psychotherapy, you are dealing with the child. But you are dealing with a damaged child, a child who is in a very difficult situation, for example a child who is always described by her mother as so unattractive; a child whose mother always says: "I know what you're really like".

MP: That child is given a false sense of his or her identity.

SM: Yes. So, the child we would be working with is a delusory child and fortunately that child's self is empty of inherent existence; it doesn't really exist, it's a phantom. One of the Tibetan teachers I heard said: "Well, if all problems weren't delusions, then how could I help you?" I could say that Buddhism gives me a deep faith that the child that the patient thinks he is, is a child he doesn't have to be. A man I saw recently, I said to him: "You can't conceive of yourself as being able to rear a child. You see yourself as a very small, vulnerable child everyone kicks around and everyone is determined to get into trouble but no one can see any good in that child. But you think you are so small and weak and so intimidated that you just have to comply with their requirements and to live perpetually in fear." But I also said: "You're not really that child at all. You hold down a sophisticated professional job; you have tremendous adult faculties, tremendous academic and professional achievements. If we look at all the adult things you do, you can't possibly be that child." I don't know but for me that's always a practice of emptiness. I think the whole session is an exercise of emptiness.

MP: How did that man take your idea?

SM: He said: "Oh, I can see". But he is the kind of patient who takes in an interpretation with a minimum of resistance and is very tolerant, but has a minimum of understanding and a minimum capacity to play in it and act on it, unfortunately.

MP: If I understand correctly, your aim in psychotherapy is to recognise emptiness in the Buddhist sense, that is, to free the patient from the false or delusional identity that has been projected onto him or her since early babyhood and to get to the core identity of the patient, whatever it is?

276   THE BUDDHA AND THE BABY

SM: I suppose, in a sense, it's a game. I suppose I pretend to myself that I've realised emptiness and everything that comes to mind for me is perceived on what they call a valid basis. I suppose I pretend I'm enlightened or I pretend I'm a Buddha.

MP: You pretend or you really are a Buddha?

SM: I try to realise the idea of emptiness. I remember talking to one of the painters in the Buddhist community in North Yorkshire. She trained as a traditional Thanka painter—the Tibetan banners with religious ideas. It's a very elaborate iconography. She seemed to confirm the idea that if you have the view of emptiness, this dual view, the Madhyamika (the Middle Way), then you see things and you know them to be empty of inherent existence but you really are seeing them. The colour of the blue cup, for example, is a construct of the mind, which has this amazing capacity to create this experience of colour. It is not inherent in the cup; it's in the mind, not in the object.

MP: It's a convention we use, when we call that colour blue, isn't it?

SM: Yes, but colours are just wavelength. They are names of experiences we call blue or orange etc … My understanding is that the more you realise that you're looking at a play of phenomena that the mind creates on the basis of its sensory contact with the world, the more vivid that experience becomes, as you realise that its nature is, after all, what Bion calls "hallucinosis" (Bion, 1959a). By that, he means a projective function born of intolerance of frustration. But to me, it means a mechanism whose function is to generate experience, whether on the basis of projection or introjection, what Bion would have called simply, a function. My understanding of the "dual view" is that we see and we feel the intensity of the sensory experience, while at the same time knowing it to be purely sensory in nature.

MP: And empty in substance?

SM: Empty of inherent existence. I suppose everything that is going to happen in the session is conditional. Everything I feel, everything the patient says or does, is all a play of phenomena, which primarily should be experienced, and which is capable of being understood in as many ways as you're capable of understanding it. They only exist as phenomena.

MP: What do we mean by phenomena?

SM: I mean mental phenomena, the perceptions, impulses, sensations, and emotions which comprise our consciousness and which appear to us to include a real world out there. Of course, our minds evolved in nature to mediate between desire and reality. The point of phenomena was that they were a realistic representation of the "real world", which increased our capacity for survival and procreation and so were naturally selected. But Dharma and psychoanalysis are equally, in their very different ways, dealing with the psychopathological difficulties of this and not with its biological success. So phenomena do not exist in themselves but only in our minds as fiction exists in a book. Everything that happens in the session could be understood as something different. I interpret more and more along the lines of: "Do you think it's helpful to think of things like this?" Rather than saying: "It is like this". I no longer think that interpretations should be made with tremendous authority, with something like the infallibility of the Pope's doctrinal didacts. You can interpret much more tentatively and you could be wrong, as I learned from a supervision group years ago. I think of it as a practice of emptiness that more and more I invite the patient to speculate with me about things.

MP: An interpretation could just be a "yes" or a "no", perhaps? Now, what about combining the idea of developing the ego in psychotherapy and of *anatta* (no-self), letting go of the ego, in Buddhism?

SM: Yes, I have been thinking a lot about this. *Anatta* means not-self, no *atman*, no spirit, which is Brahma, the Ultimate Existence in Hinduism. To me, no-self is precisely the concept of emptiness: the two are branches of emptiness: emptiness of the object and emptiness of the self. No matter where I look, I can't really find me or it. I distinguish between ego strength as a psychoanalytic concept and egotism as a narcissistic, self-congratulation. So if I cultivate the belief in myself, a narcissistic belief that this self of mine is something wonderful, then I'm going deeper and deeper into a delusion and indeed into attachment in the worse sense of attachment. I think the real psychoanalytic meaning of ego is not egotism at all. I think that the essence of ego in psychoanalysis

278   THE BUDDHA AND THE BABY

is the ability to implement the reality principle. Ego is the agent which distinguishes what is real, in order to mediate between the id and reality. Ego is simply the function of telling true and false.

MP: And this is very Buddhist!

SM: Exactly. It's so basic and such simple stuff. If you take ordinary psychoanalysis and you just think about what these things really mean, then the ego has to do simply with the ability to face facts in the depressive position.

MP: It's amazing: such a simple clarification and yet so deep! From the way you see it, the ego in psychoanalysis and the non-ego in Buddhism are very similar.

SM: I think that, if you study this on the Buddhist side, in Buddhist terms and practice, it puts a lot of heart into your work as a psychotherapist.

MP: In therapy, we should have no memory and desire (Bion, 1967), but in reality the target is to help the child or adult patients to accept the reality, to develop an ego strength that allows the patient to face separation, illnesses, old age, as well as pleasure and fun, and to see them all as fleeting conditions. Quite similar, this is, to Buddhist practice.

SM: T. S. Eliot said: "Humankind cannot stand very much reality" (1959). Putting too much reality onto a patient by what seems quite an obvious interpretation can be too much, and patients can go mad or run away. Reality is very well, but you have to think about interpretations the patient is ready for. They say you should only ever teach emptiness when you have been requested to do so. You should never impose that on people because it's a disturbing idea. Some people find the idea of emptiness very frightening. I think it is John Steiner, the Australian psychoanalyst, who talks about how important it is to the patient that the analyst understands him (Steiner, 1994). What is subtle in Steiner is that he says the patient sometimes wants the analyst to do the understanding and to keep it to himself, and sometimes he wants the analyst to give the patient understanding of himself. They are two completely different ways of being understood: "You understand me, that's so wonderful, I don't have to understand myself, I'm just

THE CHILD IN THE ADULT   279

a child"; and: "you understand me and can help me understand myself". I am very aware of this especially with borderline patients. Trainees often want to interpret to reassure themselves, but the patient is desperately evacuating material, beta elements (Bion, 1959), and the trainee's job is to contain them, not to interpret as the patient will experience that as a destructive intrusion.

MP: Yes, a sort of maternal reverie, that is, to have the understanding but not share it with the patient, as yet.

SM: The patient feels held just by the understanding they feel is there in the analyst. Patients often cannot bear interpretations nor can have a real dialogue. This can be a narcissistic position, in which it is impossible for the patient to accept that the analyst has something to give. This would put the patient in the intolerable position of being a vulnerable child who needs from the other, that is, the parental object.

MP: Yes, I can see how this infantile omnipotence and omniscience would prevent that adult patient from accepting dependency and vulnerability and the need for the other. Perhaps the link with Buddhism here is in the total acceptance on the therapist's part, of the reality of the present state of the patient, without forcing interpretations, which will be felt as intrusively persecutory and will be spat out, like unwanted milk.

SM: The issue of attachment is connected with the ego issues. Buddhist attachment addresses our belief that having this or being that thing will be the cause of happiness. We believe that it is real, solid, and that is going to work, but it doesn't work. There is what they call the suffering of change: if the meal you've just eaten was really so good for you, then eating another one should be twice as good. I suppose attachment, in the Dharma, means attachment to the wrong object. If you were attached to virtuous objects, as they call them in Buddhism, that attachment would be encouraged, for instance, a determination to reach enlightenment in this lifetime because I can't bear the suffering of sentient beings.

MP: They would say that is still attachment, I believe?

SM: Well, yes, craving blocks the very thing you're trying to have. To be un-attached means to be there already, that is, that you already have what you really need and there's nothing to crave for, which would really be thought to be a cause of happiness. So you do need to have a determination to get there. I think that attachment the way that Bowlby means is almost the opposite of attachment to something that you crave, in the way that the Dharma describes. I guess for Bowlby, attachment is a matter of the mother's environmental provision being adequate to support a secure attachment by the infant. For him, surely, this is a matter of the quality of the mother, not of the disposition of the infant. It's all very well for Bowlby writing about the adequacy of the mother as an object to attach to, but I think about Klein and how much she says about how much the infant can bear to overcome his own narcissism and to make an attachment. The narcissism, which craves all the agency the mother has and all her power and wisdom, I think of as the attachment the Dharma sees. That infant wants to do all the things that Mum can do. He wants all the power and knowledge that the breast has. He wants to be able to feed himself whenever he wants. I think of all that as attachment, you know, the belief that one can have it all oneself and do it all oneself. That is what the Dharma calls craving and attachment. I think that the ability to be what Winnicott (1968) calls "a speck in the universe", to be small, needy, and vulnerable as an infant, who accepts dependency, is the opposite of attachment, as the Dharma sees attachment, even though it is secure attachment, as Bowlby sees it. This looks like another semantic contradiction as we saw thinking about the ego. I think the Dharma teaches that those things which we constantly crave and we believe will make us happy, mostly won't really make us happy because that often changes into suffering. I think it also teaches that to crave what we cannot acquire is to put ourselves into a wasteful and suffering state of mind. Geshe La [La is the diminutive of reverence by which disciples call their teachers, thus Geshe La for Geshe Kelsamg or Gen La for Gen Thubten] calls it, dismissively, ordinary mind. He prefers to see us identify with the Buddha nature, our potential for enlightenment. Second of all, they won't make us happy because they are a very temporary respite from suffering. The real way to be happy is to stop suffering and you do not stop suffering by acquiring objects that you crave: you only compound the suffering. It's the opposite: you will be happier, the more you

THE CHILD IN THE ADULT   281

let go of. In the Dharma, the way to the cessation of suffering is wisdom, the realisation of emptiness. That ego we seek to satisfy by possession, security, pleasure, and status is a beast that can never be satisfied, a hydra whose last head can never be excised. The greatest moments are moments when you think: it's just great to be here; what else could one possibly want except to be here. I suppose this is the aim of the session for both the therapist and the patient: we should both be here and witness what is taking place completely. So I would call that a meditative practice; a practice of mindfulness, a practice of wisdom in the sense that we require ourselves every moment of the session to understand that these things aren't inherently real: they are unreal things that we have to understand.

MP: So the ideas of attachment in psychology or psychotherapy and in Buddhism are very, very different: a healthy and necessary attachment versus an attachment based on craving and grasping.

SM: I think so. So many things are misleading simply because we use the same words for very different things, particularly for ego and attachment.

MP: That's very clearly put, Steven!

SM: There's another thing that I read somewhere where Klein says that the patient in psychoanalysis should not or must not regress. It sounds contradictory, but I'm sure she does say so. So how can this be that it is so important to relate to the child in the patient so much that I have a patient who wouldn't respond to anything that an adult would understand and I have to talk to him in terms a child would understand before he would answer? So I thought, it's because what regression really means is that we become nothing but a child and so we have no protection from craving and desire and all the penalties of that. Regression means literally and actually becoming a child and limiting our mental capacities to a child's capacities.

MP: This is very interesting and makes me think of a child patient of mine, who has regressed in the sessions to just being the terrified and nearly dying infant in the incubator, which he was seven years earlier, when he was born. I could not keep any thinking

282   THE BUDDHA AND THE BABY

about the seven-year-old boy part of him present in the session. I had to have his real, concrete mother coming to the session temporarily to overcome this impasse of total regression in order to preserve treatment altogether.

SM: The adult patient has to know the child in her- or himself; it has to be present in the room, but it has to be known by an analytic ego in the patient. This is how I think of it: I'm trying to get the patient to think with me as an adult involved in analysis about the child in him that is feeling vulnerable, persecuted, scared, hateful. I'm inviting him to think about this child and how much this child needs to be known and cared for.

MP: What about a very disturbed patient, who similarly to my little boy, may be in the grip of the psychotic side of his personality and could not keep that thinking ego in the room?

SM: I had a very good consultant psychiatrist, Colin McEvedy, who used to come out on compulsory admissions under sections of the Mental Health Act, and he would sit down with a patient and would say: "Stop being mad and tell me what's going on", and the patient would sort of shake himself and proceed to talk sensibly.

MP: So he managed to talk to the non-mad side of the patient.

SM: He seemed to do so. It was like enacting the equivalent of a paradoxical injunction in which you get in there and be mad along with the patient and get into the whole fragmented system they're operating and let the patient be the one who calls a halt to the madness. It's like little children saying to parents: "You stop being so silly".

MP: A reversal of roles, then.

SM: I knew a psychiatric nurse who had to take a patient to court. They would get in the hired car and the patient would pretend to be the nurse and the nurse to be the patient. The driver of the car would never know that it was the other way round! So I can imagine going into the psychosis as far as the psychotic can bear until the psychotic himself says: "Come on, let's start making sense here". But I don't really know, it's just a fanciful idea. So going back to regression: it's paradoxical as it's both regression to a psychic

THE CHILD IN THE ADULT   283

organisation and an emotional experience, and yet there's also an adult patient who has an analytic understanding and sympathy for that child.

MP: How does that relate to Buddhism?

SM: I don't think it does, except that, I think, Buddhism has a great expectation that much of what we realise would be the stuff that children have which we've lost. A lot of the achievements of Buddhism are the regaining of something that we had in childhood.

MP: Like the acceptance of reality in the here and now?

SM: Absolutely yes: play, simplicity, present, innocence of selfishness, what Winnicott (1954) calls pre-ruth: a child in his very early development has no conception of needing to show consideration for the object and hence no guilt about it. I think that Buddhism sees the value in regaining that innocence but having to do it in a knowing way. I think Buddhism and psychoanalysis both take the child for granted. A patient in long term treatment had to go on being very self-destructive until that child had been noticed. He had to go on suffering until people understood that something was wrong. For years and years, the only thing that would do any good in his treatment was that we should understand that he, as a child, was never noticed, like so many patients when they were children. No matter how hard or well that child does, he's never really been noticed by the parents, who were having their own difficulties. He therefore feels that he must be an awful person.

MP: The projection of stuff onto children is so much in contrast with the emptiness you were talking about earlier on! On a more personal level: did you ever have any particular or special experience as a result of your meditation practice?

SM: No, I just felt very clear and good quite often. When I was at the centre for a course, I found that I would get into this very calm, accepting state of mind, affection and benevolence came easily to me and lasted. I felt philosophical. As soon as I went back to London, I returned to feeling anxious and driven and mean. But I found that if I did the recitation, I would regain the good feelings I had in the centre. I've now stopped my daily practice

284 THE BUDDHA AND THE BABY

but I retain the good feeling it gave me of warmth and solidity, what I think Klein would call having a good internal object and which the Buddhists call knowing our own Buddha nature: I kept everything they gave me. But not practising daily means I'm not getting any better. It seems a shame because it's quite a remarkable teaching. An early therapist of mine, Ilse Seglow, said to me: "You cannot be a psychotherapist and a Buddhist", and of course for ten years I could. But later when I met Paddy, we both started the formal teacher training course at the Dharma Centre every Saturday. We found that doing serious, formal studies on Saturday morning, leading to exams, after a week of working as a psychotherapist, was too much. You need a rest. So we stopped it. It was hard to keep up both practices. I'm afraid that finding Paddy after my divorce made me happy and then I had no motivation to practise. When Paddy died, I found that although I missed her, I still felt good enough to live but did not have the will to return to further my practice in Buddhism.

MP: But it looks that you practise your Buddhism also in your work, don't you, Steve?

SM: Well, mostly, in every single session, I recognise things through the Dharma and take refuge in it and in the community of other Buddhists and in the Buddha himself. I am also inspired by the ten perfections of the Bodhisattva to practise patience, giving, wisdom, and dedicate the merits of that practice to my enlightenment for the sake of all sentient beings. To have these basic human functions of maturity named and listed and to be instructed to acknowledge them as accumulating merit makes it easier to behave myself in the consulting room and even out of it.

MP: Hence, I always think of you as a Buddhist psychotherapist as you called yourself earlier on. And on this note, I'd like to end and thank you very much for your thoughts on how the child is on stage in your psychotherapy with adults.

References

Bion, W. R. (1959). *Attention and Interpretation*. London: Tavistock.

Bion, W. R. (1962). *Learning from Experience*. London: Tavistock.

Bion, W. R. (1967). Notes on memory and desire. *Psycho-Analytic Forum, 2*: 272–273; 279–280.

Chogyam Trungpa (1976). *The Myth of Freedom*. London; Shambala.

Eliot, T. S. (1959). *Four Quartets*. London: Faber & Faber.

Govinda, A. (1957). *Foundations of Tibetan Mysticism*. London: Rider Books, 1969.

Sartre, J. -P. (1943). *Being and Nothingness*. New York: Pocket Books, 1992.

Steiner, J. (1994). Patient-centred and analyst-centred interpretations: some implications of containment and countertransference. *Psychoanalytic Inquiry, 14*: 406–422.

Winnicott, D. W. (1954). The depressive position in normal emotional development. *Collected Papers: Through Paediatrics to Psycho-Analysis*. London: Tavistock, 1958.

Winnicott, D. W. (1968). Communication between infant and mother, and mother and infant, compared and contrasted. *Babies and Their Mothers* (pp. 98–101). London: Free Association Books.

EPILOGUE

Many issues have been approached in this book and some enlightenment provided by the contributors. We see how both Buddhism and psychotherapy address forms of human suffering but propose different ways to reduce or end it. Both practices support finding one's own way to liberation from suffering via experiential learning. The unconscious is not analysed and the transference relationship is not given much attention in Buddhism, while its understanding and analysis are the hard core of psychoanalysis. Although Buddhist meditation is not another form of psychotherapy, or psychotherapy a form of religion, there can be meditative aspects in psychotherapy and therapeutic outcomes in the practice of Buddhism.

The Buddhist perspective on attachment is somewhat different from, but not antagonistic to, Bowlby's thinking. He found that a secure, early bond between the infant and his or her mother or main carer formed the backdrop to the capacity for loving attachment throughout life and thus of healthy mental development. Buddhism, too, sees the mother–infant relationship as a prototype of empathy, love, and compassion but considers attachment from a different point of view. What Buddhism calls "attachment" is mainly an attitude of clinging to a belief or to be stuck

288 EPILOGUE

in one's own opinion or state of mind, which, as mentioned earlier, distort our link with, and capacity to see and accept, reality as it is; thus keeping us in a state of delusion.

The existence of a self and how to establish a healthy self are central concepts in psychotherapy. Mothers and babies, children, adolescents and adults enter psychotherapy because there are areas of their life that are problematic, uncomfortable, or unfulfilled and they need a new ability to manage them. Perhaps there are parts of themselves not apt to living; their ego is unable to fit in and is in need of repair. Buddhism places these questions on a different level by going beyond the sense of existence of a self, but it can be very hard for Westerners to penetrate the concept of *anatta*, that is, no-self, no-soul. *Anatta* is intended not as an absence of self in conventional terms; it does not mean that we have no self; Buddhism starts from acknowledging the existence of a self. We need to have a well-established self, a self that is separated from, not fused with, the object in order to be able to transcend the self itself, to go beyond it to realise the impermanence and emptiness of it all.

Coltart tried to explain this by linking it with Winnicott's theory of true and false self. The Buddha "would perfectly well have understood a therapy directed towards dismantling a constrictive False Self and encouraging the awakening and growth of the True Self" (Coltart, 1996, p. 134). This is something that cannot be understood intellectually, she continued, but can only be experienced or realised as a result of hard and intense meditation practice. The realisation of the "Void" or "Emptiness" in Buddhism, "must not be confused with a loss of self or dissolution of ego boundaries", writes Epstein (1998, p. 126). Buddhism goes beyond the dualistic approach, that is, relative versus absolute; temporal versus eternal; full versus empty; internal versus external, and so on. It affirms that the true and ultimate nature of human being is beyond the "affirmation and negation" of the existence of a self (Abe, 1998, p. 185).

Psychoanalyst Jung, in a conversation with Zen philosopher Hisamatsu, said that the self "is unknown because it indeed designates the whole of a person, both conscious and unconscious" (Muramoto, 1998, p. 42). These authors have tried to make sense of, and reflect on, the concept of no-self, but, as for many other concepts in Buddhism, it is the experience and the persistent practice of meditation which lead to the apprehension and emotional understanding of such concepts. As we have been seeing in the dialogues in this book, a way of understanding

EPILOGUE   289

anatta is that nothing is independent or self-existing but everything is dependent on everything else and everything is conditioned. The self is essentially unsubstantial, impermanent and devoid of inherent independent existence. This is what Buddhism calls "dependent origination", that is, that everything is dependent on other conditions (Abe, 1998, pp. 184–185). Buddhism emphasises interconnectedness, human commonalities and not the building of a separate and independent self. Human beings are—according to Buddhism—composed of five aggregates or *khandas*: matter, sensation, perception, mental functioning, and consciousness; nothing is there—that is, there is no-I—beyond them. The changing nature of these five aggregates makes the idea of a conventional self, or I, something in constant flux, impermanent, unsubstantial, and with no separate self, exempt from cause and effect, from change and death; there is no absolute self or god in Buddhism. In its way of aiming at transcending the self, Buddhism is mostly a spiritual tradition, while psychotherapy aims at the building of a solid ego to foster healthy living. This is where the two traditions may be seen to be incompatible. However, this may not be as straightforward as it appears. Psychotherapy, too, aims at building awareness and an experience in the patient of both the dependence on others and on the conditions of the external world that affect and influence all of us.

An essential stance to foster contact with moments of emotional truth during the therapeutic encounter is for the analyst to have "a faith that there is an ultimate reality and truth—the unknown—[and that] such faith is unsustained by any element of memory and desire" (Bion, 1970, pp. 31–32). Such an attitude can be linked to the idea of *anatta*, when the therapist relinquishes memory and desire and sits silently in the session and is there with the patient. This state of letting go implies that the therapist's needs and wish to cure, to be helpful, successful, right in interpreting, and so on, have to be put aside. The therapist has to let go of any clinging to memories about the patient, the previous session, patterns of being, psychoanalytical concepts, and so on, in order to be in the present moment, fully aware and receptive to what goes on, to the flowing of thought, words, sensations moving from the patient to the therapist and vice versa. This requires a meditative attitude and the quieting of the therapist's ego. The therapist's ego functions are still there but in the background, as humus nourishing the therapeutic encounter. The therapist's meditative stance allows both thoughts to arise in him and free associations in the patient. These thoughts may then be communicated to the patient and this facilitates the patient's unconscious mind to become conscious.

In this whole process, a moment of "O" may be reached in the session and the truth or reality for patient and therapist be glimpsed at that specific moment. Both the psychotherapist and the patient can experience aspects of *anatta* in the process of psychotherapy. Perhaps the difference is that the therapist relinquishes certain ego functions to focus on the patient, while the patient has an emotional experience of his dependency on, and interconnectedness with others as well as of the impermanence and transience of his states of mind.

The apparently less reconcilable aspect of *anatta* and the repairing and fostering of a functioning ego are possibly bridged, when the therapist puts aside her or his ego to approach the patient free of memory and desire and opens fully to the impact of the encounter, of the projections, and to the truth, "O" (Bion, 1965) emerging at a particular moment in the session.

Buddhism believes that the "full acceptance of the impermanence of everything leads to an experience of peace and the ability to truly cherish life" (Safran, 2003, p. 29). In Buddhist terms, impermanence is linked to the attitude of not grasping and non-attachment, which implies an acceptance of impermanence. We allow our thoughts, things, and life to come and go. Everything passes: happiness and misery pass, therefore to live in the present moment and in the full awareness of ourselves without attaching to our reactions of happiness or misery gives us a full, intense experience of it. It captures the sense of the old Roman saying: *carpe diem* (live deeply in the fugitive moment).

Freud (1916a, p. 305), during a "summer walk through a smiling countryside in the company of a taciturn friend and of a [...] young poet" was struck by the former's lack of joy in such beauty. He thought that contemplating the transient nature of beauty and of existence can lead to a state of mourning that all that we value and cherish is intrinsically transient. This can give rise to despondency or to a greater appreciation of what we cherish. The determining factor is whether we are able to accept the intrinsic transience, not avoid the mourning that is linked to this acceptance and to let mourning come to an end. Life and love can then be resumed.

In Kleinian terms, the capacity to accept the loss of the object and to look after it creatively inside oneself constitutes a depressive state of mind (the term "depressive" is used very differently from depression). A depressive state of mind includes an acceptance of impermanence, and such "full acceptance" defines the so-called depressive state of mind. However, movements from a persecuted to a depressive state of mind have to be worked through again and again (Britton, 1989) and so "full acceptance" of impermanence is itself impermanent. Similarly, in Buddhist practice, deep moments of insight, intuition, and enlightenment are repeatedly experienced and the full acceptance of impermanence develops over time. It seems that acceptance of impermanence and the depressive position are similar and they both require emotional maturity, a sense of separateness, awareness, and responsibility of one's states of mind, feelings, and projections in the full acceptance of the passing of time and of the inevitability of death.

As we have been told by the contributors in this book, the practice of meditation can widen and deepen one's capacity to observe, to be in touch with the patient's body–mind experiences, to foster one's loving kindness and compassion (from the Latin: *cum pateo*, i.e., to suffer with), to broaden the countertransference in its emotional and physical aspects, as many contributors to this book have shown. Therapeutic tools and insight can also feed the process of meditation; they help to name, recognise, understand, and accept some disconcerting states and the awareness that emerge during meditation. In this respect, the practices of Buddhism and psychotherapy can come together in a mutually enhancing way in clinical practice.

References

Abe, M. (1998). The Self in Jung and Zen. In: A. Molino (Ed.), *The Couch and the Tree* (pp. 183–194). London: Constable.

Bion, W. R. (1965). *Transformations*. London: Maresfield Reprints.

Bion, W. R. (1970). Reality sensuous and psychic. In: *Attention and Interpretation* (pp. 26–40). London: Maresfield Reprints.

Britton, R. (1998). Before and after the depressive position Ps(n) > D(n) > Ps(n + 1). In: *Belief and Imagination* (pp. 69–81). London: Routledge.

Coltart, N. (1996). *The Baby and the Bathwater*. London: Karnac.

Epstein, M. (1998). Beyond the oceanic feeling: psychoanalytic study of Buddhist meditation. In: A. Molino (Ed.), *The Couch and the Tree* (pp. 119–130). London: Constable.

Freud, S. (1916a). *On Transience*. SE 14, pp. 303–307. London: Hogarth.

Muramoto, S. (1958). The Jung-Hisamatsu conversation. In: A. Molino (Ed.), *The Couch and the Tree* (pp. 37–51). London: Constable, 1998.

Safran, J. D. (2003). Psychoanalysis and Buddhism as cultural institutions. In: *Introduction to Psychoanalysis and Buddhism* (pp. 1–34). Boston: Wisdom.

INDEX

acceptance and commitment therapy (ACT) 13
Adelson, E. 15
Adolescent Psychiatrist 77
Adorno, Theodore 198
Adult Attachment Interview 23, 148
Alexandra Palace 194
Alice in Wonderland (Lewis Carroll) 26
Alvarez, Anne 191
    Technique 176
Amaravati Buddhist Monastery 109
Anna Freud Centre 45, 190–191
anti-depressant medication 220
anxiety 209, 225
    in children 114, 136–137
    in new mothers 146
    in pregnant mothers 14–16, 25
    thermostat 58
attachment xxii–xxv, 7–8, 21–24, 36–38, 48–49, 59, 73–75, 82, 84–87, 100, 116–117, 135–138, 148, 152, 165, 174–176, 188–189, 195, 201, 203, 205, 209–210, 221, 229–230, 242–243, 257, 260, 277, 279–281, 287, 290
attending mind 100

bare attention xxi, 6, 14
Bartram, P. ix, 93–94, 96
Batchelor, S. 110–111, 117
Being and Nothingness (Jean-Paul Sartre) 274
Bick, E. 174, 190
Bion, W. R. xviii, xxv–xxvi, xxix, 7, 44, 73, 82, 104, 117, 139–140, 151, 154, 161, 173, 180, 182, 189, 193–194, 244, 269, 272, 274, 276, 278–279, 289–290
Blue, L. 54
Bobrow, J. xxvii, xxix
Bollas, C. 105

294 INDEX

Boston School of Psychotherapy 101
Bowlby, J. 74, 84, 266, 280, 287
Bremner, J. 163
Buddhism
  and children, xvii–xviii
  and psychoanalytic
    psychotherapy xix–xxiii
  and suffering xxiii–xxv
Buddhism Without Beliefs (Stephen
    Batchelor) 110
Buddhist meditation xix–xxii, xxviii,
    55, 60, 67, 110, 170, 188, 228,
    233, 287
Buddhist monasteries 14, 31, 152, 243
Buddhist organisation 70

Carroll, L. 26
Carroll, Nick 189
Cassel Hospital 56
Cassidy, J. 148
Castaneda, Carlos 267
Cavalli, Alessandra 213
Chaskalson, Michael 204
Child & Adolescent Mental Health
    Service 114
Ching, Tao Te 58
Chödrön, P. xvii, 161
Chogyam Trungpa Rinpoche 73, 159,
    265
Clear Vision Trust 129
Coltart, N. xvi, xix, xxi, xxv–xxvi, 6,
    14, 62, 95, 159, 161, 198, 242,
    288
container–contained process/model
    44, 82
Corrigan, E. 208
Cutting through Spiritual Materialism
    (Chogyam Trungpa
    Rinpoche) 159

Dalai Lama xvii–xviii, xxviii, 47,
    59–60, 67, 78, 82, 85–86, 88,

    105–106, 159, 165, 179, 206,
    209, 211, 271
  finding the new 2
  thinking xviii
Dalai Lama neurons 69
DBT 13
deintegration 214
Devi, Akasha 121, 131
Dhamma Revolution, a peaceful
    127–128
Dharma 33, 180, 224, 265, 268–271,
    273–274, 277, 279–281, 284
Dharma Centre 55, 284
Dharma, interpretation of 14
Doing Time, Doing Vipassana
    (Vipassana Research
    Institute) 6, 164, 205
Dowling, D. x, 43, 46, 130

Eastern
  community-based society 16
  concept of emptiness 139
  notion of thinking xxvi
  philosophies 60, 112
  religions 56
    and psychological health 210
  spirituality 12, 158
  traditions 193
EBD school 55
ego 6–7, 19, 21, 33, 36, 47–48, 59–60,
    72, 82–83, 86, 88–89, 96–97,
    99–100, 104, 106, 116–117,
    129–130, 134, 162–165,
    173–175, 180, 190–193,
    209–211, 214, 245, 247–248,
    254, 258–259, 277–282,
    288–290
  Buddhist 72, 112, 163
Eigen, M. xxii, 193, 199
Eliot, T. S. 278
Emanuel, R. xi, 179, 183, 189, 195,
    204–205

Emotional Intelligence (Daniel Goleman) 69
empathy neurons 69
Epstein, M. xx, 180, 192, 240, 244, 288

felt-sense 249–250
Fleischman, P. R. xx
Fraiberg, S. 15
Freud, A. 45
Freud, S. xxiii, xxvii, 72, 94, 100, 105, 200, 208, 244, 290
Fromm, E. xx, 82
Full Catastrophe Living (Jon Kabat-Zinn) 71

Gaia House 110
Gendlin, E. T. 249–250
George, C. 23
ghosts in the nursery 15
Gibran, K. 61
Glover, V. 24
Goldsmith, Joanna 213
Goleman, D. xvii–xix, xxvii, 69, 211
Gordon, P. -E. 208
Goulder, C. xi, 1
Govinda, Lama A. 270–271
Grotstein, J. S. xxvi, xxix–xxx

Hahn, A. 194
happiness
    achievement of 152
    cause of 279–280
    importance of 59
    search for xxiv
Happiness (Matthew Ricard) 60
Hautman, G. xxv
Hayes, S. C. 13
Heaven and Hell (Aldous Huxley) 267
Hitchhiking to Heaven (Lionel Blue) 54
Hoxter, S. 163

imprisonment 253
interconnectedness 7, 48, 119, 122, 130, 195, 289–290
International Meditation Centre 231

Jon Kabat-Zinn MBSR model 134, 201

Kabat-Zinn, J. 71, 144, 201, 241, 249–251
Kafka, F. 197
Kaplan, N. 23, 148
Kelsang, Geshe 268
Keltner, D. 206
King, Martin Luther, Jr. 29
Klein, M. 6, 72, 175, 198, 213, 266, 280–281, 284
kleshas 73
Kundalini yoga xxii

Laing, R. D. 81
Lama Anagarika Govinda *see* Govinda, Lama A
Lanyado, Monica 80
Lao Tzu 60
Lawrence, D. H. 4
Linehan, M. M. 13
Lion's Roar 170–171
Longchen 170
love 105–106

Main, M. 23, 148
Manjushri Dharma Centre 268
MBCT *see* mindfulness-based cognitive therapy
MBSR *see* mindfulness-based stress reduction
McGilchrist, I. 257
McKenzie, V. 14
meditation 33, 35 *see also* Buddhist meditation; Vipassana meditation

296 INDEX

Meltzer, D. 163, 185, 194
Mental Health Act 282
Merton, Thomas 159
mindfulness-based cognitive therapy
(MBCT) 12–13, 134, 201
mindfulness-based stress reduction
(MBSR) 71–72, 250 *see also*
Jon Kabat-Zinn MBSR
model
Molino, A. xx–xxi, xxv–xxvi, xxxiii
"Mourning and Melancholia"
(Sigmund Freud) 105

nameless dread 244
narcissism 112, 173–174,
180, 280
narcissistic self 163, 277
New Buddha Way 44
New Kadampa Tradition 30

Ogden, P. 251

parent–infant psychotherapy 3, 46,
146–147
parent–infant relationship 36–38
perceptive identification 105
Plum Village 31
Porges, S. W. 206, 251
Powrie, R. xiii, xxii, 6, 9, 146
Pozzi, M. xiii, xv–xvi, 59, 69–70
projective identification xxv, 154,
237–238, 276

radical acceptance of suffering 13
Rahula, W. xxv, 153
Ramachandran, V. S. 69
real world 277
reorganisation of the right
hemisphere 258
Revel, J. -F. 60
reverie xxviii–xxx, 102, 104,
151, 279

Rey, Henri 266
Ricard, M. xvii, xxviii, 60
Rilke, R. M. 1
Rinpoche, Sogyal 44, 67, 69, 74
Roth, Priscilla 112
Royal Albert Hall 30–31
Rudolf Steiner Camphill Residential
Children Home 122

Sampson, Margaret 55
Sangharakshita 126–128, 130
Sartre, J. -P. 12
Schore, A. N. 247, 258
Segal, H. 101, 105
Segal, Z. V. 13
Seglow, Ilse 284
Shannahoff-Khalsa, D. S. xxii
Shapiro, F. 254
Shapiro, V. 15
Siegel, Daniel 203
Sinason, V. 215
Skype 41
Steiner, J. 2, 266, 278
Stern, D. 19, 101
Strosahl, K. D. 13
Studies on Hysteria (Sigmund
Freud) 72
Suzuki, D. T. xxvi
Suzuki, S. 44, 198

Table Mountain 9, 20
Tagore, R. 143
Tao TeChing 60
Tapping technique 184
Teasdale, J. D. 13
"The curative factors in
psychoanalysis" (Hanna
Segal) 101
The Mind Object (Corrigan & Gordon)
208
The Philosopher and the Monk
(Matthew Ricard) 60

INDEX   297

The Present Moment in Psychotherapy and Everyday Life (Daniel Stern) 19
The Prophet (Kalil Gibran) 61
The Sanity We Are Born With (Chogyam Trungpa) 73
The Three Princes of Serendip 50
The Tibetan Book of the Dead 12
Thich Nhat Hanh xx, 13, 30–32, 38–39, 44, 47–48, 110, 145, 154
third wave of mental health therapies 13
Thoughts for the Day 54
Thoughts without a Thinker (Mark Epstein) 180, 240
Tibetan Buddhism 12, 31, 67, 126, 153, 159, 179, 268
Trungpa, C. 73, 159, 265
Tustin, Frances 56

Vipassana meditation xxii, 6, 100, 164, 205
Vispassana Research Institute xxii

WAIMH (World Association of Infant Mental Health) congresses 9, 12, 17
Wallace, Allan 50
Walpole, H. 50
Weber, S. L. xxvii
Weddell, D. 163
Welwood, J. xix
Western Buddhist Order 30, 126
Western society 87, 159
Williams, G. 75
Williams, M. 204, 250
Williams, M. G. 13
Wilson, K. D. 13
Winnicott, D. W. 3, 9, 46–47, 64, 208–211, 245, 280, 283, 288
Wittenberg, I. 163
Wittenberg, Jonathan 56
Wolgers, Roger 253
Wordsworth, W. 45

Zen Buddhism 110, 158
Zen Mind, Beginner's Mind (Shunru Suzuki) 44